3000 8000
St. Louis Community College

D1031638

WITHDRAWN

St. Louis Community College

Library

5801 Wilson Avenue
St. Louis, Missouri 63110

Christianity and the
Rights of Animals

Christianity and the Rights of Animals

Andrew Linzey

Crossroad • New York

1987

The Crossroad Publishing Company
370 Lexington Avenue, New York, N.Y. 10017

Copyright © Andrew Linzey 1987

All rights reserved. No part of this book may be reproduced,
stored in a retrieval system, or transmitted, in any form
or by any means, electronic, mechanical, photocopying,
recording or otherwise, without the written permission of
The Crossroad Publishing Company.

Printed in the United States of America

Library of Congress Cataloging-in-Publication Data

Linzey, Andrew.
   Christianity and the rights of animals / by Andrew Linzey.
      p.   cm.
   Includes 16 church statements on animals, 1956–86.
   Bibliography: p.
   Includes index.
   ISBN 0-8245-0876-9   ISBN 0-8245-0875-0 (pbk.)
   1. Animals, Treatment of—Religious aspects—Christianity.
   I. Title.
HV4708.L564 1987   87-21768
179'.3—dc19   CIP

Contents

To my wife, Jo, to whom I owe more than I can say

Acknowledgements

Thanks are due to the following for permission to quote from copyright material: the Division of Christian Education of the National Council of the Churches of Christ in the USA, for Scripture quotations from the Revised Standard Version of the Bible, copyrighted 1946, 1952, © 1971, 1973; Oxford and Cambridge University Presses for extracts from the New English Bible, second edition © 1970; SCM Press and Macmillan Inc. for extracts from *Ethics* by Dietrich Bonhoeffer, ET N. H. Smith, 1971; Geoffrey Bles Publishers (Garnstone Press) for extracts from 'Vivisection' by C. S. Lewis from *Undeceptions: Essays on Theology and Ethics* edited by Walter Hooper, 1954; David Higham Associates for extracts from 'Still Falls the Rain' by Edith Sitwell from *The Penguin Book of English Christian Verse* edited by Peter Levi, 1984; and Element Books for extracts from *Animals and Ethics* by Edward Carpenter *et al.*, 1980.

Many people have helped me over the years to shape this book by criticism and discussion. I wish I could acknowledge them all. But I must record some. Carolyn Barry kindly typed the manuscript with forbearance and skill, despite her many other commitments. Dr P. A. B. Clarke from the University of Essex read some of the final drafts of the book and offered me friendly and erudite criticism. I owe two special debts. The first is to Professor Tom Regan from North Carolina State University, who visited Essex University to lead a major conference on the Rights of Animals in May 1986, and whose intellectual grasp of these questions is without rival in the movement. Discussion with Tom enabled me to clarify a range of basic issues and encouraged me to take up my pen again. The second debt is to Dr Peter J. Wexler from the University of Essex, who read the entire manuscript. He gave generously of his time to save me from all sorts of errors—both logical and linguistic—and provided indispensable stimulation and encouragement. Without his help the manuscript would have been immeasurably poorer than it is. In the end of course the responsibility remains my own.

I have dedicated the book to my wife Jo, for whom the sentence from Romans chapter eight, verse twenty-two, concerning the groaning and travailing of creation, awaiting liberation, has recently acquired a new and personal relevance.

Andrew Linzey
Feast of St Francis of Assisi
4 October 1986.

Introduction

Animal Rights—Ten Years Back

During my student days, perhaps before and certainly since, I have frequently found myself perplexed by Christian attitudes to animals. For many Christians, animals are a non-issue. Generations of moral textbooks testify to the lack of interest in non-human creatures generally and the treatment of animals in particular. 'We have no duties of charity nor duties of any kind, to the lower animals, as neither to sticks and stones' is the judgement of one nineteenth-century Jesuit;[1] and that we do not have *direct* duties to animals remains, as far as one can see, the official Roman Catholic position.[2] Such indifference and misjudgement (as I saw it) led me during my time as a theological student to write my book *Animal Rights: A Christian Assessment*, published by SCM Press in 1976. It came out when I was a freshly ordained curate working in Dover. The book was strongly polemical, as I suppose all such first works written in reaction to perceived indifference tend to be. In it I defended, contrary to almost all the Christian tradition as I saw it, the idea that animals had moral status and in particular that no convincing reasons could be advanced for denying rights to them. 'If the reader can find no fault with the reasoning in these pages, then he is as a rational and Christian being committed to an acceptance of the rights of animals.'[3] This was determined stuff all right.

The intellectual roots of the book stretched back to a time of intense questioning and discussion in the late 1960s, helped in particular by John Harris and Roslind Godlovitch who were postgraduate philosophy students at Oxford. It was they who edited the first major contemporary work on animals and their treatment, *Animals, Men and Morals*, published by Gollancz in 1971. *Animal Rights* tried to present this philosophical case for the right treatment of animals in terms comprehensible to Christians. It began by resisting the traditional Christian arguments against animals—namely that they were devoid of immortal

1

souls; that they felt no pain; and that humans had a divine right, commonly called 'dominion', to use them as they wanted. Sentiency (consciousness and the ability to feel pain) was advanced against the traditional notions of 'personhood' or 'rationality' as the best basis for rights—a basis which should include all mammals and the higher animals which we often treat so badly. Subsequent chapters of the book argued the case for treating animals as we would treat most fellow human beings, with responsibility and with regard for their intrinsic value. A final chapter spelt out the need for a theology of creation that took non-human animals seriously.

Enthusiasm and Hostility

Reaction to the book was in many ways surprising, even overwhelming. Despite the fact that I was barely ordained and in theological terms a nobody, the book was taken up and reviewed all over the place. Reviews were almost all of one or two sorts: enthusiastic or hostile. 'Few curates', began David L. Edwards in the *Church Times*, 'have appeared with a more accomplished first performance in theology, on a subject less hackneyed.'[4] 'It could scarcely be bettered and may do something to end our ambivalence—or indifference,' claimed the *Expository Times*.[5] 'It should be read by all Christians' was the generous judgement of *The Franciscan*.[6] 'A learned and painstaking work', reported the *Catholic Herald*,[7] and so on. On the other hand, Hugh Montefiore in *Theology* was adamant that the argument from sentiency 'confuse[d] feeling with moral obligations' and that the work was 'open to fundamental criticisms' of a theological and ethological kind.[8] W. D. Paton in *Crucible* accused the book of 'dishonesty' in its arguments against experiments on animals.[9] *The Tablet* found the argument for the extension of rights to animals 'less than compelling ... all the details ... do not succeed in adding up to a cogent piece of argumentation'.[10] In addition to the sharply divergent reviews, the letters seemed unending. Over a thousand were received during the first three months of publication, to which should be added the many unannounced visitors and the numerous telephone calls. My recollections of this period range from elation to bewilderment. Most of all, I remember the fatigue involved in trying to do the job of a parish priest on one hand, and the work of 'unofficial chaplain to the animal welfare movement' (as someone then dubbed it) on the other.

It became clear that for some at least the subject of the book had touched a raw nerve. The Christian tradition was not quite so indifferent as I had supposed. Indeed, my postbag had shown that for some, traditional attitudes to animals were a stumbling-block to faith. There were, it appeared, a sizeable number of individuals who were frankly uncomprehending of indifference to the world of animal pain. On the other side, there were others alarmed by the notion that God could really be concerned with anything other than the closed world of human/divine relations. That a priest, of all people, should spend time fostering concern for other suffering creatures was thought, in those quarters, to be faintly ridiculous.

Perhaps the most heartening aspect of the book was the way in which its central argument about rights was taken up and developed by philosophers in a variety of ways. Tom Regan from North Carolina State University, for example, examined my argument at length and offered a critical defence.[11] In particular his own modified argument based on 'the subject of a life criterion' forms the major intellectual plank of his *The Case for Animal Rights*[12]—a work which earns him, rightly in my view, the title of intellectual leader of the animal rights movement. On the other hand, Raymond Frey of Liverpool University has repeatedly taken the rights argument to task in attempts to show its incoherence and unsatisfactoriness.[13] I am in both these people's debt, as will become clear. On the wider stage, *Animal Rights* coincided with a whole range of new publications, many of them by philosophers. Peter Singer's *Animal Liberation* was published later the same year and Stephen Clark's *The Moral Status of Animals* in 1977. Major work was also produced by Mary Midgley in *Beast and Man* (1979) and especially *Animals and Why They Matter* published in 1983. Together with the RSPCA, I organized a two-day Symposium on 'The Rights of Animals' in 1977 which brought together many of this new generation of writers; their contributions were published in 1979.[14] On the popular front, many hundreds of animal societies in Britain came together to co-ordinate 1977 as 'Animal Welfare Year', which attracted enormous publicity.[15] Soon after, a number of philosophers, scientists and lawyers formed the International League for Animal Rights and 1978 was designated 'World Animal Rights Year'. Sunday 15 October saw the first ever proclamation of a 'Universal Declaration of the Rights of Animals' at UNESCO House in Paris. This document was an ambitious and comprehensive attempt to establish 'the equality of the rights of humans and non-humans, all of whom have an equal claim on life and equal standing in nature'.[16] It was perhaps not surprising that for Frey at least this new emerging interest amounted to a 'deeply felt, philosophical orthodoxy on rights, animals and vegetarianism'.[17]

In many ways reaction from the theological community was more muted and less enthusiastic. And yet some real steps were taken in the 1970s towards putting animals on the agenda of the churches. The General Synod of the Church of England, for example, passed by an overwhelming majority a motion welcoming Animal Welfare Year in 1977 which urged concern 'for the due *rights* of sentient creatures in God's world' and that we should 'make more widely known the plight of many animals and birds today'.[18] Moreover, in 1977 Donald Coggan, then Archbishop of Canterbury, accepted the Presidency of the RSPCA and sent a forthright statement to its Annual General Meeting. 'I am happy to follow the lead given to the Church by the London vicar who called the meeting in 1824 which led to the Society's foundation,' he wrote. 'There have always been and still are many Churchmen, both lay and ordained, who have seen it as part of their Christian profession to work for animal welfare.' More directly, 'Animals, as part of God's creation, have *rights* which must be respected. It behoves us always to be sensitive to their needs and the reality of their pain.'[19] Arguably no Archbishop before or since has gone further. Robert Runcie, the present Archbishop, has echoed this concern in two important statements in 1981 and 1982. 'In the end lack of respect for the life and well-being of an animal must bring with it a lowering of man's own self-respect: "inasmuch as ye do it to the least of these little ones ye do it unto me".'[20] There are signs then that the concern for animals which has so dominated the agenda of moral philosophers for over a decade, is beginning to be felt within Christian churches.

Various Deficiencies

And yet despite all the discussion which *Animal Rights* created, it became clear within a short while that it suffered from various deficiencies. It *was* too polemical. It suffered, as does much in the animal movement, from a surfeit of moral zeal. Most of all, it failed to grapple sufficiently with the theological tradition about animals that we have inherited. It offered moral critique with insufficient theological understanding. It barely scratched the surface of some genuinely difficult theological issues which underlie not only talk about rights but also our general perception of the non-human. 'It is easy enough', I wrote recently, 'to point the finger of blame at apparently uncaring theologians but it is much more difficult to try to wrestle with the ideas presented and to try to have some insight into why they were led to the conclusions they were.' In a passage especially aimed at myself, I added:

> This is a responsibility that should not be shirked. To be a Christian is to inherit almost two thousand years of scholarship, study and spirituality, some of the profoundest thinking in almost every area of human life. We have a responsibility to understand that tradition; not to agree with it all, but to understand it . . . Our task, as I see it, is not the negative one of rejecting bits and pieces of the tradition we think are erroneous, but the positive one of discerning, judging and evaluating this tradition in order that what we pass on may in turn be tested, judged and discerned. We have a duty to listen to and wrestle with the tradition even and especially when it appears to be saying things we regard as mistaken.[21]

Since 1976 therefore I have worked both on the formal level of academic research[22] and in my reading generally to grasp more clearly what the tradition has been saying and to engage with it. In this process I have made some surprising discoveries; often expecting the worst, I have come to discover the best, and the best the Christian tradition has to offer cannot, I judge, be bettered elsewhere. Christian theology provides some of the best arguments for respecting animal life and for taking seriously animals as partners with us within God's creation. It may be ironical that this tradition, once thought of as the bastion of human moral exclusivity, should now be seen as the seed-bed for a creative understanding of animal liberation. I am only sorry that I did not see all this before and that such an important movement should be served by such a poor advocate. What follows is a belated attempt to remedy my shortcomings and to pay back some of my debts.

My intention has been to write a simple, concise and well-documented discussion for the general reader, free of technical language and abstruse argument. This apparently simple task has proved to be considerably more difficult than I had initially supposed. I am now only too painfully conscious of the book's limitations and how it falls short in a variety of directions. Ideally I would like to have spent another ten years reflecting upon some of the serious questions thrown up by the whole issue of animal rights before launching again into print. The issue, however, is so timely and so few theologians have entered seriously into a discussion of it, that I have felt constrained to respond to the invitation to write. If the book serves discussion it will have been worthwhile.

1 Blessing and Curse

Understanding properly the nature of the creation around us and our part within it has become an increasingly pressing issue. And yet understanding creation is not the work of a day, nor yet of six. It is for some if not most Christians a deeply mysterious thing. Believing in God the Creator does not automatically solve the riddles and puzzles in creation, even if it gives us some vital clue to the question of meaning. At heart the problem is this: creation is deeply ambiguous. It seems to affirm and deny God at the same time. We can find both evidence for God and simultaneously against him. The truth of God is not written all over the created world so that anyone who is not deaf, dumb, blind or stupid can grasp it without difficulty. Only by being amazingly blinkered to pain, misery and suffering can we say that all empirical evidence leads to God. By grappling with two biblical themes, blessing and curse, we can begin to understand this two-sidedness of creation.

The Divine Generosity

As it has been understood through centuries of tradition, blessing (*barak*) stands especially for three things. Firstly, *generosity*. God does not *have* to create anything; that he does so is sheer grace. That God gives, and delights in giving, is the hallmark of the God as revealed in Jesus Christ. In contemplating the self-giving of Jesus, his life, death and passion, we are able to see more clearly what it means for God to give abundantly, without reserve and without meanness of measure. 'Praise the Lord for he is good,' is the great conviction of the Judeo-Christian tradition. 'Sing to our God for he is loving: to him our praise is due.'[1] And this generosity is the glory of God. 'We praise Thee, O God, for Thy glory displayed in all the creatures of the earth,' writes T. S. Eliot. 'For all things exist only as seen by Thee, only as known by Thee, all things exist only in Thy light.'[2] To affirm creation as blessing is to go far beyond what sense-experience may dictate to us, it is to enter the world of faith illumined by the generosity we see lived in the life of Jesus Christ. Notice how the generosity of God knows no bounds. 'How many are your works, O Lord!' exclaims the Psalmist, 'In wisdom you have made them all. The earth is full of your riches.'[3] To affirm the generosity of God is to celebrate creation as gift and to know ourselves as participators in divine beneficence. This we do along with all creation. 'All things affirm Thee in living,' writes Eliot. 'The bird in the air, both the hawk and the finch; the beast on the earth, both the wolf and the lamb; the worm in the soil and the worm in the belly.'[4] When the Old Testament pictures the non-human creation in relation to God it is not surprising that the dynamic of praise is frequently articulated. The secret of the world as creation given by the generosity of God is not one from which animals and birds, even inanimate creatures, are excluded. Indeed, they sing 'the Lord's Song' throughout creation in an exemplary way.[5] It is 'all mountains and hills, all fruit trees and cedars, beasts, wild and tame, reptiles and birds on the wing' that precede humans in the self-evident praise of their Creator.[6] Even more directly, in the first creation saga, the animals and birds are blessed alongside human beings and blessed with the same blessing. Commentators on Genesis are often disposed to overlook the fundamental closeness presupposed by the inclusion of land animals with man in the creative work on the sixth day. As Karl Barth points out, 'O Lord, thou preservest man and beast' is a thread running throughout the whole Bible.[7] It appears to find continuity even in the strange verse from Mark's Gospel where the ministry of Jesus begins after a period in the wilderness with 'the wild beasts'.[8] Blessing then means first of all grasping the insight that *all* creation proceeds from the creative, generous hand of God. Human or non-human, animate or inanimate, we all share the profound beneficence of God in his creative work.

Intrinsic Value

Secondly, *value*. To affirm the blessedness of creation is to affirm an independent source of its worth. In this sense *all* creation has an irreducible value. Whatever else it may be necessary to say about creation must not allow us to dislodge this fundamental insight. All being, all *ousia* affirmed in the incarnation, has glory because it partakes of divine glory. Nothing that God has made can be in the last resort really alien to him. Whatever the precise construction laid on the Johannine verses about God 'so loving the world', it must not lead us to a devaluing of the goodness of the created order as God intended. All creation, large and small, intelligent and unintelligent, sentient and non-sentient has worth because God values it. 'For thou lovest all things that exist', declares Wisdom, 'and hast a loathing for none of the things which thou hast made, for thou wouldst not have made anything if thou hadst hated it.'[9] Moreover, it is the Spirit immanent in creation that gives life and in so doing develops all beings into their particular fullness. 'Thou sparest all things, for they are thine', continues Wisdom. 'O Lord who lovest the living . . . thy immortal spirit is in all things.'[10] There are many intimations in the Old Testament of the care and love of Yahweh for the non-human, and this despite the clearly pre-eminent place given to humans in creation. The Lord's answer to Job, faced as he is with terrible and unmerited suffering, points to the mysterious and providential hand of the Almighty which extends to all living beings. It is difficult not to see, in this humbling answer to Job which compares him unfavourably with a crocodile, some mocking of the anthropocentric notion that the world should be naturally pleasing to man:

> Can you draw out Leviathan with a fishhook,
> or press down his tongue with a cord?
> Can you put a rope in his nose,
> or pierce his jaw with a hook?
> Will he make many supplications to you?
> Will he speak to you soft words?
> Will he make a covenant with you to take him
> for your servant forever? . . .
>
> Behold, the hope of a man is disappointed;
> he is laid low even at the sight of him.
> No one is so fierce that he dares to stir him up.
> Who then is he that can stand before me?

And notice how this section ends with a resounding affirmation of God's prior ownership of all things:

> Who has given to me, that I should repay him?
> Whatever is under the whole heaven is mine.[11]

There is no better place than Job to look for a lesson in how God cares equally for all creatures and how the Almighty opposes the vanity that places human worth and well-being before everything else in creation.

The Freedom of Being

Thirdly, *freedom*. Blessing empowers creation to be. It is in this sense that Barth speaks of blessing as 'authorisation', the freedom of the creature to be itself before the Creator.[12] If the immanence of God in creation gives it life on one hand, it is the transcendence of God that enables the creature to be truly itself in relation to its nature, on the other. Approached in this way, the transcendence of God which is sometimes ridiculed as the 'absent God' actually has positive meaning for all creatures. God does not constantly violate creatures through dictatorial control or mechanistic interference. Creatures can move and act and be themselves with full integrity. We see this most clearly in the way in which non-humans, as well as humans, share something of the divine creativity in the process of reproduction. Together with us they *pro*-create life and in doing so participate in fullness of life. And yet, it has to be said that humans are freer in their relationship to God and, because of this, freer in their relationship with all other creatures as well. This special freedom of man, and therefore his particular responsibility, will be described later. But we need here only emphasize the inherent nature of creatures who are blessed to be. And what are they to be? The simplest answer is the most profound: they are to be with God. They are to enjoy their life with him according to their creaturely being. This, after all, is the goal of the first creation saga, namely the Sabbath. Creation, as envisaged by the Priestly writer, has as its goal peaceful coexistence with God in a state of perfect freedom. Alas, for many appreciation of the Sabbath both as a practical sign of belonging to God and as a recuperative experience is frequently slight. But there it is central to the first creation saga, and what is more, it is to signify for us the whole future of creation as such, that we come from God and belong to him forever. Notice here how it is quite impossible to articulate the meaning of the Sabbath except in inclusivist terms, that is, in terms which include the whole created order. We are far away from the highly individualistic notions of our relationship with God that have so dominated Christian theology for centuries. Our liberation as children of God is to be found at precisely the point where we expect it least, namely as fellow creatures in God's creation, looking forward to consummation and fulfilment. Jürgen Moltmann may not be far wrong when he suggests that in the Sabbath experience the whole point of creation is pre-figured and made manifest.[13]

Divine Disappointment

Now let us turn to the notion of curse (*arar*). Again in direct contrast to our previous elaborations, we can unravel three layers of meaning.

Firstly, *displeasure*. If God is delighted with the world, he is, if we take the biblical narratives seriously, also frequently disappointed. The world of creation signals promise, hope and expectancy and yet it is a promise tragically unfulfilled. Classical Christian theism teaches that the wickedness of man throws the system of intending order into disorder, harmony becomes engulfed in meaninglessness and teleology lapses into futility. Quite *how* we explain all this is more than difficult. I shall not be concerned here with the various theories of man's fall from grace, except to indicate, in fidelity to the story, that the Fall involves not merely a dislocation of man's relationship with God and his fellow humans but also with the entire created order. This is shown graphically in the second saga which portrays the enmity between woman and serpent.[14] The old order of harmony is lost and a new order of violence affecting every level of existence comes into being.

This cosmic dimension to sinfulness is frequently so embarrassing to theologians that it is conveniently overlooked or ignored altogether. And yet it contains a vital key to appreciating the lostness not only of humans but also the equally valid tradition about the necessary redemption of all creatures. The divine displeasure means simply that creation in its entirety is no longer pleasing to him. Creation now stands in an ambiguous relationship to God. True, the relationship is not completely broken and God is not unfaithful. But that which *now is* stands in inevitable contrast to what *should be*. Whatever the limits of anthro-

11

pomorphism, we have to posit something like divine disappointment and displeasure in order to convey the urgent and tragic sense of loss of which Genesis speaks. Eden changes from a place of 'harmless sport' between animals and man, as William Cowper portrays it, to a situation where 'sin marr'd all' and where 'each animal of every name, conceived a jealousy and an instinctive fear' of 'the loathed abode of man'.

> And in that hour,
> The seeds of cruelty, that since have swell'd
> To such gigantic and enormous growth,
> Were sown in human nature's fruitful soil.
> Hence date the persecution and the pain
> That man inflicts on all inferior kinds,
> Regardless of their plaints.[15]

The language, like much of Genesis, is poetic, and all the more powerful for that. For Christians it is part of a long tradition of seeing something quite radically wrong with the world as we now experience it. The God who loves his creation can hardly be indifferent to its cruelty. 'The Bleat, the Bark, Bellow & Roar', writes William Blake, 'Are Waves that Beat on Heaven's Shore.'[16]

The Sad Uncomprehending Dark

Secondly, the notion of curse means that creation, while valuable, can become *devalued* or, even at times, valueless. The logic of this insight is inescapable. The very power which authorizes creation to be itself can be turned by human will against itself and therefore into self-negation and violence. This 'risk of creation' as it has been called,[17] is central to the Christian view of a God who creates freely, that is, in hope and with possibilities in mind but no certainties guaranteed. Notice how in the Genesis sagas it is the act of violence on Cain's part that provokes the despair of God.[18] Again, prior to the Flood it was the violence of the earth that made God 'sorry that he had made man'. This condemnation, however, while centred on man because he alone has choice and is therefore accountable, extends to all living things, 'man and beast, reptiles and birds'.[19] In this way the biblical narrative underlines the radical alienation from God which the whole created order has to suffer. And suffer it has since, and in no small measure. 'Still falls the rain', writes Edith Sitwell, on 'the wounds of the sad uncomprehending dark',

> The wounds of the baited bear,—
> The blind and weeping bear whom the keepers beat
> On his helpless flesh . . . the tears of the hunted hare.[20]

Like it or not, it is on us human beings that the primary responsibility falls for this 'sad uncomprehending dark'. And however difficult we may find this as an adequate explanation of cosmic evil, we cannot resist the fact that it is indeed the human species alone that is now responsible for the massive devaluing of creaturely life through exploitation and greed. At the very least, as a story with a contemporary moral Genesis cannot be faulted. The problem is that we have yet to grasp the moral point. Adam 'would not have used the creatures as we do today', writes Luther. Before the corruption of nature we would have used animals principally 'for the admiration of God and a holy joy'.[21] That this suggestion may strike us as romantic is a sign of our lost innocence.

Travail and Futility

Thirdly, curse becomes '*bondage*'. It is altogether a piece with Paul's theology that the suffering of creation could not simply be seen as the result of human waywardness; there just had to be some divine providential purpose behind it all. Thus Paul propounds the startling thesis that creation 'was subject to futility, not of its own will but by the will *of him who subjected it in hope*'. This in turn opens up the whole possibility of freedom for everything that 'groans and travails'. And what is creation to be freed from? From 'bondage to decay' or perhaps more accurately from 'the shackles of mortality'.[22] It is to be freed to be eternally itself for God. In this way the salvation of man can be seen as encompassing the redemption of all creation. The curse which Jesus Christ takes upon himself reverses the natural order of mortality not only for human beings but for the 'sad uncomprehending dark' of innocent creatures. This belief in the inclusive redeeming capacities of God in Jesus Christ, while frequently put to one side by biblical scholars,[23] is actually essential in order to understand the contradictions of the world as we know it. It is

13

true that the 'biological and zoological sciences present us with the most terrible picture of the evolutionary process', as Harry Williams observes. 'But if the universe has been created by a good God and is supposed to reveal His glory, if, in St Paul's words, God has shown His invisible nature to be clearly perceived in the things which have been made, isn't it frighteningly strange that the created order should so often completely contradict everything we believe God to be?'[24] And yet in turn this contradiction is not total or absolute. Curse does *not* entirely replace blessing. We also know that nature is *not* simply red in tooth and claw. There are also possible signs of mutual aid, apparent altruism and co-operation in the natural world.[25] Blessing and curse live side by side. Our whole universe testifies to the *complexity* of light and darkness. 'Thy glory is declared even in that which denies Thee,' grasps Eliot in a moment of genius, 'the darkness declares the glory of light.'[26] It is light which enables us to see the darkness.

In general, the challenge to us is how human beings can themselves become a blessing rather than a curse to creation, or to be more precisely theological, how we can co-operate with God the Spirit in the freeing of creation to be itself for God. There are doubtless many implications here to wrestle with, but I shall choose three of primary importance: (i) respecting; (ii) valuing, and (iii) letting be.

Reverence for Life

(i) That we should honour and respect the life of creation because God made it, is hardly a new idea in the Christian tradition. And yet it has frequently been lost in the shuffle of theological ideas from one century to another. Perhaps the most notable exponent of respect for life in this century, namely Albert Schweitzer, has certainly received a poor press so far. The reasons for this are varied and complex, partly because Schweitzer's work on Jesus has necessarily made him a controversial figure in the area of New Testament studies. More directly still, 'reverence for life' has undoubtedly been misunderstood by almost all its critics as meaning the absolute inviolability of *all* life under *all* circumstances. Viewed from this perspective, Schweitzer can certainly be written off as inconsistent or cranky.

And yet, as Schweitzer himself makes clear, reverence is not to be interpreted as law, but as attitude, feeling and disposition.[27] Reverence commends itself in this context as the general ethical response of Christians to the grace of created life. It is a 'principle of the moral' in the sense that this is where our thinking and activity must conjoin if we are to recognize the grace of our own life as well as that of other created lives. 'The time is coming', he writes, 'when people will be astonished that mankind needed so long a time to regard thoughtless injury to life as compatible with ethics.'[28]

This does not mean of course that we do not have to make some difficult and painful choices about which life in practice we have to kill in order to live. Schweitzer is no romantic (in a disparaging sense) about the natural world. He speaks of how creation is 'a ghastly drama of the will-to-live divided against itself' and how we all have to proceed as far as we are able to take responsibility for what we can. 'Whenever I injure life of any sort, I must be quite clear whether it is necessary,' writes Schweitzer. 'Beyond the unavoidable, I must never go, not even with what seems insignificant.'[29] What Schweitzer's thought means for us today is that we need to become radically sensitized to the natural world. Our general posture must always be one of reverence for other forms of life. In this it seems to me that Schweitzer makes a case of compelling significance for the Christian conscience. What does it mean to be human, if it is beyond our wit and will to honour the life given by the Creator? John Woolman, the Quaker divine, in true Schweitzerian spirit writes of how he 'was convinced . . . that true religion consisted in an inward life, wherein the heart doth love and reverence God the Creator and learn to exercise true justice and goodness not only toward all men but also toward the brute creatures'.[30] The notion of 'inward' spiritual life is striking here. For, as I have tried to show elsewhere,[31] much in the spiritual life can be phoney if we do not lay before ourselves the goal of becoming sensitive, generous, feeling people. Of course it is possible to sentimentalize the created order by being cognizant of only its blessing rather than its curse. But to live without any fellow-feeling for other creaturely inhabitants of God's good world is to live a deeply impoverished kind of life. It is spiritual immaturity that leads us constantly to stress our dominance to the exclusion of fellow-feeling and

15

togetherness. It is our task to enter into something of God's joy in his process of creativity. 'If thy heart be straight with God, then every creature shall be to thee a mirror of life and a book of holy doctrine,' writes St Thomas à Kempis, 'for there is no creature so little or so vile, but that showeth and representeth the goodness of God.'[32] Yes, it is the *goodness* of God we must encounter and rejoice and celebrate, if we are to have any hope of confronting the bad. My own conviction is that there must come a time when Schweitzer is recognized by the Christian Church along with all its other doctors, saints and martyrs as expressing something both urgent and vital to the Christian faith.

Anthropocentricity or Theocentricity

(ii) Many theologians are now beginning to see how central is the insight that creation has value.[33] This, it has to be said, comes after many years in which the Christian tradition has understood the value of creation primarily in term of its utility to ourselves. A list of names can be compiled, as Robin Attfield shows,[34] of notable Christians who have seen creation made specifically for human use. They include: Origen, Peter Lombard, Aquinas, Luther, Calvin, and even Karl Barth.[35] There can be little doubt that it is the approach of these thinkers which has vastly influenced the treatment of animals for the worse. Keith Thomas has shown the direct link between theological notions of utility and the correspondingly inferior status of animals—a status which amounts to little more than nothing in most cases. Thomas cites, for example, the popular 'country house' poems of the early seventeenth century which supposedly reveal the purpose of animals and birds:

> The pheasant, partridge and the lark
> Flew to thy house, as to the Ark.
> The willing ox of himself came
> Home to the slaughter, with the lamb;
> And every beast did thither bring
> Himself to be an offering.[36]

Even now, the notion that animals 'exist for our sake' has strong resonances throughout popular Christianity. It is only right that theologians should now mock 'the folly' of this notion, but such belated protests would carry more weight if they were offered in a spirit of some penitence.[37] Folly it must be that sees the whole world as our plaything, but it has also been a *grievous* folly for those who have had to suffer it. We suffer least the folly inflicted on others when it affects us not at all. No wonder that the rationalist and vegetarian Voltaire could claim against Christians that 'those who believe absurdities will commit atrocities'.[38]

And yet it is also true that some Christians have celebrated a non-instrumentalist view of nature and animals in particular. Not only St Francis of Assisi of course but also numerous others have championed the claims of animals. St Basil the Great prayed for the salvation of man and beast, St Chrysostom urged the duty of kindness to animals and St Isaac the Syrian spoke of the core of piety as the 'charitable heart' which is revulsed by animal suffering of any kind.[39] To these figures (and the many others cited throughout the book) needs to be added the strong Christian support for the animal protection movement from the eighteenth century onwards. It often comes as quite a surprise to Christians to learn that it was an Anglican cleric, Arthur Broome, who called the first meeting which led to the formation of the SPCA (later to become the RSPCA) in 1824 and that he ended up in prison trying to pay for the Society's debts.[40] As I have argued at length elsewhere,[41] there are strong grounds for regarding this non-instrumentalist view of creation as more coherently required by orthodox doctrine than its utilitarian alternative. The challenge of the doctrine of God, the free, generous Creator, is that we have to value what he values and respect what he has allowed into being. We are to value life *because* of the Lord of life. And once we have begun to do this our anthropocentric horizons can be replaced by a theocentricity or 'God-centredness' in which we have to live each day in the realization that we are not the centre of all that is valuable. 'Where the love of God is verily perfected and the true spirit of government watchfully attended to,' wrote John Woolman in the seventeenth century, 'a tenderness toward all creatures made subject to us will be experienced, and a care felt in us that we do not lessen that sweetness of life in the animal creation which the great Creator intends for them.'[42] This insight is one that we have to learn afresh in each generation.

There are, however, powerful cultural as well as theological reactions which operate against the inclusion of other creatures as objects of value. The most important of these is the right perception that animals in their own violence and disorder represent the forces of the demonic. Sensitive humans who see the almost casual play of cats with their terrified victims or who witness the varied ways in which one species devours another, frequently respond by perceiving in other life forms the very moral evil in which humans themselves frequently excel. No wonder that we commonly use pejorative terms to describe other creatures whether human or non-human: 'animals', 'beasts' or even 'brutes'. One cannot help but be slightly bemused by the reference in the marriage service of the *Book of Common Prayer* to 'brute beasts that hath no understanding', since many mammals seem to know more about monogamous relationships than some *homo sapiens*. Even Walter Hilton, along with many other spiritual writers of his time, suggests that people who forsake God 'forshape themselves from the worthiness of man, and turn them[selves] into diverse beasts' likeness'.[43] When we are tempted to react in this way, we need to remember that animals as well as humans share the curse as well as the blessing of creation. Despite the extraordinary history of animals being made responsible for their 'misdeeds' before medieval courts, we should recognize that humans alone are properly responsible. In contrast to Hilton, the central point is that humans alone are free to reject God. There *may* be blessings, like mutual aid, even perhaps altruism among animals, but there are also very real curses, like suffering and predation, for which animals themselves are not responsible. It is perhaps for this reason that many biblical passages speak of the hope of future peaceful coexistence not only between humans but also between humans and animals, even between animals and animals. 'I will make a covenant on behalf of Israel *with the wild beasts*, the birds of the air, and the things that creep on the earth, and I will break bow and sword and weapon of war and sweep them off the earth,' says the Lord, 'so that *all living creatures* may lie down without fear.'[44] The biblical view seems to be that we most help the accursed creation by co-operating with God and therefore living together in peace.

Contemplating the Harmony

(iii) The attitude of 'letting be' is not to be understood as a sign of intending indifference to the world of creation. We have, as I

18

shall shortly expound, *active* responsibilities to animals in particular, but we can only find the right context of our activity if we have grasped the prior commandment to all life to be itself as it is, as God intended. Specifically and practically, creation can often only be itself if we surrender our hubris and meddling. There is of course a right use of power over creation and we do well to acknowledge that, but our first task has to be not to spoil what God has made. We 'should not spend the creatures on our lusts', writes George Fox. We should 'do good to them'. We must in this way express humility within the world of life. 'For nothing brought you into the world, nor nothing you shall take out of the world, but leave all creatures behind you as you found them'.[45] If we are to share the blessing of God for his world, we must begin by not making his blessing a curse. We turn the world against itself when we will not even let be that which works for good within the disordered creation we inhabit. If we cannot do good, at least we must refrain from harm. This minimalist implication is surely not enough, but if it is at times all of which we are capable, then so be it. If we cannot 'love all God's creation, the whole of it and every grain of sand'; if we cannot 'love the animals, love the plants, love everything' then at the very least, as Dostoyevsky claims, we must not 'trouble' creation: 'do not torture them, do not deprive them of their joy, do not go against God's intent'.[46]

Even this, of course, is no small matter. But it has to be the *attitude* with which we begin. But how far do we take it? As far as possible to all that lives. If there is to be a special case made out for animals, based in turn on their special relationship with God and ourselves, this must never be seen as a sign of the general unworth of creation. All that lives within creation has some kind of claim upon us. Cowper makes the point finely:

> I would not enter on my list of friends
> (Though graced with polish'd manners and fine sense
> Yet wanting sensibility) the man
> Who needlessly sets foot upon a worm.
> An inadvertent step may crush the snail
> That crawls at evening in the public path;
> But he that has humanity, forwarn'd,
> Will tread aside, and let the reptile live.[47]

And yet of course the kind of world, cursed as it is, in which we live does make it impossible to respect all kinds of life all the time. This point needs to be grasped at the outset. As Cowper himself accepts, a 'necessary act incurs no blame'.[48] What is defended here is that in general terms all blessed creation should evoke from us attitudes of respecting, valuing and letting be. But much more, and that more strongly, needs to be said in defence of animals and it is to this issue that we shortly turn.

Before we do, it is appropriate that we should link the spiritual attitude of 'letting be' with the long tradition of contemplation. Contemplation, in short, is the rejection of 'having', 'possessing' and 'claiming for oneself', in order to value what is given and experience a harmony with it. We sense God *through* the created order and rejoice as he rejoices. 'If you have heard the singing of the birds or the running of the stream, or the voices of the children as you came to church,' in the words of F. D. Maurice, 'then recollect that it was Christ who caused you to hear them.'[49] There is spiritual goodness as well as moral evil in creation. It is both glorious and bestial. We do ourselves no good if we shut our minds to the 'dearest freshness deep down things' which Gerard Manley Hopkins so eloquently describes. It is because the Holy Spirit 'over the bent world broods with warm breast'[50] that contemplation is such a rewarding experience. Creation thus signals the possibility of encounter with Creator. 'For I have learned to look on nature, not as in the hour of thoughtless youth', wrote William Wordsworth. Rather he has made a discovery, he speaks as one who has felt a 'presence that disturbs . . . with the joy of elevated thoughts'. And what is this discovery? Of nothing less than:

> A motion and a spirit, that impels
> All thinking things, all objects of all thought,
> And rolls through all things.[51]

Perhaps Thomas Merton was right. In a world of feverish activity and incessant desire for manipulation, contemplation of this kind can become a prophetic sign. 'We have more power at our disposal today than we have ever had', he writes, 'and yet we are more alienated and estranged from the inner ground of meaning and love than we have ever been'.[52] Not surprisingly he saw our destruction of the world of nature, and the use of animals in factory farming in particular, as a sign of 'the increasingly destructive and irrational behaviour of technological man'.[53] The task of letting creation be itself is thus part of the response of faith. Perhaps it is only when we have found ourselves as creatures of God that we can find enough inner self-confidence and freedom to allow other creatures similar freedom to be. The lesson seems to be that our future may depend as much upon our ability to be sensitive to what is given in creation as upon our capacity to manipulate and control it.

2 Dominion and Covenant

An Ambiguous Tradition

Despite the doctrine of God the Creator and the scattered concern for the non-human creation throughout the Christian tradition, there can be little doubt that the Christian religion is today deeply anthropocentric. Almost all preaching, teaching and moralizing centre on human beings and their relationship to God or to fellow humans. For the most part it has simply been assumed that God is not very much interested in anything else but the human species within the world he has made. It has frequently been assumed that humans have the pre-eminent place and that their position, intellectually and morally, gives them rights, even *absolute* rights over animals in particular.

'By divine providence', argues St Thomas Aquinas, animals 'are intended for man's use in the natural order', and hence 'it is not wrong for man to make use of them either by killing or in any way whatever'.[1] This scholastic position remains, as far as one can see, the official Catholic line. It still finds a voice in moral textbooks of all sorts, even those published as recently as 1960. Animals, it is said 'can claim nothing at our hands; into our hands they are absolutely delivered'.[2] But of course it is not only the Catholic tradition in its moral theology at least that gives animals the thumbs down. The Reformers, for all their rejection of the tradition, did not appear to question scholasticism in this regard. We sense with Calvin in particular a theology accommodating itself to preconceived notions. It is 'because we know that the universe was established especially for the sake of mankind, we ought to look for this purpose in his [God's] governance also'.[3] Luther appears to agree. After the Fall and the Flood 'the animals are subjected to man as to a tyrant who has absolute power over life and death'. But is this God's design? Yes, supposes Luther, indeed it is his 'gift', showing how God is 'favourably inclined and friendly towards man'.[4] Both these traditions so central to Western theology unite giving man a neo-despotic role in creation. Eastern theology, at least in some respects as we shall see, appears to fare better. But the comeuppance in the Western tradition is to be seen in the Reformed tradition where the theological giant of our time, Karl Barth, posits that the doctrine of creation means 'in practice anthropology, the study of man',[5] while for the Catholic tradition Pope Pius IX in the nineteenth century forbade the opening of an animal protection office in Rome on the basis that humans had no duties to animals.[6]

Faced with such powerful statements of unconcern by distinguished or authoritative exponents of the Christian faith, it is perhaps not surprising that many, concerned for animals, dismiss the tradition as irremediably 'speciesist' or even embrace one of the other currently feasible world-views on offer.[7] If they are hostile to Christianity, it is because, not without some justification, they assume that Christianity is hostile to their own moral insights. Peter Singer, among the leaders of the animal movement, is frequently dismissive of the Christian tradition. 'It is beyond dispute', he writes, 'that mainstream Christianity for its first 1,800 years, put non-human animals outside its sphere of concern.'[8] Richard Ryder writes of the 'whole Judeo-Christian tradition' as viewing animals 'principally or solely . . . as food, as clothing, as beasts of burden and as sacrificial victims'.[9] Maureen Duffy appears to agree.[10] While Lynn White Jr speaks of the Christian doctrine of creation as being responsible for 'the historical roots of our ecological crisis',[11] many an animal liberationist would go further and see the Christian Churches as agents of animal oppression.

But what people concerned for animals have to face is that for the most part, it is not that the Christian tradition has faced the question about animals and given unsatisfactory answers, rather it is that the question has never really been put. We do not have books devoted to a consideration of the theological significance of animals. We do not have clearly worked-out systematic views on animals. These are signs of the problem. The thinking, or at least the vast bulk of it, *has yet to be done*. Even Aquinas, Calvin and Luther work essentially in an *ad hoc* manner when it comes to animals. It is not the animal issue which is their sole or even

23

major concern in their writings and thus in almost all cases they cannot be said to have a worked-out position. It is easy, really too easy, to interpret the silence of the Christian tradition as indifference. Those guilty here include myself.[12] Of course there has been real indifference, but the more complete picture is different. While it is certainly true that some theological arguments, like the ones just outlined, are still used to justify cruelty and callousness, it must be remembered that almost all human thinking, secular, utilitarian, rationalist as well as Christian, has been guilty of what Mary Midgley calls 'the absolute dismissal' of the claims of animals.[13] When, therefore, Singer with some justification accuses Christianity of failing to grasp the moral status of animals, it has to be asked: Where prior to the modern period are the secular, rationalist philosophies which embrace animals? One or two doubtless, but not many. Atheism is as historically guilty as Christianity of perpetuating speciesism. Even today secularism, and utilitarian philosophy in particular, is hardly united in its defence of animals; indeed some would claim that humanistic utilitarianism is one of the main enemies of animal rights.[14]

In opposition to Singer, Ryder and Duffy, we must protest against the notion that Christianity has been uniquely or uniformly justifying of animal abuse. Much of the evidence is ambiguous and like so much in the Christian tradition points both ways. Attfield is surely right that the attempt to incriminate the whole tradition flies in the face of substantial evidence.[15] It is not my purpose, however, to whitewash the tradition and to pretend that powerful negative factors are not arrayed against animals from within. But it has to be asked: How within is within? Not all that is claimed for Christianity has the authenticity of the gospel. Discernment is essential. On the face of it much appears contradictory. Theologians have held that animals were made *both* for our use and *at the same time* for the glory of God. Theologians have commended vegetarianism *and also* justified carnivorousness. Theologians have spoken of respect for life *and also* justified some barbarism towards animals. There is clearly a potential minefield here, and it is entirely understandable, if erroneous, that some have concluded that there is no specifically Christian view of animals anyway. 'It is necessary for me to say something about the Christian attitude to the non-human,' writes Stephen Clark, and concludes in the following line: 'There isn't one.'[16] But it is surely too early to give up. After all, the present interest in the theology of liberation must be partly due to the slow and painful growth of Christian consciences concerning the iniquity of slavery and the equal rights of coloured people. The line attributed to William Temple deserves to be savoured: 'Theology is still in its infancy.'

This becomes most clear when we begin to analyse two of the biblical concepts that have largely influenced Christian thinking about creation: dominion and covenant.

Dominion or Despotism?

Earlier we referred to Aquinas' view about the place of humans and their absolute right over creation. This assumption, as we should properly call it, derives in fact from natural philosophy concerning the *order* of creation. We are able to 'observe' that 'the imperfect are for the use of the perfect', because 'the plants make use of the earth for their nourishment, and animals make use of plants, and man makes use of both plants and animals. Therefore it is in keeping with the order of nature, that man should be master over animals.'[17] This is Aquinas' *interpretation* of the meaning of dominion (*radah*) in Genesis. Without doubt, it is also the classical rendering of this verse. It is to be found almost everywhere in the Christian tradition. Centuries later, when writing of the enmity between man and mouse, Robert Burns exclaims: 'I'm truly sorry man's dominion/has broken nature's social union.'[18] Dominion means, in short, despotism or 'tyranny', as Luther suggests. But the difficulty with this line of interpretation, common and widespread though it has been throughout the Christian tradition, is that it conflicts with a great deal of scholarly evidence. Indeed, it would be difficult to find one reputable biblical scholar who now defends the traditional interpretation. Why is this? There seem to be three basic reasons.

In the first place, we misread the first saga if we fail to grasp the essentially *dependent* nature of man's lordship. God certainly gives man power over creation, to use it and even to control it. But it is out of keeping with the theology of the saga for man to have that absolute power which belongs necessarily to Yahweh alone. It is vital to understand the giving of dominion within the context of the making of man 'in God's image'.[19] To be like God is to share something of his prerogative but also his moral nature. 'Responsible authority is God-like,' summarizes C. F. D. Moule, and this is precisely the point.[20] When commentators like Aquinas and Luther go on to link man's prior position in creation with the intention of God to allow for the exercise of *absolute* power, they clearly lapse into error. Secondly, understanding the context is vital. As John Austin Baker has shown, what is being shaped in the saga is the early theology of kingship. Man is to be a king in creation. But this kingship was rather different from popular notions today. The king was to share the power of God but was strictly accountable to him. He was the one especially commissioned to maintain the kingdom (the reign) of peace and righteousness, that is, *God's* order, not his own. Man is thus determined to be 'God's perfect viceregent' in creation, 'under whom nature is fertile and peaceful and all she was meant to be'.[21] The point is nicely summarized by Gustaf Wingren: 'The more he [man] exercises dominion, the more he obeys',[22] Thirdly, for those who are still disposed to regard these further interpretations as sophistications, there is one crucial piece of internal evidence to account for. Subsequently in the saga, man is commanded to be a vegetarian. 'I give you all plants that bear seed everywhere on earth, and every tree bearing fruit which yields seed: they shall be yours for food.'[23] If what is presupposed by the giving of dominion is the exercise of absolute power, including life and death, as Aquinas suggests, it is surely extraordinary that this precise power should be subsequently denied. Keeping God's peace within creation and not harming life to the extent of not killing for food, indeed living off the superfluity of vegetable life, is hardly consonant with licensed 'tyranny'. Thus dominion, as John Austin Baker indicates, is 'poles apart from the kind of egotistical exploitation which it suggests to our ears'.[24] Indeed the care and harmony supposed by the first saga is rendered even more explicit in the second. Man is created specifically to look after creation, 'to till it and care for it'.[25] Again man's power is expressed by the way in which the animals come to him and he 'names them', but before too much is read into this verse, it should be remembered that man also names the woman with whom he is to live in harmony.[26]

And yet could it really be that for centuries the Christian Church has misunderstood its own Scripture? Those acquainted with the art of theology may well find it less difficult than others to answer in the affirmative here. The process of theological reflection is always dynamic, always moving towards a fuller realization, by the grace of the Holy Spirit, of biblical truth. In this process there can be steps backwards as well as forwards. It would be wrong to be too self-righteous about Aquinas. From his perspective what he was trying to work out was the nature of creation in the light of the truth that God has destined it for order rather than chaos. He thought it 'quite unreasonable' to suppose that the nature of animals was 'changed by man's sin'.[27] Thus in his actually quite radical rejection of classical theism in its doctrine of the cosmic Fall, he had little option but to suppose that the order as we now know it for animals was actually the order as purposed by God and therefore morally acceptable. But at a deeper level what brings Aquinas to his view more clearly than anything else is his insistence upon man's rationality 'which makes him like the angels'. In other words what we see in Aquinas, and in so many subsequent exponents of the Christian tradition, is the notion of the pre-eminence of the rational, human soul. 'Accordingly intellectual creatures are ruled by God,' he argues, 'as though he cared for them for their own sake, while other creatures are ruled as being directed to rational creatures'.[28] This view, taken over almost completely from Aristotle and Augustine, sees creation, not as in the biblical sagas as one of monarchy, but of hierarchy. Instead of the biblical picture of one divinely appointed steward for the rest, we have a rigid conception of order with animals and plants in a necessarily subordinate position. 'The truth seems to be', as Attfield postulates, 'that the tradition which holds that in God's eyes the non-human creation has no other value except in its instrumental value for mankind has Greek rather than Hebrew sources.'[29] Aquinas, then, for all his intellectual brilliance, leaves Christian theology with a bitter legacy. His influence is vast in many ways: the conception of hierarchy confuses the biblical notion of monarchy and gives animals a strongly subordinate status; the stress on soulfulness, and the division of creatures into rational and therefore incorporeal souls or otherwise, has led to a disparagement of the spiritual status of animals, in neglect of the biblical material; and last but not least, the view that what we do to animals need not be governed by moral constraints—all these helped support years of indifference and wantonness towards animal life. Here, if nowhere else, we learn the social and political significance of theology.

A Christological Challenge

But the most important question has yet to be posed. It is striking that for centuries Christians have taken the notion of dominion at its face value without asking the further crucial christological question: How, morally speaking, should we exercise our power over animals? Elsewhere I have tried to deal with this question in detail and I shall only summarize the essential point now.[30] If God wants us to share his lordship, what kind of lordship might this be? For Christians the question can only be answered in terms of Jesus Christ, the unique self-revelation of God. But what is revealed here in terms of the morality of the exercise of power? God's power is expressed in powerlessness, in condescension (*katabasis*), humility and sacrificial love. When it comes to wanting to know the attitude that Jesus may have taken to a range of pressing moral issues today, we are often at a loss to know precise answers. But we can at least be clear about the contours even if the details are missing. The lordship of Christ is expressed in service. He is the one who washes dirty feet, heals the sick, releases individuals from oppression, both spiritual and physical, feeds the hungry, and teaches his followers the way of costly loving. Whereas 'in the world the recognized leaders lord it over their subjects', it should not be so among his disciples: 'whoever wants to be great must be your servant, and whoever wants to be first must be the willing slave of all'.[31] Compassionate teaching can of course be paralleled elsewhere, but what is central to Jesus is that his life and his teaching are one. He expresses, is one with, indeed is inseparable from, the love of God. Now if this central thrust of the gospel is true, then we are surely faced with a challenge. If God's self-revealed life in Jesus is the model of how Christians should behave and if, crucially, divine power is expressed in service, how can we disregard even 'the least among us'? It may be that in the light of Christ we are bound to say that the weakest have in fact the greater claim upon us. In some ways Christian thinking is already orientated in this direction. What is it that so appals us about cruelty to children or oppression of the vulnerable, but that these things are moral betrayals of relationships of special care and special trust? Likewise, and even more so, in the case of animals who are mostly defenceless before us. Slowly but surely, having grasped that the notion of dominion means stewardship, we are now for the first time capable of seeing how demanding our lordship over creation is really meant to be. Where we once thought that we had the cheapest ride, we are now beginning to sense we may have the costliest responsibilities.

In sum: Jews and Christians have been right to point to man's God-given power over the non-human. Where they have been wrong in the past is in interpreting what this power means. If full weight is given to Christ as our moral exemplar, our power cannot be understood as legitimate except as service, which is necessarily costly and sacrificial. Lordship without service is indeed tyranny.

The Neglect of Covenant

When we turn to the notion of covenant (*berith*) on the other hand we face a different situation. Whereas the notion of dominion has been overplayed as regards the non-human, the insight of covenant has been considerably underplayed. The twin ideas of covenant and election and their importance for reformed theology are most massively focused for us in this century by Karl Barth. He takes as his major interpretive theme of all creation doctrine the covenant between man and God, which in turn relates to God's own election of the humanity of Christ within himself. According to the biblical witness 'the purpose and therefore the meaning of creation is to make possible the history of God's covenant with man', writes Barth, 'which has its beginning, its centre and its culmination in Jesus Christ'.[32] But what about the non-human? What part do they play in God's creative design? Barth agonizes and sometimes appears to offer positive explanations of their place. In general, however, he is emphatic that an agnostic response is preferable. 'We may entertain beautiful and pious thoughts . . . concerning the independent reality of animal and vegetable existence', he writes, but 'man is not addressed [by God] concerning animal and vegetable life, nor life in general, but concerning his own human life'.[33] In this way the biblical message of the covenant becomes anthropocentrically, or more accurately anthropomonistically, conceived. As regards the life, status and destiny of the non-human, we have to accept that these things are beyond human knowing. Animals are in some ways an 'enigma'.[34] Barth in his approach reflects the massively anthropomonistic theology that has dominated Christianity for centuries. Perhaps it is not surprising that Schweitzer likened the issue of animals in Western philosophy to a newly cleaned kitchen floor which had to face the muddy paws of the dog who comes in from the garden.[35]

And yet Barth's thought is all the more difficult and surprising because the biblical witness actually points in the opposite direction. 'I now make my covenant with you and your descendants after you', says the Lord after the Flood, and expressly includes 'with every living creature that is with you, all birds and cattle, all the wild animals with you on earth'.[36] This indication, and many others, of an inclusive covenant needs to be taken a great deal more seriously by scholars and theologians. Of course it is true that the major events recorded in Genesis onwards mainly concern human beings and their destiny. But it is surely a mistake to overlook these verses as though they convey nothing of divine purpose and intention.

But, what does it mean for other living beings to share the covenant relationship with human beings? In Barthian theology, covenant means nothing less than the election of God. God elects humanity within himself in the person of Jesus Christ. God becomes *one* with humanity. God is therefore the agent making possible both community and redemption. Can these things really be claimed for animals as well? Let us take the notions of community and redemption in turn.

Covenant as Community

In order to grasp how various biblical writers understand the inter-species community of humans and animals, we need first to understand that all life, *nephesh*, is a gift from God. It belongs to him alone. Even within the permissive tradition that allows killing for food, this *nephesh* may not be appropriated by man, because it belongs to God.[37] Humans clearly have some preeminence over all other forms of life because of their divine-like responsibility, but animals are not different kinds of life. They have of course differing forms, but it is the Spirit which is the basis of all life, however differentiated. Thus Barth is undoubtedly right that there is no biblical basis for denying 'soul' or 'spirit' to animals; quite the reverse.[38] There are a variety of ways in which this 'common life' of animals and humans is expressed: animals, for example, are classed with humans by their creation on the sixth day.[39] Animals too are blessed with the same blessing with which humans are blessed.[40] In this way, we have seen how both humans and animals are therefore subject to the same hope and judgement, that is, *both* are blessed and cursed and therefore *together* are subjects of divine judgement and mercy. 'On man and beast', says the Lord, 'my anger and my fury shall fall.'[41] This theological relatedness is given an explicitly christological interpretation by many New Testament writers. 'All that came to be was alive with his life,' writes John.[42] 'In him everything in heaven and on earth was created,' maintains Colossians.[43] Noah's ark has become the symbol of the view that we are all in one boat together, but it is also worth reminding ourselves that in 1 Peter, for example, the ark is also used as a type of the Church itself.[44] Edward Irving is one of the few systematic theologians who have seen the vital connection between the life of the world and the work of Christ. Speaking of the curse in Genesis, Irving understands death as 'execution of the sentence'. What then is life? 'Life we hold . . . [to be] the purchase of Christ's sacrifice made from the foundation of the world,' he writes. 'Whether you regard the life of any individual or the life of the race of men, or the life of animals,' he continues, 'it is all a fruit, a common fruit of redemption, a benefit of the death of Christ.'[45] What Irving seems to suggest here is that the process of transforming death into life involves the self-giving of Christ at every level of existence, indeed life at all levels is impossible without it.

The second point to grasp in interpreting the idea of covenant as community is the subsequent moral relatedness of man and animals. Because of the sense that all life had a common origin, it is not surprising that Hebrew law had various humane provisions about animals. 'When you see the ass of someone who hates you lying helpless under its load . . . you must give him a hand with it.'[46] Similarly, so that it can eat, the ox should not be muzzled 'while it is treading out the corn'.[47] On the Sabbath too, animals should not be worked, but allowed rest.[48] In general, animals are not to be used cruelly or exploited without any regard for their worth in the sight of God.[49] Even the cattle of Nineveh were of account to the Lord.[50] 'A righteous man cares for his beast,' says Proverbs, 'but a wicked man is cruel at heart.'[51] Rabbinic interpretations of verses from Deuteronomy forbade 'a person to partake of food unless he had first fed his animals'.[52] Now while it would be foolish to look to the Old Testament for a charter of animal rights, what can be clearly gleaned from these examples is that the human use of power must be subject to certain constraints for the sake of the animals themselves. What we see in Exodus and Deuteronomy especially is an emerging sense that some of those basic obligations owed to fellow humans should extend to animals as well. 'We should be prepared to show pity and mercy to all living creatures.' writes Maimonides, 'except when necessity demands the contrary.'[53]

The sense of moral community can be illustrated by the lives of many saints and poets. 'When he [St Francis] considered the primordial source of all things', writes St Bonaventure, 'he was filled with even more abundant piety, calling creatures no matter how small, by the name of brother or sister because he knew that they had the same source as himself'.[54] The crucial theological point here is that the Fatherhood of God enables us to see all other creatures as brothers and sisters. The notion of covenant always contained within itself the seed of this development. It is seen even more clearly in Eastern Orthodoxy, where 'awareness of man's cosmic vision has never been lost to sight, has never ceased to be an integral part of man's redemption'.[55] Because man is seen as a microcosm of the whole created order, his redemption signals the destiny of all created things.[56] 'Surely we ought to show kindness and gentleness to animals for many reasons', writes St Chrysostom, 'and chiefly because they are of the same origin as ourselves'.[57] We have yet to learn the necessary depth and subtlety of this covenanted fellow-feeling and empathy towards animals. Feelings of togetherness, even of love, however, must be distinguished from sentimental self-seeking love. It would indeed be a poor spirituality that excluded love for the non-human, but Christian love is best characterized by its altruistic nature. In other words we should love our fellow creatures not for our own sake but for their own. Robert

Browning clearly includes them within our most intimate relations:

> God made all the creatures and gave
> them our love and our fear,
> To give sign, we and they are His
> Children, one family here.[58]

Covenant as Redemption

Browning's reference to 'fear' brings us appropriately to the second implication of covenant, namely redemption. The relationship of enmity between humans and animals is sometimes assumed to be the meaning of the covenant for the non-human after the Flood.[59] And there can be little doubt that the situation subsequent upon the Flood makes grim reading. 'The fear and dread of you shall fall upon . . . everything that moves upon the ground.'[60] But in this it is difficult not to see Genesis depicting the state of general enmity which still persists within creation subject to the Fall of man himself. Moreover, the subsequent covenant promised in Hosea offers release from these conditions of fear both within and between species.[61] In this way many passages in the Old Testament speak of a return to Eden. It is as if the early Hebrews saw the violence and disorder present within creation and knew that such a state of affairs could not under God's providence remain forever. There just had to be a better kind of world. When the messianic age dawns not only will 'the leopard lie down with the kid' and the 'calf and the young lion . . . grow up together', but quite precisely:

> They shall not hurt or destroy in all my holy mountain;
> for as the waters fill the sea,
> so shall the land be filled with the knowledge of the Lord.[62]

For many New Testament writers the covenant becomes embodied in Jesus Christ, whose work of reconciliation extends to all things. The 'hidden purpose' of God in Christ was 'determined beforehand'. It consists in nothing less than the bringing of 'all in heaven and on earth' into 'a unity in Christ'.[63] Notice how here in Ephesians, as with Colossians and Romans, creation is in some mysterious way foreordained and elected in Christ. We shall discuss elsewhere the sacrifice of Christ which makes the new covenant possible, but at this point we need only to grasp that its design is wholly inclusive and thus continues the deeply cherished Jewish hope of restoration.

And yet it is surely extraordinary that this message of cosmic redemption should have been so sorely eclipsed by centuries of Christian theology. 'Christ', writes St Athanasius, is 'the Saviour of the Universe'.[64] For modern theology, however, the dominant, if not exclusive, concern has been for human beings. Indeed Hans Küng seems to represent anthropocentricity at its narrowest when he claims an absolute identification of God's will with human welfare.[65] We do well, however, to recognize that God the Creator, Reconciler and Redeemer has interests and goals beyond the human species. We are after all only one of millions of species which God has created. 'Shatter, my God,' writes Teilhard de Chardin in a moment of protest, 'through the daring of your revelation the childishly timid outlook that can conceive of nothing greater or more vital in the world than the pitiable perfection of our human organism.'[66]

Perhaps the strongest reason why anthropocentric theology has maintained such a hold on doctrine is due to the central belief in the incarnation. It is commonly thought that the incarnation is God's special 'Yes' to human beings, and in Barth's words the expression of an eternal decree that the 'Logos did not will to be an angel or animal but man'.[67] But it is surely extraordinary to understand God's 'Yes' to man as 'No' to creation. There may well be good grounds for seeing in the particular election of one man, Jesus Christ, the focus of divine activity and therefore the unique and central place of humans in the cosmos. But since the *ousia* assumed in the incarnation is the *ousia* of all creaturely being, it is difficult to resist the conclusion that what is effected in the incarnation for man is likewise effected for the rest of the non-human creation. In accord with Ephesians, Robert South explains that the purpose of incarnation was 'to cancel the essential distances of things, to remove the bounds of nature, to bring Heaven and Earth, and (what is more) both ends of the contradiction, together'.[68] If this is true, we have good grounds for affirming the incarnation as God's 'Yes' to materiality, to nature and to non-human species in particular.

And yet there is some sense in which the massive concentration on man within the Christian tradition can be justified. Since it is through man's curse that the creation has become estranged from its Creator, it is only right that one important step along the road to recovery and wholeness is that man himself should be redeemed. The salvation of human beings is in this way a pointer to the salvation of all creation. Almost certainly, however, we should go further than this. For it must be the special role of humans within God's creation to hasten the very process of redemption, by the power of the Spirit, for which God has destined it. T. F. Torrance writes perceptively of man's 'task to *save* the natural order through remedial and integrative activity, bringing back order where there is disorder and restoring peace where there is disharmony'.[69] There is a danger here of course that we ascribe *too much* power to humans to save creation. It is the Christian view that nothing much can be achieved without the inspiration and activity of the Holy Spirit. But in the light of its history the question that must be posed for moral theology is whether we have allowed *enough* for the Holy Spirit and man's co-operative effort in the work of peace-making. To this question we shall shortly turn.

The question may be raised: What kind of redemption are we to hope for concerning the non-human creation? The general answer is given by F. D. Maurice when he writes that 'as we hope for ourselves, so we hope for all those creatures who not for their own fault have been made subject to misery and death, who are not sinful as we have been'. He argues that death cannot be lord of any creature since death 'did not make them', and that he who has made them is 'stronger than death'.[70] In this way we return to our opening insistence that life itself is a gift from God. It belongs to him alone, and for all the time of our mortal pilgrimage together we do well to remember that set in fellowship with the non-human, we await the world that is to come. For unless the many classical voices are to be set aside, we must conclude that the world as we now know it is not the only possible world. God as Holy Trinity—Father, Son and Holy Spirit—is not yet finished with creation and is always moving it on to new possibilities of renewal and redemption. 'In his way to union with God,' writes Lossky, 'man in no way leaves creatures aside, but gathers together in his love the whole cosmos disordered by sin, that it may at last be transfigured by grace.'[71] Human beings must be healed because it is *their* violence and disorder which has been let loose on the world. Through humans, liberated for God, we can glimpse the possibility of world redemption. Can it really be so difficult to grasp that the God who performs the demanding and costly task of redeeming sinful man, will not also be able to restore the involuntary animal creation which groans under the weight of another's burden?

Animal Souls

And yet some will surely question: Can animal souls become Christian doctrine? It is worth reminding ourselves that Aquinas never denied the existence of animal souls as such. Indeed all living beings, vegetable and animal as well as human, were thought of as possessing 'souls'. Aquinas, however, differentiated between different *kinds* of souls: 'vegetative' for vegetables, 'sensitive' ones for animals, and 'rational', incorporeal souls for human beings. Hence rationality becomes the all-important factor in determining our immortal soulfulness, a faculty which Aquinas denied to the non-human.[72] There are a variety of ways in which one can take issue with Aquinas here. In the first place it is by no means clear that animals lack rationality altogether and certainly many higher mammals show goal-directed activity.[73] Secondly, one can surely question the biblical basis for this scholastic view. For where in the Bible are we given the necessary information concerning these vital distinctions between different forms of life? The evidence, if it is there in the biblical material, is at best indirect, based largely upon assumptions relating to the giving of the divine image in man. Both these criticisms can take us some way and I have certainly used one or more of them at some time or another.[74] But the really important objection to Aquinas' position, it now seems to me, consists in taking issue with the philosophical view which it entails, namely that rationality is the key to spiritual status. In this Aquinas simply takes over the tradition already inaugurated by Aristotle and Augustine, but whether it is fully mainstream Christian doctrine is open to serious doubt. According to this view, intelligent existence is *real* existence. 'Those who believe that man's chief and highest end is to glorify God and fully enjoy him for ever', writes Alec White-house, 'are frequently disposed to treat as fully actual, and to envisage as finally actual, only what is incorporated into the activity of rational agents'.[75] These people, not unfairly described by Whitehouse as 'aristocrats of the mind' are 'unwilling to be comfortably or uncomfortably at home along with the world's minerals, vegetables and animals'.[76] Physicality is at best an encumbrance and at worst a threat. Spiritual existence, now and forever, exists in transcendence from the world of matter rather than in its renewal and redemption.

This approach, deeply embedded though it is within much popular Christianity, is desperately difficult to reconcile with the biblical notion of world-embracing redemption. For this reason alone it should be treated with some reserve, but more precisely it conflicts at heart with the doctrine of God the Creator. It leads inevitably, and has led historically, to the disparagement of materiality and in particular of the worth of non-human animals. If therefore the question is asked: Should we adopt animals as soul-bearers within this particular world-view?—the answer must be negative. We shall not serve animals well by trying to secure for them a place even within an enormously popular, but at heart deeply erroneous world-view. To my mind all claims for incorporeal soulfulness, human or animal, detract from God the Creator and have the danger of telescoping the work of the Spirit in creation into the fusing of individual souls. It is worth reminding ourselves, for example, of the humbling speculation of Ecclesiastes:

> For the fate of the sons of men and the fate of beasts is the same; as one dies, so dies the other. They all have the same breath, and man has no advantage over the beasts; for all is vanity. All go to one place; all are from the dust, and all turn to dust again.[77]

Notice here that it is the 'same breath' of the Spirit which unites man and animals in covenant fellowship. Whatever hope there might be for a future life for humans applies equally to animal life as well.

It is in *this sense*, and this strictly, that we can affirm (to use past language) 'animal souls', though preferably we should speak of 'animal redemption'. We affirm the hope of future life for animals as we affirm that the Spirit is the basis of their breath; we affirm the necessity of redemption as we ponder with the biblical writers how it is that God's moral goodness will triumph over moral evil. 'If there is any sentient being which suffers pain, that being', writes Keith Ward, 'must find that pain transfigured by a greater joy'.[78] It is quite impossible to posit a *loving* Creator who allows the life he has created, loved and sustained to be thrown away as worthless. 'Immortality, for animals as well as humans, is a necessary condition of any acceptable theodicy', concludes Ward.[79]

Perhaps the best exposition of this view is found in the sermon on 'The General Deliverance' by John Wesley. In good scriptural fashion he links the present bondage of creation with the all-pervading influence of man's fall from grace—an influence, it should be noted, which actually extends to cutting off divine communication to animals. Will creation remain in this condition? 'God forbid that we should affirm this', replies Wesley. He particularly stresses the need for a deliverance that will give to animals 'the vigour, strength, and swiftness which they had at their creation, but to a far higher degree of each than they ever enjoyed'.[80] It is important that we see, however, that this divine providence does not bypass man in the sense that he can leave everything in God's hands. To suppose this would invoke forsaking the biblical notion that man has a special commission on earth. He is the surrogate king who in obedience to the Lord of all must pursue, by the spirit of true kingship, the unfolding reign of peace and love which is breaking into the world and which comes to special focus in the work of Christ. We shall return to the particulars of this commission shortly.

And yet we cannot suppose that the nature of this hope is not such as to impose upon humans a burden of perception. It could be that one of the really important challenges that the Christian faith has to present to the world is the need for the recovery of hope that we can really bring about by God's Spirit a world-embracing redemption. This is indeed a *demanding* perception, requiring that we adapt the world to a view of God rather than adapting God to our view of the world, which so often happens in liberal theology today. No person knew better the demands of this hope than Alfred Tennyson, who wrestled with Christian revelation in the light of the discoveries in his own day which pointed to the *disorder* as well as order present in creation:

> Oh yet we trust that somehow good
> Will be the final goal of ill,

To pangs of nature, sins of will,
Defects of doubt, and taints of blood;

That nothing walks with aimless feet;
That not one life shall be destroy'd,
Or cast as rubbish to the void,
When God hath made the pile complete.[81]

3 Sacrifice and Peace

We have seen how difficult it is for Christians to look at the world as it now is and not hope for a better one. Creation, while still the object of the Creator's love, is radically estranged from him. Because of this, creation itself frequently becomes the focus of both love and fear. It represents to us the order that now is as well as the order which could yet be. Something has 'to give' as we say; or more precisely something had to be given in order that wholeness and redemption might be possible. The world cries out for redemption, but how shall this redemption be secured? Grappling with this question requires us to consider two further biblical themes: sacrifice and peace.

The Rationale of Sacrifice

Understanding animal sacrifice (*zebach*) in the Old Testament is notoriously difficult. Why is it that Noah's first response to God after the Flood consists in taking 'clean' (that is, non-carnivorous) animals and offering them as 'burnt offerings'? What is meant by God 'smelling' (that is, literally breathing in) these 'pleasing odours'? And why is it that this response leads God to the reversing of his curse and the promise that he will never again 'destroy *every living creature* [animals as well as humans] as I have done'?[1] At first sight, the practice is surely paradoxical: God is seen to delight in the gratuitous destruction of the creatures he has made. Doubtless for many centuries this has been the dominant, popular view. Animals are there seen as simply expendable as signs of human penitence. According to this view, sacrifice consists almost entirely in the death of the subject, indeed it is the slaying nature of sacrifice that most characterizes it. And yet this view is obviously open to all kinds of difficulties. For if the *destruction* of life is the core of sacrifice, how can God *receive* what is offered? If death is the end of animal life, what is there to offer? Moreover, why (in this particular instance at least) does the offering of sacrifice lead to the establishment of blessing for all living creatures both human and animal? The only way forward in grappling with the rationale of the practice of sacrifice has to be to move away from the simple equation of sacrifice with the infliction of death.

'In modern discussions of the significance of Old Testament sacrifices', writes Frances Young, 'it is frequently claimed that the animal victim died as a substitute for the offerer.' And yet as Young shows this idea is 'unfounded'. The central issue is whether the essential feature of the act of sacrifice 'was the death of the victim or the offering of lifeblood'.[2] But what did it mean to offer lifeblood (*nephesh*) to the Creator? First of all, it meant that all life was a gift from God and therefore belonged to him. Secondly, the act of return to the Creator was probably understood (by those who practised it) as the offering of life. Thirdly, and perhaps most importantly, the practice of sacrifice thereby assumed that the life of the individual animal continued beyond mortal death. In these ways it is possible to understand the historic practice of sacrifice as affirming the value of the individuals slain and not simply as their gratuitous destruction. The tradition of sacrifice did not *necessarily* involve a low view of animal life.

And yet it would not be fair to the Jewish tradition to suppose that the practice did not pass without objection and protest. 'What to me is the multitude of your sacrifices?' says the Lord in Isaiah. 'I have had enough of burnt offerings of rams and the fat of fed beasts; I do not delight in the blood of bulls, or of lambs, or of he-goats.'[3] What the Lord requires is not substitutionary sacrifice but the exercise of justice. 'The prophets stressed the uselessness of the sacrificial system without moral virtues', writes Young, 'and the superiority of justice, mercy and love to all forms of material offering.'[4] Although it is true that much of this criticism is directed against the corresponding lack of justice or against the efficacy of the sacrifices themselves, it is surely puzzling that this same tradition, which was so vastly indebted to the practice, could also indulge in such severe criticism of it. Young shows that there is a developing moral critique from Deuteronomy to the Prophets which is reflected in the Psalms as in later Wisdom literature. In particular there also grew up the powerful notion that innocent human suffering during persecution was a means of atonement and thus that the proper sacrificial victim was 'a servant of God without moral blemish'.[5] Before we reach the time of Christ, there are strong signs that, under the weight of widespread criticism, the sacrificial system was beginning to wane. 'So it was that Judaism was able to develop from a religion in which sacrifice played a most important part to a religion in which sacrifice had no place'.[6]

The Challenge of Jesus

It is only in the light of this that we can see both the continuity and the challenge of Jesus. Whatever the justification for animal sacrifices, the Christian Church effectively abolished them. In this it is difficult not to see the hand of Jesus. Few scholars have reflected, for example, on the radical significance for the animals themselves of the well-known incident concerning the cleansing of the temple of 'those who sold pigeons' and by implication all those who traded animals in the temple precincts.[7] When it is combined with the later passage in Mark concerning the ineffectiveness of sacrifice,[8] we are able to see Jesus as expressing the continuity of moral protest illustrated so well by the prophets themselves. Moreover, there is no hint in the Gospels of Jesus' support for the practice of sacrifice itself; neither he nor his disciples practised it. In this, and the subsequent theology of sacrifice, Jesus clearly posed a radical challenge to the tradition. Although sacrifice was arguably on the wane, the advent of the followers of Jesus was to hasten the decline of an already questionable practice. It is surely tragic in this regard that the one major monotheistic religion which has grown up since Christianity, namely Islam, should have inherited a disagreeable aspect of historical Judaism, namely a sacrificial practice which modern Judaism as well as Christianity has rejected.[9]

The challenge of Jesus, however, is deeper than simply the rejection of animal sacrifice, important though that is. Christians came to see Jesus alone as the true form of sacrifice acceptable to God. 'He entered once for all into the Holy Place, taking not the blood of goats and calves but his own blood, thus securing an eternal redemption'.[10] I have written elsewhere concerning the significance of Christian sacrifice,[11] and there is need only to reiterate two fundamental points here. The first is that the offering of Jesus is not simply that of blood, so as to suppose that

God is appeased either by the simple giving of lifeblood, animal or human. Rather what is offered in Jesus is the giving of what lifeblood signifies, namely the whole of life itself. In Christian conceptions of sacrifice we move, as with later Jewish tradition, from exclusive focus on blood to the sacrifice of justice and especially love. Christian sacrifice is characterized by its emphasis on the free, loving offering of God the Son to God the Father. We are not dealing here with an angry God who desires to overrule the wishes of his Son, but the free offering of life as required by love itself. Notice also, how in orthodox theology it is God who sacrifices himself for us and thereby secures the redemption which humans can barely approximate. The Trinity is for Christians that community of sacrifice within which the marks of suffering remain and through which *all* suffering can be transformed by joy. Edith Sitwell gives this point imaginative expression when she pictures the 'Christ that each day, each night, nails there' in our suffering world and how 'He bears in his Heart all wounds'.[12]

The second point to grasp about Christian sacrifice is that it involves the sacrifice of the higher for the lower and not the reverse. Not only is sacrifice to be freely chosen rather than imposed, but also it is they who have much who are to give to those who have little. Or to be more precisely theological, the omnipotence and power of God are expressed through condescension (*katabasis*) and powerlessness. 'Have this mind among yourselves, which is yours in Christ Jesus, who, though he was in the form of God, did not count equality with God a thing to be grasped, but emptied himself, taking the form of a servant'.[13] So fundamental was this idea to the followers of Jesus, that selfcostly loving rather than simply being a pattern to admire became the model to emulate, indeed the one true model of Christian discipleship. In this way the disciples of Jesus 'filled out' his suffering by themselves becoming 'a living sacrifice' which was to be their new form of 'spiritual worship'.[14]

The Sacrifice of Love

Thus Christian faith was born in the realization that God himself had become our sacrifice in Christ and that in following his way of loving service a new kind of redemption was made possible for the world. In all kinds of ways, Christians are still grappling with what this kind of loving sacrifice must mean for them in the world today. But for the most part, if not the exclusive part, Christians still conceive this service in narrow anthropocentric terms. To some degree this was inevitable since humans themselves sorely need redemption, and perhaps without it cannot even begin to embrace a wider vision. And yet as Victor Hugo wrote we 'must also be civilized towards Nature'.[15] The radical challenge to current Christian notions of sacrifice is that they have been too sharply drawn and are far too forgetful of the 'least among us'. We do well to remember that animals are frequently the most vulnerable, defenceless and weak among us. We use our power over them in ways that illustrate that we have not grasped the radical spirit of Christian sacrifice. We think of them as existing for us, whereas it seems to me that the truer, scriptural notion is that we are made for them. It is our task to sacrifice ourselves not for our own sake but for the will of him who seeks to unite all things in himself.

While dogmatic theology has been slow to extend the spirit of Christian sacrifice to animals, there are signs that this insight has not been lost within the saintly tradition. Frequently hagiographers are bemused by the 'antics' of even celebrated saints who go out of their way to express concern for the non-human, 'preaching the Gospel to them', celebrating their gift of life and being scrupulous even in the smallest matters where their life and well-being are concerned. This 'wildness' and 'folly' gave St Francis of Assisi 'a profound rapport with all living things'.[16] As in their own day, these 'fools for Christ' are apt to be despised and ridiculed, and many today who care for animals are similarly despised. But who can deny that these 'fools' preserve for us an essential element of the gospel of sacrificial love? The moral point is aptly put by Austin Farrer. 'If Jesus is willing to be in us, and to let us show him to the world, it's a small thing that we should endure being fools for Christ's sake'.[17] Happily this 'folly' is still enjoined today in the Principles of the Society of St Francis. They are to follow Christ 'in the way of renunciation and sacrifice' and by so doing exemplify loving service to the world. Moreover, they 'must remember that they follow the Son of Man' who 'loved the birds and the flowers', and particularly 'They will rejoice in God's world and all its beauty and its living creatures, calling nothing common or unclean.'[18] In this the Christian tradition has much to learn from the modern-day followers of St Francis. The recent signs of concern among them for the lost tradition of cosmic awareness and the welfare of animals in particular should be heeded.[19]

And yet St Francis was not the first, and certainly not the last, Christian saint to recognize the spiritual unity of all God's creatures and to befriend them. Several of the Georgian saints, for example, many hundreds of years before Francis, were distinguished by their love of animals. 'St John Zedazneli made friends with bears near his hermitage' and 'St Shio employed an obliging but rather inefficient wolf to guide the donkeys which brought supplies to his lonely grotto'.[20] In particular, the stories of St David of Garesja and his protection of deer and birds from the hunters of his day abound with moral protest. 'He whom I believe in and worship looks after and feeds all his creatures, to whom He has given birth,'[21] is his reply to those who wish to kill them. The early Celtic saints too, who lived in Ireland, Wales, Cornwall and Brittany in the fifth and sixth centuries after Christ, showed extraordinary consideration to animals, not only befriending them, but also praying for them and healing them of injury.[22]

The point to be grasped from the saintly tradition is that to love animals is not sentimentality (as we now know it) but true spirituality. Of course there can be vain, self-seeking loving, but to go (sometimes literally) out of our way to help animals, to expend effort to secure their protection and to feel with them their suffering and to be moved by it—these are surely signs of spiritual greatness. Such, at least, is the verdict of countless numbers of story-tellers and sages within Christendom. We do well to listen to them if our present vision of God's Kingdom is not to be severely diminished. Moreover, it is worth recollecting how for many saints the exercise of Christian loving towards the non-human creatures was an intensely practical affair. There is no general romanticizing over the state of the world, only an enhanced and deepened awareness of God the giver of all life. 'Are you not also creatures created by my God?' asked St Catherine of Genoa of living things in her garden. 'Are not you, too, obedient to Him?'[23] The Christian tradition can, at best, liberate people from a desperately imprisoning narrowness of moral vision. The decisive question is not: What can such and such a thing do for me? but rather: What further goodness does the Creator of all require of me? Arguably, it is the Christian founders of the RSPCA, people like William Wilberforce, Richard Martin and Arthur Broome, who are the moral heirs of St Francis. The first 'Prospectus' of the Society, published in 1824, begins by asking questions of which St Francis would surely have approved: 'Is the moral circle perfect so long as any power of doing good remains? Or can the infliction of cruelty on any being which the Almighty has endued with feelings of pain and pleasure, consist with genuine and true benevolence?'[24] Benevolence, as I go on to show, is not enough. But it is surely the point at which we ought to begin. Benevolence, or in modern language generosity, is one proper response to a generous Creator.

In sum: Jews were not wrong to look at sacrifice as the means of moral reparation in a world lost and fallen. However awful the practice of animal sacrifice, it at least pointed in the right direction. The sacrifice of the true paschal lamb, however, not only abolishes the need for animal sacrifice but also, and crucially, offers a new understanding of sacrifice itself. In the self-costly giving of Christ we have the pattern of living for those who follow him. What Christians have yet to learn is how costly and inclusive this sacrificial loving must be. The least among us should have the greater claim. Even, and especially, the animals are to become our 'brothers' and 'sisters' in Christ.

The Prince of Peace

We now turn to our next biblical theme, namely peace (*shalom*). Peace, as we have seen, should have been established by the institution of the covenant. Peace is both a gift from God, a sign of his blessing, and also inseparable from the covenant relationship itself. And yet the early Hebrews knew that while they spoke of peace, 'there was no peace'.[25] Accordingly they were neither pacifists nor vegetarians. This does not mean that the taking of any life, human or animal, was a small or insignificant matter, indeed quite the reverse. The taking of human life could only be justified in special circumstances, and the slaughter of animals for food required special justification. Thus after the Fall and the Flood, animal life may be taken for food, only if the *nephesh*, the lifeblood, was drained and thereby returned to God. For humans had no right to take the actual life of an animal, because it did not belong to them but to God alone.[26] Moreover, all killing for food, except in this way and in obedience to this command, was judged unlawful. 'Only after the Fall and the Flood were human beings authorized to eat flesh,' writes Attfield, 'as if the society which transmitted and edited the Genesis narratives was uneasy about meat-eating and sensed that special justification was needed.'[27] Thus Old Testament attitudes have a remarkable tension and ambiguity when it comes to killing for food. On the one hand such things could not possibly be compatible with the perfect designs of an omnipotent Creator, but, on the other, living in a fallen world required some kind of concession, some accommodation to the needs of sustenance and survival.

Even the Prince of Peace himself appears to acquiesce in the need for killing. Jesus certainly ate fish and possibly meat, depending upon the view taken of the Last Supper and whether it was a 'Passover meal' in the Jewish tradition.[28] It is certainly possible that John the Baptist was a vegetarian, but as Clark points out, Jesus' disciples did not fast like those of John the Baptist.[29] Some have claimed Jesus as an ascetic, or even as an Essene,[30] but the evidence points firmly in the other direction. Some animal societies in America have argued that Jesus must have been a vegetarian in order to fulfil Old Testament prophecies like this one from Isaiah: 'Behold a virgin shall conceive, and bear a son, and his name shall be called Emmanuel. He shall eat butter and honey, that he may know to refuse evil, and to choose the good.'[31] But it is difficult not to interpret this argument, in the light of the gospel records as a whole, as wish-fulfilment. However, we do face the problem that much of what Jesus might have said about animals is simply not recorded in the New Testament. This has frequently led to the view that Jesus was indifferent to animals and cared nothing for them. This view, too, is unsupportable. Such evidence as we do have indicates that Jesus upholds the basic Jewish attitude that the created order is God's work and is therefore essentially good. Indeed John Austin Baker goes so far as to suggest that the parables of Jesus encourage 'care and concern for animals'.[32] It certainly seems that Jesus endorses as right the breaking of the Sabbath for animals that must be fed and watered or for the seeking of lost sheep that otherwise would surely perish.[33] But there is clearly a

47

danger in extrapolating from New Testament texts anything other than the clear intention of the author; in both cases the issue in dispute is Sabbath observance and not animal welfare. Likewise there is something ludicrous in Augustine, for example, claiming that the incident concerning the Gadarene swine shows how Jesus felt about pigs:

> Christ Himself shows that to refrain from the killing of animals and the destroying of plants is the height of superstition for, judging that there are no common rights between us and the beasts and trees, he sent the devils into a herd of swine and with a curse withered the tree on which he found no fruit.[34]

In his far-fetched interpretation, it is difficult not to see Augustine supporting his already existing view that there are no common rights between humans and beasts. The point is that Jesus does not *send* the demons into the pigs; demons by their very nature prey upon the defenceless, whether humans or animals. We have to face the fact that when it comes to determining Jesus' actual attitude to animals, in the records as we now have them at least, we have to work largely from hints and guesses. But these are on the whole certainly more positive than negative. The rejecting attitude towards animal sacrifices is, I judge, far more significant than most scholars have so far allowed. But also the well-known sayings concerning sparrows,[35] in an age when they were certainly sold for less than a penny, surely underlines the fact that they do have value to God. In this at least, and the comparison between Solomon and the glory of the created world,[36] we do have Jesus' support for the idea that 'God's providential care extends even to the most insignificant animals'.[37] Attfield goes so far as to suggest that the Johannine verse concerning the *good* shepherd laying down his life for the sheep 'must have influenced its readers' attitudes to actual flocks as well as to the pastoral care of Christ for his followers'.[38] Whatever the likelihood of this, it does seem in keeping with the whole outlook of Jesus that the demands of shepherding should be seen as actually more costly than was frequently supposed.

The Kingdom of Peace

In a number of striking ways, the New Testament continues and develops the hope of the Old concerning the ultimate peace of creation itself. Melchizedek, who is seen as a type of Christ, in Hebrews is 'king of Salem' that is, 'king of peace'.[39] There are surely hints of the universal peace that is supposed to accompany the advent of the Messiah in the birth narrative of Luke, where he is described as the one who guides 'our feet into the way of peace'.[40] Again in the Beatitudes in Matthew, the 'peacemakers' have an esteemed place as 'sons of God'.[41] Moreover, the work of reconciliation promised in Colossians has peace as its aim through the blood of the cross.[42] But this peace which is received by faith in Christ Jesus is a peace which we have to manifest in our lives. 'If possible,' writes St Paul, 'so far as it depends upon you, live peaceably with all'.[43] In these ways the New Testament writers continue the same kind of proleptic vision of the Kingdom: it is here now as a possibility and yet it must be worked at through discipline and perseverance. The connection in Christ is that he inaugurates living in peace as the present possibility of the future which is yet to come.

In reply to a question concerning the Kingdom of peace, Donald Soper replied that while Christ was neither a teetotaller nor a vegetarian, 'I think probably, if He were here today, He would be both.'[44] There may be grounds for thinking that Jesus would regard vegetarianism as more serious than teetotalism, but in any case Soper's reply focuses for Christians the difficulty in living between two worlds, or more precisely between two kingdoms. For to be committed to Jesus involves being committed not only to his earthly ministry in the past but also to his living Spirit in whose power new possibilities are being continually opened up for us in the present. All things have yet to be made new in Christ and we have yet to become perfect as our Father in heaven is perfect. Making peace (*shalam*) is a dynamic possibility through the power of the Spirit. When it comes to formulating moral judgements in our own day, we need to take as our authority the whole nature and character of God as revealed in Christ and in the work of the Holy Spirit. We do not have from Jesus the detailed prescriptions which we would like, perhaps erroneously, to possess. Christ did not legislate on animals, or for that matter on many other moral issues either. John Habgood tells us of the 'popular misconception, especially apparent among people who write angry letters to bishops, that the teaching of Jesus was simple'. 'In fact he very rarely gave a straight answer to a straight question.'[45] This means that for the most part, and animal welfare should be included in this area, we have no alternative but to work out our own salvation and that of the redemption of all creation too, in the power of the Spirit but with fear and trembling. There are no prepacked answers to detailed questions from the life of Jesus currently available.

Making Peace with Creation

And yet despite the fact that the creation is ambiguous and that the witness of Scripture is often less explicit than we would like it to be, and despite the fact that Christian insights cannot easily be turned without injustice into moral maxims, nevertheless there is one thing of which we can be sure. It is, as Stanley Hauerwas puts it, that 'nonviolence is not just one implication among others that can be drawn from our Christian beliefs', rather 'it is at the very heart of our understanding of God'.[46] At the heart of our understanding because God has made it comprehensible in Christ. The way of sacrificial loving, of living for others—in short, peace rather than violence—is pre-eminently the Christian way. There may well be, and frequently are, disagreements among Christians as to the limits and possibilities of living such a kind of life in the world as we now know it. Christians are always entitled to say that the world constrains the fullest realization of any moral imperative. But Christians should never say that this world as it is, is all that we have to contend with and that God is satisfied that we stay as we are. For creation is a dynamic entity; it belongs to a dynamic God who has not yet finished with his creation. If we cannot see it whole, one reason has to be that it is not *yet* whole. Trinitarian theology necessarily holds before us the possibility of a world which is in the process of being made. Even if we have grasped something of the work accomplished in Christ, we have yet to have the vision of what is to be achieved by the Holy Spirit. Hauerwas is right when he insists that the Church 'must learn time and time again that its task is not to *make* the world the kingdom, but to be faithful to the kingdom by showing to the world what it means to be a community of peace'.[47] In this way the Church has to be seen to be faithful to the gospel of peace which it has inherited, and what is more, to the Spirit of peace in our own time. Alas, Hauerwas fails to see that living in peace extends beyond human frontiers, indeed that it is especially the work of the Spirit to witness to a new *world* order and to encourage us to make peace wherever there is discord within *all* creation. For the work begun in Christ has yet to be completed. 'For the creation waits with eager longing for the revealing of the sons of God', writes St Paul.[48] How can there be peace for the human creation, in our hearts or in our communities, while the non-human creation is mortgaged to violence? Brother Ramon makes the vision clear:

> The whole creation groans in pain
> Travails in birth and burdened sore . . .
> Awaiting consummation's hour—
> Christ's healing and transforming power.
>
> So men of God are drawn to prayer
> By the indwelling Spirit's call
> And men of faith and love arise
> Reversing thus the cosmic fall;
> Redeeming man's aridity,
> Renewing earth's fertility.[49]

We need to consider how far we are *now* capable by the power of the Spirit of living free of violence and making peace with creation.

4 The Claims of Animals

The Religious Debate about Animals

The history of animal welfare, or rather the lack of it, makes grim reading. It is astonishing that just over 150 years ago, people in Britain, as now in many other countries, could do whatever they wished to animals without any legal constraints at all. In London as late as the 1850s 'it was no unusual happening for a horse to be beaten to death'.[1] Not only were bull-baiting, bear-baiting and cock-fighting prevalent in town and country but also arranged fights between dogs and cats, or dogs and monkeys were common. 'Cattle, sheep and pigs brought to London for slaughter were killed in underground cellars, the sheep being literally thrown out of the carts, where the animals lay bruised and injured for days at a time.'[2] Calves, pigs and other animals were killed by slow methods, especially bleeding to death. Arabella's advice to Jude in Thomas Hardy's famous novel makes this clear: 'the meat must be well bled and to do that he must die slow . . . I was brought up to it and I know. Every good butcher keeps un bleeding long. He ought to be up till eight or ten minutes dying, at least.'[3] The first ever attempt at legislation was made in 1800 when Sir William Pulteney sponsored a Bill to outlaw bull-baiting on the grounds that the practice was 'cruel and inhuman'. It failed narrowly in the division by two votes. Commenting on its failure, *The Times* was adamant that the attempt was misconceived since 'whatever meddles with private personal disposition of a man's time is tyranny direct'.[4] Twenty-two years had to pass before Richard Martin's limited Bill to prevent the cruel treatment of cattle was finally given royal assent. It was the first Act of its kind passed by any parliament.[5] People are frequently apt to forget how painfully slow has been the progress of reforming animal legislation—a process, of course, that is by no means complete and which faced then as now fierce opposition and frequent ridicule. In particular, the first inspectors of the SPCA had regularly to face threats and intimations of violence and it appears that these have continued well into this century.[6]

Although it has to be acknowledged that many Christians were on the side of the status quo, it is remarkable that so many Christians opposed the common cruelty of their time. 'Clerical denunciations of brutality to beasts' writes James Turner, 'flowed on unabated in what had become a routine'.[7]Some of the most influential Christians of the eighteenth and nineteenth centuries opposed cruelty and lent their support to various humane movements. Among these William Wilberforce and Lord Shaftesbury have a special place. 'To delight in torture and pain of other creatures', argued Shaftesbury, 'is wholly and absolutely unnatural, as it is horrid and miserable.'[8] Many preachers joined the ranks of one of the largest and most influential protest groups of the age. The Clapham Sect held that bull-baiting 'fostered every bad and barbarous principle of our nature'.[9] The moral revulsion at pain inflicted on animals is reflected in a whole range of publications, books, tracts and leaflets, published from the seventeenth century onwards.[10] Queen Victoria herself wrote: 'No Civilization is complete which does not include the dumb and the defenceless of God's creatures within the sphere of charity and mercy.'[11] Indeed royal support and patronage helped the then SPCA, founded in 1824, to gain increasing acceptance. It is surely significant that, though for mixed motives, the new Society could adopt a declaration in 1832 that its proceedings 'are entirely based on the Christian Faith and on Christian Principles'.[12] There were important signs then that a minority of Christians at least had come to see that man's treatment of animals was a matter of moral concern.

And yet it is also clear that the early debate about animals was dominated by a whole range of specifically religious justifications for animal abuse. These justifications divide broadly into five categories: (i) they 'belong to us' or are 'our property'; (ii) the non-human 'have no souls'; (iii) animals are violent and frequently cruel to each other; (iv) they cannot feel pain; and last but not least (v) animals have no rights. For well over a century, and in some cases until the present day, these arguments have carried weight, sometimes considerable influence, and we do well to consider them.

Animals as Human Property

The story is told of how Lord Erskine, one of the pioneers of animal welfare legislation, remonstrated with a horse-beater on Hampstead Heath only to be met with the reply: 'Can't I do what I like with my own?'[13] The question illustrates a widely held moral position in the eighteenth century. Animals, it was assumed, had no independent moral standing. Whatever claims they had could be completely subsumed under human interests. In short: animals were human property, and when bought they had no independent claim against their owners. The rights of owners were absolute. Thus the first legislation in 1822 was specifically passed 'more with the intention of safeguarding animals as property rather than protecting them from suffering'.[14] The animals in question were domestic horses, oxen and cattle, and the Act was directed against those 'having the care or custody' of them in order to meet the argument that those who owned animals (as distinct from those who had to look after them) should be free of legal constraints as far as their welfare was concerned.[15]

The argument may not appear at first to be a specifically religious one. And yet Catholic moral textbooks until the present day speak of how we 'have no duties of justice or charity' towards animals, only 'duties concerning them and the right use we make of them'.[16] The right of humans to use animals is almost absolute, qualified only by the condition that wanton cruelty to animals which may encourage cruelty to humans should be avoided. Animals are frequently listed under 'human property' in the textbooks. The moral question only arose in so far as humans use their property in an unjust way—for example, by infringing the rights of other humans. It is difficult not to see a theological underpinning of human interests here in the way in which animal life is so subjugated to human needs. This tradition, however, antedates the eighteenth century; what we see in debates in this period is the use of a previous theological prescription to justify current abuse. The 'argument' from property had become, not an *argument* at all, but an inherited social *assumption*. The assumption does not involve the holder in any necessary debate about animals. Rather it simply refuses to accept that animals have any claims that should be debated. In this way, moral discussion is simply precluded from the outset. It has to be said that what characterizes many of the early parliamentary debates about animals is precisely this absence of moral argument, at least as we sometimes understand it today.[17]

Can anything be said in favour of this assumption? As an interpretation of Genesis, as we have seen (pp. 25–8), it is simply mistaken. What characterizes the biblical material, both Old and New, is the contrary view that all life, human and animal, belongs to God. Even within the 'permissive' tradition that allows animals to be killed for food, there is no assumption that animals should be viewed simply as human property, as appendages to human interests, or indeed that humans should have absolute rights over them. If God is the Creator of all, it must follow, in a primary and decisive sense, that everything created belongs to him alone. He alone *owns* them. How then are we to understand the Catholic attitude in this regard at least? One clue is given in the strikingly odd suggestion found in Catholic textbooks to the effect that animals are not directly created by God. Hence even in this century, *A Catholic Dictionary* of 1924 holds that the lower creation are 'not created by God, but . . . derived with their bodies from their parents by natural generation'.[18] This, of course, is an absurdity. It results from an exaggerated interpretation of the so-called special creation of man in Genesis 2, and a neglect of the fact that humans, like animals, are created from the dust of the ground and that the Spirit is the basis of life in both cases. In this way, extraordinary as it appears, it is possible to argue that animals do not belong to God because God did not, directly or indirectly, create them. Whether this position arises from a specific desire to subordinate or relegate the claims of animals is difficult to know. But what is certain is that the suggestion that animals are not, like us, creatures of God, indeed fellow creatures in his world, undoubtedly weakens their status and makes the case against abuse infinitely weaker.

It is difficult not to hope that the Catholic tradition will amend and reform itself in this matter.[19] But since the textbooks go on, generation after generation, repeating the same line about humans having no duties to animals, except in an indirect sense as property, we cannot at present be sanguine. It is terribly difficult not to convict Catholic tradition in this regard of moral culpability. More important, however, than trying to apportion blame is that Christians now see the force of the insight that animals do not belong to human beings. To believe in God the Creator of all necessarily involves positing that 'in him *all* things were created, in heaven and on earth, visible and invisible, whether thrones or dominions or principalities or authorities—*all* things were created *through* him and *for* him'.[20]

The Soulless Non-Human

The suggestion that animals might have immortal souls was rejected by one seventeenth-century preacher as an 'offensive absurdity'. 'The life of a beast', said another, was 'long enough for a beast-like life'.[21] This view, supported at least in part by Aristotle, Augustine and also by Aquinas, remained the dominant view in the eighteenth century and with only minor, although important, objectors until the present.[22] It is perhaps worth noting, however, that something like the same question could be posed concerning women. Aquinas, for example, held that 'in a secondary sense the image of God is found in man, and not in woman; for man is the beginning and end of woman'.[23] Aquinas here was concerned with the right ordering of creation and yet the suspicion that women were 'near the animal state', as Keith Thomas indicates, has persisted throughout the tradition. Some preachers went as far as to expound it,[24] and George Fox apparently met a group of people who believed that women had 'no souls, no more than a goose'.[25]

The parallel may not be quite as frivolous as it appears. The cases of women and animals have at least one thing in common: low spiritual status has led to low moral status. And this of course has been the implicit argument used with great effect throughout Christian centuries to deny animals proper moral status. In short: 'they have no souls' implies that they are not worthy subjects of moral concern. As we have seen, however, it is by no means clear that immortal souls in the traditional sense can with sufficiency be denied to animals. There are good reasons for questioning not only the scholastic framework in which immortality is denied animals but also the biblical basis for the whole notion of immaterial souls.

But let us suppose for a moment that it could be shown that animals lack immortal souls, does it follow that their moral status is correspondingly weakened? It is difficult to see in what sense it could be. If animals are not to be recompensed with an eternal life, how much more difficult must it be to justify their temporal sufferings? If, for an animal, this life is all that he can have, the moral gravity of any premature termination is thereby increased rather than lessened. The argument was succinctly put by Humphry Primatt as early as 1834. Humans, he says, have hope of a future life. But

> what *hope* is there to support and comfort the brutes under their affliction? They are incapable of *hope*, because they can neither reflect nor foresee. The present moment is an eternity to them. All their happiness is in this life only; they have neither thought nor hope of another. *Therefore, when they are miserable, their misery is the more insupportable.*[26]

This argument, and the similar one advanced by C. S. Lewis,[27] seems unanswerable. At a deeper level both may be seen as pointing to the greater difficulties inherent in justifying animal pain in contrast to the infliction of human pain. In the first place, animals cannot *choose* to sacrifice themselves. *Every* case of cruelty is necessarily an act of coercion. Humans can choose to suffer for worthy goals, even sometimes for unworthy ones, but in either case it is, or rather can be, an act of chosen sacrifice. When it comes to animals, that choice being lacking necessarily points to the greater difficulty in justifying it. Secondly, as Brigid Brophy indicates, animal suffering can never be softened by an intellectual appreciation of the circumstances. The animal in question necessarily suffers 'the raw terror of not comprehending what is being done to it'.[28] Since we may suppose that an animal lives closer in some respects to its own instincts than many humans now do, any interference with its life, unless done with regard to that animal's ultimate interest or benefit, necessarily violates its life in a way that constitutes greater harm than in the case of human beings. These important differences concerning the justifiability of inflicting pain or deprivation on animals need constantly to be borne in mind. They necessarily act against any all-too-easy defence of animal pain by those who want to inflict it for their own however high-minded purposes.

In short: if we invoke the traditional argument against animals based on soullessness, we are not exonerated from the need for proper moral justification. Indeed, if the traditional view is upheld, the question has to be: How far can any proposed aim justify to the animal concerned what would seem to be a *greater* deprivation or injury than if the same were inflicted on a human being?

Warfare Among the Non-Human

We turn now to the third argument that animals themselves are violent and frequently cruel to each other. Once again we are not really dealing with an argument, but with an assumption. The assumption, simply put, is that nature is inherently violent, and that to extend human compassion to it is to import human values into an amoral system. By doing this we make ourselves foolish.

This assumption crucially hinges upon our perception of nature and animals in particular. Our very use of language to describe animals, as we have seen, betrays our bias. We sometimes think of humans as well as animals as 'brutes', 'beasts', 'dumb animals' or even as 'bestial'. 'Animal insults remain a feature of human discourse today', argues Thomas. But he reminds us that 'they have lost the force they possessed in an age when beasts enjoyed no claim to moral consideration'. 'For to describe a man as a beast was to imply that he should be treated as such.' What Thomas shows is how, as more accurate information became available, the low perceptions of animal life, as reflected in language, themselves began to change.[29] We now know that while animals kill, they are seldom indiscriminate killers. Moreover they are rarely in our terms 'cruel'—how can they be if they are truly amoral?[30]

And yet there is no getting away from it, animals do not live wholly at peace with other animals. Nature is a predatory system. And however *we* accept the need for other species to eat and survive, for the species being eaten it is another matter. Harry Williams says that his favourite verse from the Psalms is: 'The lions roaring after their prey do seek their meat from God,' but wryly comments, 'I wonder what appeal it would have for me if I myself or somebody I loved dearly were the meat.'[31]

How then are we to account for this violence in the natural world? Brigid Brophy, writing as a non-Christian, calls it the 'Darwinist's dilemma' or, less grandly, a 'conundrum'. If she locks up her cat in order to feed pigeons in safety, is she behaving 'condescendingly' to the cat species? Is she setting up a barrier of 'moral superiority'?[32] Brophy rightly says we must accept this moral responsibility as actually part of our superiority. But it is difficult to see how in either naturalistic or Darwinian terms violence within the natural order presents a *moral* problem. If there is no God, no moral source of the universe as we know it, violence is not a problem to be sorted out, it is simply a fact to be accommodated. Strictly speaking, violence in the natural world can only be a moral problem for those who believe in God. Frankly speaking, the difficulty for Christians is how to reconcile a loving, holy Creator with a created world that operates a parasitical system with suffering and pain as an inherent feature of it.

It is not surprising, therefore, that some Christians have despaired of trying to make moral sense of the natural world. If God allows such suffering, why should he be concerned about it? There are plenty of answers to the problem of suffering in the Christian tradition, but few of them very satisfying. 'Some Church Fathers held that the various orders of creatures in the world corresponded to various degrees of perfection and imperfection. Origen, for example, held that all creatures were originally created equal and free but received their present status "as rewards or punishments for the manner in which they used their free will". Thus "as befits the degree of [the individual soul's] fall into evil, it is clothed with the body of this or that irrational animal".'[33] In this way beastliness becomes the actual penalty for misuse of free will. Such a view gives us a revealing insight into the low view of animal life held at least at one point in church history. What it lacks in compassion for animals is made up by ingenious theophysical speculation.

Some more contemporary Christians have met the problem by simply denying that God is concerned with pain in the animal creation. They take as their starting-point the prevalence of pain within the natural order as revealed by the natural sciences and offer theological justification for it. Far from being an evil, argues Andrew Elphinstone, pain is actually a 'companion to the very earliest biological ventures into life' and is the raw material for our spiritual journey to newer and greater heights of maturity.[34] According to Peter Geach, God shows 'mere indifference to the pain that the elaborate interlocking teleologies of life involve'. The Creator does not possess 'the virtue of sympathy' with suffering animals.[35] However intractable the problem of pain, we cannot help but view these voices as theological retreats from the issue in question. They meet the 'facts' as their authors think them to be in the natural world at the expense of the doctrine of a loving, holy God, for belief in such a morally outrageous deity would surely itself be immoral.

But is there a moral answer to the question about animal suffering? How can we hold that God is in some sense responsible for the world as it is and also hold that animal suffering is an evil? The question when posed in this way is not substantially different from the same kind of question that may be asked concerning human beings and their own suffering. The issue, sharply put, is not, Why is there animal pain, suffering and misery? but, Why is there any pain at all? The Christian answer to the problem about animals' pain can therefore only be of the same kind as to *all* questions of pain and suffering. And the Christian answer in substance is this: In Christ, God has borne our sufferings, actually entered into them in the flesh so that we may be liberated from them (and all pain and all death) and secure, by his grace, eternal redemption. In principle, the question of how an almighty, loving God can allow suffering in a mouse is no different to the same question that may be posed about man. Of course there are important differences between men and mice, but there are no morally relevant ones when it comes to pain and suffering. It is for this reason alone that we need to hold fast to those cosmic strands of the biblical material which speak of the inclusive nature of Christ's sacrifice and redeeming work. Again, poets and imaginative artists seem able to understand this vision in a way that frequently eludes the dogmatic theologian. Joseph Plunkett, born in 1887 and executed after the Easter Week Rising in 1916, illustrates the sentiment well:

> I see His blood upon the rose
> And in the stars the glory of His eyes,
> His body gleams amid eternal snows,
> His tears fall from the skies.
>
> I see His face in every flower;
> The thunder and the singing of the birds

Are but His voice—and carven by His power
Rocks are His written words.

All pathways by His feet are worn,
His strong heart stirs the ever-beating sea,
His crown of thorns is twined with every thorn,
His cross is every tree.[36]

To hold this imaginative vision of Christ suffering all pain and all disorder in the universe is not to lapse into the formal heresy of patripassianism—the notion that God the Father *eternally* suffers in his Son.[37] Rather, all that needs to be claimed is that in his incarnation, passion and death, Christ takes to himself all suffering and disorder wherever it is present and thus saves all creation from itself. By taking flesh, *all* flesh is assumed and thus redeemed. St John of the Cross makes the point forcefully. By 'uniting Himself with man, he united Himself with the nature of them all'. The sheer profundity of his thought is expressed in this line: 'To behold [all creatures] and find them very good was to make them very good in the Word, His Son.'[38] It is the anthropomonistic notion that God in Christ only cares for humans—and nothing for the sparrows or the birds of the air or the beasts of the field—that compounds our difficulty when it comes to unravelling the mystery of animal pain.

And yet some will surely question: Why should pain be inherent in the *structures* of the world as we know it? Parasitism is after all no irregular feature of creaturely life; rather it seems almost essential to it. But there is no answer to this question if the biblical tradition concerning fallen creation is to be completely eschewed. It is surely for Darwinian animal rightists to answer the question: How can one defend the rights of animals in a creation that does not admit of them? For the Christian, however, the world of nature *cannot* simply be read as a moral textbook. According to classical Christianity all creation is fallen, not just the human species but all structures of all life are fundamentally at variance with the designs of the Creator. Now this perspective does not furnish us with any ready-made explanations of how it all came to be, save that human wickedness involves the whole creation of which humans are a part, and that there is a connection between human sin and creaturely corruption.[39] Christians are free to adopt, revise or reject some or even all of the currently fashionable world-views on offer, including the one most currently in favour that God works *through* evolution, moving it by the Spirit to new peaks of spiritual possibility. All that is vital is that Christians do not eclipse the possibilities for the non-human creation by insisting that while God can transform human existence, he is sadly incapable of doing the same to animal existence. We simply must not put limits on what are the 'unfathomable riches of Christ'. We do not know precisely how God in Christ will restore each and every creature. But we must hold fast to the reality witnessed in Christ that our creaturely life is unfinished reality—that God is not yet finished with us.

Animals as Automata

We now turn to our fourth objection, that animals are not sentient (understood as the capacity to experience pain) and are therefore incapable of suffering. We have assumed throughout our discussion so far that animals do indeed feel pain, but however well-founded we now think this assumption to be, it is not one that has been self-evident throughout the tradition. While in the Old and New Testaments there is no suggestion that animals do not feel pain as we do, scholastic theology, in its clear emphasis upon the lack of rationality in animals, paved the way for the Cartesian view that animals had insufficient self-consciousness to experience suffering. According to Descartes, animals 'act naturally and mechanically like a clock which tells the time better than our own judgement does'. Although he admits that their bodily organs are 'not very different from ours', animals have no mind; they are devoid of reason.[40] And if we ask how we can know this, the answer, as with the previous arguments, is theological: Animals have no rational *soul*. Descartes' discussion is a classic piece of *a priori* theological speculation stemming from the idea that only humans possess immaterial, rational souls. And, of course, if one accepts the exclusive link between human rationality and soulfulness on one hand, and the experience of consciousness and pain on the other, his conclusion is entirely logical. This argument has served a number of different needs within the tradition. In the first place, it has helped theologians make the special, if not exclusive, claims for human nature which many feel almost instinctively are right. It is surely only a small step from the notion that man is made in God's image to the question: In what faculties or capacities does this 'image' manifest itself? Once one has begun along this route, the Cartesian argument has much appeal. Indeed much theological discussion since Darwin has been laboriously concerned with ways in which we can establish the special uniqueness of human beings *over and against* animals, to the detriment of other insights like common creation and blessing. Descartes has to be seen within a tradition that seems sometimes to have taken upon itself the role of defending human superiority in almost any way and with almost any kind of argument. This is not to suggest that an important case cannot be made for human superiority, especially in the matter of moral sense. But what we witness in Karl Barth, for example, is someone going to quite extraordinary lengths to defend even naturalistic arguments beyond their possible theological utility.[41]

In the second place, Cartesian scholasticism has enabled Christian theology to answer our previous question concerning theodicy: that is, explaining God's will in relation to the suffering non-human creation. The explanation, put simply, is that since suffering, pain and misery in all levels of existence below man are nothing more than idle anthropomorphic projections, there is no moral case to answer. If, to take a case in point, Descartes was right that 'when swallows come in spring, they operate like clocks',[42] it can hardly be a moral question if we choose to take their eggs, wreck their nests or shoot them down in flight. We may *think* that we do wrong, but they cannot be wronged in this way, because they do not *think* (and consequently experience pain). 'There is no *prejudice*', writes Descartes, 'to which we are all more accustomed from our earliest years than the belief that dumb animals think.'[43] We do not know whether Descartes specifically thought that by dispensing with pain and suffering in the animal world he was vindicating God from a potential charge of injustice or indifference. But what is clear is that Descartes has provided grounds for many subsequent apologists in the tradition who want to deny animal pain for various reasons, and in this way supported the suspicion, which is still common, that animals 'don't really feel things like us'.

If we look at this century alone, we can find serious echoes of

Cartesian thought about animals. C. E. Raven, sometime Professor of Divinity at Cambridge and a biologist by training, was highly reticent about the possibility of animal pain. He wrote in 1927 that 'it may be doubted whether there is any real pain without a frontal cortex, a foreplan in mind, and a love which can put itself in the place of another; and these are attributes of humanity'.[44] Illtyd Trethowan could conclude in 1954 that 'beasts do not suffer as we do'. In any case 'we know too little about their psychology for it to present us with any real problem'.[45] As late as 1966 we still find theologians repeating what Descartes said, even in spite of the emergence of considerable biological evidence to the contrary. F. van Steenbergen suggests, in another work, that we are the 'victims of a serious illusion' when we interpret animal cries as expressions of pain. 'It appears to me', he writes, 'that an examination of instinctive animal behaviour reveals a very interesting, and indeed very mysterious, psychism, but one that is devoid of any consciousness of any kind.' The problem of animal suffering is therefore an empty one, since 'unconscious suffering' is a contradiction in terms.[46] It is perhaps not surprising that A. R. Kingston concludes that 'with few noble exceptions theologians have done far more to discourage than to stimulate a concern for the lower creatures', and also: 'British theodicy, although not formally denying animal suffering, has often virtually done so by reducing its intensity almost to zero.'[47]

Is there an answer to this Cartesian objection to animal welfare? The first and most obvious one is biological. The *Animals and Ethics* committee (of which I was a member) comprising biologists, veterinarians and theologians reviewed the evidence about pain and came down strongly on the side of those who argue that animal pain differs only *in degree* from human pain. In the case of the lower invertebrate animals like the cockroach, worm and slug it 'becomes difficult and finally impossible' to assess whatever pain, if any, they may experience.[48] We simply do not know. But when it comes to the higher vertebrate animals which are warm-blooded, such as birds, whales, mice, and all the large land animals, there can be no real doubt. Indeed the Report argued that 'we find a vast amount of evidence that animals can suffer from stresses such as anxiety, boredom, discomfort, frustration and fear'.[49] These views, far from being contentious, can be claimed as the current consensus among biologists. Perhaps we should be grateful to scientists that at least in this area they have shown theologians the folly of their ways. It is significant that one of the most influential of the contemporary exponents of Cartesian dualism, namely H. D. Lewis, quite explicitly repudiates Descartes when it comes to his view of animal consciousness. 'We have to ascribe intelligence of some kind to brutes', he writes, and therefore assume some mind/body duality in these creatures too:

> I do not think anyone can seriously question the basis of this argument. The oddity is that anyone should have thought that a purely physical or mechanistic account could be given of the lives of brutes ... None of this need be questioned for a moment, and if Descartes himself did question it, that was more a concession to the prevailing views about the material world in his day.[50]

The second answer is theological. It is simply not possible to extrapolate from the biblical material the notion that God wished to create man as an *entirely* different form of life. We have already reviewed in brief the evidence for this view. To recapitulate: Genesis posits what may be termed greater and lesser circles of intimacy with God, and therefore greater and lesser degrees of spiritual freedom, but there is no absolute dividing line between man and beast. Both are created in the same way and similarly blessed. This seems to me of enormous significance. Spirit (*ruach*) is the basis of all living, breathing, blood-filled beings in a specific way that is true of man and which cannot be denied to other species. Thus life, *nephesh* itself, is not just an individual gift but a common possession by virtue of the fact that it is given to all. And yet there are circles of closer intimacy. In this way, we are right to judge that those beings closer to us have spiritual potentiality similar to our own. I would even go further and be open to the possibility that the gift of the Spirit in animals may be such as to allow in *some* respects for greater spiritual awareness than humans and for even greater cognizance of pain. To affirm this is not to deny man's central place in creation as the microcosm of the Spirit, but it is to question whether we have to affirm humankind as the sole possessors of each and every kind of spiritual possibility. Indeed, it could be that since some creatures have not fallen in the direct way in which man has done, that some residual potential in them may yet be actualized by the Holy Spirit. St Basil the Great indicates something like this when he argues that through the Spirit 'paradise is restored'. 'We can observe as in a glass, the beauty of the goods stored up for us in the future but now anticipated in faith as though they were already here'. But if this is true of the 'first-fruits' of the Spirit given to man, how much more is this to be true of the whole creation 'groaning in travail' and also awaiting its 'adoption as sons'? It would be wrong to understand the Spirit as simply the bearer of life without also characterizing this same Spirit as active within creation, actualizing its potential for perfection. 'If the earnest is such,' asks St Basil, 'what must the perfect thing be?'[51]

The charge then against Descartes, and especially his followers, is that in their quest to uphold human soulfulness and spirituality, they have plunged non-human creation into greater materiality and, in some cases, simple misery. According to J. P. Mahaffy, the Port-Royalists 'kicked about their dogs and dissected their cats without mercy, laughing at any compassion for them, and calling their screams the noise of breaking machinery'.[52] In utter contrast, it would seem more biblical and considerably more compassionate to see the non-human creation as infused at all levels, and especially when in communion with man at a greater level, with the power of the Spirit. This means all living creatures should be seen as participating in spiritual becoming, spiritual communion and awaiting spiritual consummation. 'The whole creation prays,' writes Tertullian:

> Cattle and wild beasts pray, and bend their knees, and in coming forth from their stalls and lairs look up to heaven, their mouths not idle, making the spirit move in their fashion. Moreover the birds taking flight lift themselves up to heaven and instead of hands, spread out the cross of their wings, while saying something which may be supposed to be a prayer.[53]

Before moving to the remaining question concerning animal rights, we should perhaps note the nature of these objections. Many of them are not, strictly speaking, *Christian* objections at all, at least in the sense that they derive from considerations drawn from Christian revelation. As C. W. Hume points out, the language of incorporeal souls and the emphasis upon humans alone as the possessors of self-consciousness and rationality are undoubtedly Hellenistic.[54] Now it would be a mistake to suppose that Hellenistic categories have no place in Christian theology, or that the business of theology can now be conducted without any reference to them, but the issue that has to be posed is this: Must the Christian understanding of animals be so vastly determined by those elements which are by and large essentially foreign to its gospel? If we put the question in this sharp way, we shall also be able to see how it is that Christian theology has yet properly to begin its own task of formulating a Christian view of animals based on Scripture and tradition as well as reason. For the most part, the real work of developing an adequate theology of animals has yet to begin.

5 The Theos-Rights of Animals

The Rightless Non-Human

For Catholic theology, steeped as it is in scholasticism, animals have no moral status. If we have any duties to them, they are indirect, owing to some human interest involved. Animals are not rational like human beings and therefore cannot possess immortal souls. Even the most hard-boiled scholastic would now probably admit that animals feel *some* pain but, if so, their pain is not regarded as morally relevant or truly analogous to human pain. In consequence, animals have no rights. 'Zoophilists often lose sight of the end for which animals, irrational creatures were created by God, viz., the service and use of man,' argues the *Dictionary of Moral Theology*. 'In fact, Catholic moral doctrine teaches that animals have no rights on the part of man.'[1]

It is in this context that we have to understand the present discussion, both philosophical and theological, about animal rights. It is the persistence of scholastic Catholicism which inevitably makes rights the issue it is. When one considers the wealth of positive insight and prescription within the Christian tradition about animals, it is surely disconcerting that these negative influences should have held, and continue to hold, such prominence. The issue of animal rights is not some concession to secular thinking within theological circles but simply the latest stage of a debate that began hundreds of years ago. John Foster, writing in 1856 (against William Wyndham's opposition to early animal welfare legislation), complains of our being taught 'from our very infancy, that the pleasurable and painful sensations of animals are not worth our care; that it is not of the smallest consequence what they are made to suffer, so that they are not rendered less serviceable to us by their suffering . . . that in short they have *no rights* as sentient beings, existing for their own sakes as well as for ours'.[2] If today people concerned for animals prefer

68

the term 'animal rights' to 'animal lovers' or 'animal welfare', they are, consciously or unconsciously, linking themselves to a historic debate which is by no means concluded. It is not without significance that the 'National Catholic Society for Animal Welfare' in the United States has now become the 'International Society for Animal Rights'.[3] And yet Christians are sometimes uneasy with talk of rights, and sometimes for good reasons. What meaning can rights for animals have in a strictly theological context? I offer this three-point definition of what I shall call the 'theos'—(literally 'God') rights of animals. To affirm animals as possessors of rights means:

   (i) that God as Creator has rights in his creation;
  (ii) that Spirit-filled, breathing creatures, composed of flesh and blood, are subjects of inherent value to God; and
 (iii) that these animals can make an objective moral claim which is nothing less than God's claim upon us.

What this definition means will become clear as we consider some of the arguments commonly presented against rights—first against the existence of rights for any creature, then more specifically against non-human rights.

Arguments Against Rights

(a) Rights language is untheological

At first sight this argument appears strong. In an absolute or even relative sense creatures cannot, whatever other rights they may have, have rights *against* their Creator. 'Will what is moulded say to its moulder, "Why have you made me thus?"' argues St Paul. 'Has the potter no right over the clay, to make out of the same lump one vessel for beauty and another for menial use?'[4] St Paul's analogy here is hardly sufficient. Human beings are not simply lumps of clay, but psychosomatic entities infused with God's Spirit and uniquely capable of responding to him. But the point remains: God alone in the end has absolute sovereignty and therefore absolute rights. For if God is indeed the Creator of all things, all might, majesty, glory and power belong to him and him alone by right. Some Christians, powerfully convinced of divine sovereignty, prefer then to have no truck with any talk of rights, being so awfully conscious of the distinction between Creator and created that they can only feel a necessary diffidence and reserve about *all* moral claims for creation. Such a view must surely be respected, and it certainly serves an important function of reminding Christians that creation is not ours to do with as we like and that we do well to walk humbly within it. 'Creation is grace: a statement at which we should like best to pause in reverence, fear and gratitude,' writes Karl Barth. 'God does not grudge the existence of the reality distinct from Himself; He does not grudge it its own reality, nature and freedom.'[5] The view that always and consistently contends against *any* rights, animal or human, will always have some appeal to Christians.

But does it follow at the outset that this insistence upon God's prior right in creation necessarily rules out all talk of creaturely rights? As Dietrich Bonhoeffer shows, exactly the reverse may be the case. Perhaps it is more theological, not less, to speak of rights rather than duties, not because humans have rights against their Creator (for strictly speaking there can be none) but *because* God has rights in his creation. Bonhoeffer's argument is so relevant to our discussion that it deserves to be read in full:

> To idealistic thinkers it may seem out of place for a Christian ethic to speak first of rights and only later of duties. But our authority is not Kant; it is the Holy Scripture, and it is precisely for that reason that we must speak first of the rights of natural life, in other words of what is given to life, and only later of what is demanded of life. God gives before He demands. And indeed in the rights of natural life it is not to the creature that honour is given, but to the Creator. It is the abundance of His gifts that is acknowledged. There is no right before God, but the natural, purely as what is given, becomes the right in relation to man. The rights of natural life are in the midst of the fallen world the reflected splendour of the glory of God's creation. They are not primarily something that man can sue for in his own interest, but they are something which is guaranteed by God Himself. The duties, on the other hand, derive from the rights themselves, as tasks are implied by gifts. They are implicit in the rights. Within the framework of the natural life, therefore, we in every case speak first of the rights and then of the duties, for by so doing, in the natural life too, we are allowing the gospel to have its way.[6]

As far as I can see, Bonhoeffer was only intending to speak here of the rights of natural, *human* life. It seems that animals have not yet found their proper place in Bonhoeffer's theology.[7] And yet without any injustice to his argument it is possible, even consistent, to apply these arguments to the wider field of animal–human relationships. If 'The rights of natural life are in the midst of the *fallen world* the reflected splendour of the glory of God's *creation*'[8] it is difficult to see how only the human species can be properly envisaged here. We note two things about Bonhoeffer's argument. The first is that it involves emphasizing the priority of God's right in creation. It does not posit inherent natural rights independent of God's sovereignty, quite the reverse. By doing so it focuses attention upon God's very gift of creation and his own determination to guarantee what he has given. Secondly, the dynamic of rights flows quite specifically from what God gives and not, for example, from what 'man can sue for in his own interest'. In these ways the concerns about the priority and sovereignty of God previously enumerated are entirely met. In other words what Bonhoeffer provides is a basis for what I term the 'theos-rights' of animals. We are justified in claiming rights for them and for ourselves in the context of God's right to have what he has given honoured and respected.

From a theological perspective we might put the issue like this: God the Father gives life; God the Son in his passion, death and resurrection rescues this life from its own folly and wickedness, thereby reconciling it again to the Father; and God the Spirit indwells in this life preserving it from dissolution, working towards the redemption and consummation of all created things. By positing the rights of the creature we do no more and no less than claim God's right in his creation and the integrity of his redeeming work.

It would not of course be possible to claim that all animal rightists possess this vision of vindicating God's right in his creation. In previous work I for one insufficiently appreciated the vital theological connection between God's right and animal rights. Perhaps I deserved the trenchant criticism of Richard Griffiths to the effect that the 'search for an adequate secular basis for animal rights is bound to fail because of the overriding difficulty of establishing any rights at all (even human rights) on a purely two-dimensional plane, without including some notion of God'.[9] Clearly the Christian basis for animal rights is bound to be different in crucial respects from that of secular philosophy. But because Christians (as we see it) have a good, even superior, basis for animal rights, that in no way precludes others from utilizing the terminology. Indeed, Tom Regan has shown how convincing moral theory based on rights, as opposed to other notions like interests or duties, can be.[10] It seems to me that we should welcome the fact that workers for animals, whether Christian or not, can share something of the same vocabulary even if it has in each case a different theoretical justification.

This does not mean that rights theory is free of difficulties or that other important things do not need to be added from a Christian perspective. I shall give some account of these at the end of the chapter. But rights language is clearly here to stay. Indeed, Catholic tradition has always made good use of such language and has frequently defended the individual right to life, especially of the unborn, and even more recently the 'rights of the family' too.[11] The Lambeth Conference of 1978 was quite emphatic in regarding 'the matter of human rights and dignity as of capital and universal significance' and strongly endorsed the United Nations Declaration of Human Rights.[12]

It does seem somewhat disingenuous for Christians to speak so solidly for human rights and then query the appropriateness of rights language when it comes to animals. The most consistent position is that of Raymond Frey, who opposes all claims for rights from a philosophical perspective, or that of Christians who *consistently* refrain from all such language.[13] It is inevitable, however, that rights language should have an appeal to Christians. We have seen that for Archbishop Coggan animals, 'as part of God's creation, have rights which should be respected' and the resolution in General Synod of the same year resolved to respect the 'due rights of sentient creatures'.[14] For how can we effectively champion the inherent goodness of what God has given without using the strongest moral language available? Sadly, Ambrose Agius, writing from a Roman Catholic perspective sympathetic to animals, answers the question whether animals can have rights with four words: 'No, but God has.'[15] My answer is to change only two of them: 'Yes, because God has.' To make the point clear I shall continue to speak of the *theos-rights* of animals.

(b) Animals have no duties

'Animals cannot be said to have duties, so it is hard to give them rights,' argued Hugh Montefiore, Bishop of Birmingham, in a recent parliamentary debate. Montefiore accepted that animals have 'a moral worth', even that we have 'a moral duty to treat them with dignity and respect', but he did not accept that they had rights.[16] The reason for this view appears to be that 'there is a qualitative difference which sets humanity in a class apart' from animals. In particular what distinguishes us is our 'capacity for self-awareness, our ability to accumulate experience by the written and spoken word, our faculty for thinking conceptually and for acting responsibly towards one another and towards animals'.[17] This is finely put, and subsequently Montefiore makes clear that 'because man is said to be made in the image of God he must exercise that God-given dominion in a responsible way'.[18] But it does seem extraordinary, at least in the argument as we have it, to posit God-given human responsibility as a reason for *denying* rights to animals. (It may be objected that it is wrong to press a parliamentary speech for philosophical distinctions, but it is worth noting that Montefiore is Chairman of the Board for Social Responsibility in the Church of England and that his speech was made in the course of an important debate on the use of animals in 'scientific procedures'.) The Montefiore argument can be queried in a variety of ways. In the first place, the logic of the argument must work against those human beings, for example comatose patients or the severely mentally handicapped, who have diminished responsibility or, in some cases, no moral responsibility at all. If these classes of human beings have no duties, are they like animals to be similarly classed as 'rightless'?[19] Secondly, given the currently uncertain state of biological knowledge, while it appears true that animals have no moral responsibility towards humans, it is not as clear as Montefiore's argument requires that they do not exercise some kind of care, even some form of altruism, towards the same or similar species. Animals may well not have clear moral duties to our own kind but we cannot rule out the possibility that they exercise some form of moral concern towards others. To absolutely rule out any possibility of moral sense in animals is simply to go beyond the evidence. Thirdly, and more importantly, it is surely odd to use the argument from the exercise of God-given moral obligation *in support* of weakened moral obligation to those who are unfortunate enough not to possess a fully developed moral consciousness. In Christian terms, it seems that we can, and should, use the argument entirely the other way. For example, do not comatose patients and the severely mentally deficient have a *greater* claim upon the compassion of adult, rational and morally responsible agents? Montefiore may well dispute that he had any desire to weaken our moral regard for the non-human, and that his concern for animals has been shown in a variety of ways, but in the end his speech was *in support* of legislation allowing for painful experiments on animals, albeit with some improved safeguards.[20] As C. S. Lewis once put it, our 'very superiority ought partly to *consist in* not behaving like a vivisector', and that 'we ought to prove ourselves better than the beasts precisely by the fact of acknowledging duties to them which they do not acknowledge to us'.[21] For here is the rub: Is it any more difficult to support moral duties to animals who may possess none to us than it is to support rights for animals who do not possess duties?

At a deeper level, however, what Montefiore seems to espouse here is a form of 'contractualism' whereby we can work out our obligations on the basis of some mutual capacity. Hence, we award rights only to those beings which have duties to us. Animals in this way are excluded from the normal moral considerations which we accept in the case of fellow humans who have duties. Animals have some 'moral worth', but considerably less than all human beings (comatose or otherwise). Even in this area, as it so happens, I am not sure that we can properly exclude animals, since it is at least possible to argue (as I once did) that 'moral rights should best be accorded on the basis of *duty*' so that rights can be seen as corollaries deduced from duties towards them.[22]

But from the new perspective of theos-rights, the argument that animals cannot have rights because they have no duties is largely irrelevant. The issue is not simply what we may judge to be a sufficient contract or mutual obligation with other species, but rather what must follow from our recognition of God's right to have his creatures treated with respect. The issue crucially turns on *God's* right, who alone has the right because he alone gives life and guarantees it. In this way, in directing ourselves towards respect for what is given rather than, say, for what kind of obligation we can accommodate, the character of the moral demand is crucially altered. While rights are grounded in the existence of Spirit-filled lives, what constitutes their rights is the will of God who desires that they should so live.

(c) Animals are not persons

'Man', argues Peter Green, 'is a *person*.' Because of this, 'he possesses rights and duties'. But an animal 'is not a free, self-conscious being capable of moral choice' and consequently cannot be 'in the full sense of the word a *person*'.[23] We find here an echo of the previous argument concerning duties, since we may suppose that only 'free self-conscious beings' can have duties or at least have the fullest and most developed moral sense. But when pressed, this argument invariably rests upon rationality as the justifying criterion. In the crisp judgement of Joseph Rickaby: 'Brute beasts, *not having understanding and therefore not being persons*, cannot have any rights'.[24] In all this it is not difficult to see the now familiar argument from the rational soul of human beings presented in a different form.

One way of breaking into this circle is simply to query whether animals can be properly characterized as irrational or a-rational. Interpreting biological evidence is not without its problems, but it would not be difficult to find some good reasons for positing willed, self-conscious behaviour in many of the higher mammals. But in my experience, the argument from rationality when defended by Christians in particular has little to do with naturalistic evidence as such. The judgement of the eminent ethologist W. H. Thorpe that 'I do indeed find it essential to assume something very similar to consciousness and conscious choice in many of the highest animals'[25] will not sway them. What the argument hinges on is the deep theological conviction that human personality is especially valuable to God. At heart I do not want to dissent from this view. There are all kinds of good reasons for supposing from a theological perspective that human beings are uniquely capable, or at least to a unique degree capable, of expressing costly sacrificial love, consciously co-operating with the divine Spirit and thereby completing God's design for the cosmos.

All I would ask is that the argument from human worth should not be used in such a way as to downgrade the status of other Spirit-filled creatures. So often the affirmation of the value of human life is used as a stick to beat down the worth of the non-human. This happens in theological thinking nowadays less and less by deliberate design but almost by sleight of hand. Keith Ward, for example, while accepting that human beings are 'very unlikely to be at the centre of God's purposes in the whole of creation', subsequently affirms that 'nothing is of value unless it is experienced by some conscious being, who would choose it for its own sake'.[26] Now, I think I understand and agree with Ward that self-conscious existence has especial value to God, but where I find him difficult is in the seeming assumption that only self-conscious beings can be of value in the universe, which for most, if not Ward himself, tends to mean only human beings. The value of the theos-rights perspective is that it enables us to question the all-too-easy assumption that human personality, or human consciousness, is the only kind of value to God. This is not to deny of course that these things are valuable, even especially valuable in God's sight and I, for one, will seek to offer some defence of them. But from the standpoint of what is given in creation, we do well not to assume that God values human *intelligent* existence exclusively. Clearly 'the personal' is an important theme in Christian theology and much can be made of it. All I ask is that we do not assume that God is only interested in human intelligent existence and that all else is dross and back-up. When Rickaby wrote that we have 'no duties of charity, nor duties of any kind, to the lower animals, *as neither to sticks and stones*', he really meant it.[27] His world was clearly divided into 'persons' on one hand and 'things' on the other.

In contrast, the theos-rights perspective does not locate the value of beings in any faculty or capacity, but in the will of God, which may be deduced from the givenness of Spirit-filled individuals. It *may* be that we come close to drawing some lines in the same place, but the perspective is different. The danger with all claims for the special value of human beings is that they can be anthropocentric rather than theocentric. Ward thinks that man may not be the centre of God's purpose for the whole of creation. He may in some sense be right, although I am inclined to the view that man is the centre of God's redeeming purpose precisely because of his unique ability to co-operate with the Spirit. But whatever view is taken of the centrality of man in the universe, we do well to avoid the simple equation of human interest with God's entire purpose. 'If one's basic theological perception is of a Deity who rules all creation, and one's perception of life in history and nature one of patterns of inter-dependence,' writes J. M. Gustafson, 'then the good that God values must be more inclusive than one's normal perceptions of what is good for me, what is good for my community, and even what is good for the human species.'[28] The danger in tying all rights in an exclusive way to the possession of human personality is that one frustrates the will of God to realize the 'good' in non-human creatures. We are then no longer open to the work of the Spirit in redemption, because at the outset we have limited the moral boundaries of our concern. It may be protested that the denial of rights to other species does not necessarily entail a depreciation of their status. Theoretically this may be. But the historical evidence is against it. The supposed rightlessness of animals has meant that they have been classed as 'things' and treated as 'things'. It is for those who deny theos-rights for animals, but who also want to commend animals as proper subjects of moral concern (with all that that entails), to show how this can be done. The theos-rights perspective then does not deny that human beings have especial value to God, or that there is something important and distinctive about human personality; it simply resists the view that humans alone have special value and that theos-rights can be denied to animals on this basis. For in the end the basis of judgement should not be what *we* value but what *God* values, and more directly what God has in fact already given in creation.

(d) Vegetable rights?

The argument goes something like this: To affirm God as Creator involves positing that *all* created life has value, not only human beings and animals, but every species of life from insects to vegetables. That we draw the line say, at mammals, rather than members of the human species may appear more satisfactory but is just as subjective and arbitrary. How can we know that God values elephants *more* than he does flies, or rabbits *more* than potatoes? 'To undertake to lay down universally valid distinctions between different kinds of life', writes Schweitzer, 'will end up judging them by the greater or lesser distance from which they seem to stand to us human beings.' Very few will not recognize the dilemma which Schweitzer poses so eloquently. 'Who amongst us knows what significance any other kind of life has in itself, and as part of the universe?', he asks.[29] The force of this question will always be felt by those who opt specifically for the rights of animals. Are we not arbitrarily selecting from what is, after all, God's mysterious and wholly valuable creation?

Our first response is that if this argument is sound at all, it really must be aimed at the widening of theos-rights rather than any narrowing of them. Implicitly, and with all its difficulties of consistency, Schweitzer is really commited to the theos-rights of all living things, animals, insects and vegetables. When it comes to having to choose between which life we save and which life we take, we really have nothing objective to guide us. Whether we choose the rabbit or the child or the insect, are all essentially subjective matters with nothing substantial (save human preference) to determine our choice. No wonder Schweitzer describes the world as 'a ghastly drama of the will-to-live divided against itself'.[30] From his perspective it can be little else.

Is it true, however, that we can make absolutely no distinctions between the relative value of beings? The biblical material is certainly less than clear in this respect and there is much more we should like to know. But there are at least two ways in which we can grasp the spiritual continuity between man and beast. The first is by some appreciation of how the notion of 'spirit' (*ruach*, *pneuma*) is applied to the non-human. Ecclesiastes, as we have seen, is unambiguous about the 'spirit' of animals; the issue is not whether humans have something which animals do not, but whether the spirit of either will survive death.[31] Psalm 104 is similarly strident about the spiritual origin of beasts. When the Lord hides his face 'they die', and return to dust.

> When thou sendest forth thy Spirit,
> they are created;
> and thou renewest the face of the ground.[32]

In Joel, not only humans but also the wild beasts 'cry' to the Lord because of the barrenness of the land. In consequence the Lord responds with the promise that 'I will pour out my spirit on all flesh.'[33] It is striking how Peter, according to Acts, makes use of this very same verse to characterize the outpouring of the Spirit at Pentecost.[34] For the story of Joel is a parable of *common* loss and *common* redemption; only the Spirit of the Lord can overcome the aridity of the earth in general and the communal suffering of man and beast in particular. Perhaps it is also worth noting that it is the Spirit, according to Mark, that drives Jesus into the wilderness, where 'he was with the wild beasts' and 'the angels ministered to him'.[35] St Paul appears to pick up this same theme when he describes the non-human creation as 'groaning in travail', that is literally in labour pains, awaiting redemption. 'Not only the creation, but we ourselves, who have the first fruits of the Spirit, groan inwardly as we wait for adoption as sons, the redemption of our bodies'.[36] The picture presented seems to suggest that the Spirit itself groans alongside creation, articulating the sighing of the creatures. Luther in commenting on the verses castigates as 'blind and foolish' those who search 'into the essences and functionings of the creatures rather than into their sighings and earnest expectations'. The truth to be comprehended, he insists, is that 'the creatures are created for an end'; 'for the glory that is to come'.[37] Only from the perspective of what the Spirit will yet do, can we understand them at all.

Two further notions, 'flesh' (*basar, sarx*) and 'blood' (*dam, haima*), should be considered. According to Genesis, God makes his everlasting covenant not just with man, but 'every living creature of all flesh'.[38] Moreover, 'the life of the flesh', as Leviticus observes, 'is in the blood'.[39] Hence the special significance attached to the spilling of blood and the traditional prohibition against its consumption. The life (*nephesh*), as we have seen, must not, according to Judaism, be misappropriated in this way. The word 'flesh' not only denotes the common existence of man and animals but also their spiritual significance. All flesh shall 'come to worship' God, maintains Isaiah, and when the glory of the Lord shall be revealed 'all flesh shall see it together'.[40] Notwithstanding Paul's insistence that not all flesh is identical[41] (for the term in Paul acquires a new significance as one of that deadly triad: sin (*harmatia*), death (*thanatos*) and flesh (*sarx*) *opposed* to Spirit), all flesh envisaged in Joel and Acts is alive with God's Spirit. The significance of flesh is highlighted by two further christological considerations. Firstly, the Logos 'becomes flesh'. By so doing the Son of Man implicitly enters into a relationship of solidarity with all creatures of flesh and blood.

Secondly, Christ is seen in Ephesians as 'abolishing in his flesh' the dividing wall of hostility by his work of sacrificial love[42]—a view which has always led some to stress the inclusivity of his Passion. 'Christ shed his blood for kine and horses . . . as well as for men', argued William Bowling in 1646.[43] Perhaps we should also point to the inevitable contrast between the offering of animal blood in spiritual sacrifice and its culmination in Christ's identification of himself with the lamb slain. 'He who eats my flesh and drinks my blood has eternal life,' records St John, or even more starkly, 'my flesh is meat indeed, and my blood is drink indeed'.[44]

It would be foolish to suppose that these notions provide a watertight distinction between the life of humans and animals on one hand, and the life of vegetables and insects on the other. We do not have such a systematized view in the Old and New Testaments. And yet, it is surely not unfair or too difficult to systematize them. We may put the matter like this: through his covenant God elects creatures of flesh and blood into a relationship with himself and humanity. God pours out his Spirit upon them. While, therefore, all living things have value to God, the election of Spirit-filled creatures, composed of flesh and blood, gives them what we may call 'inherent value' by virtue of their capacity to respond to him. In some ways the nature of this relationship is already anticipated in the first creation saga. Without lapsing into the predominantly hierarchical view of creation which has dominated Christian exegesis for centuries, it is possible to understand Genesis 1 as indicating closer circles of spiritual awareness which reach their climax in man made in God's own image. Thus birds and fish are created on the fifth day and land animals are classed with man himself on the sixth. It is consonant with what we know of the Priestly writer's purpose to suppose that this developing capacity for spiritual response was something like what he had in mind.[45] When this is linked with the clearly inclusive nature of the covenant subsequently expounded, we are able to take hold of one thread, however insufficiently developed, which ties the human and non-human into a clear theological relationship.

In an earlier work, I defended the concept of sentiency (understood as the capacity to experience pain and pleasure) as the basis for the rights of animals. In this I was influenced by Bentham's argument to the effect that the crunch question is not 'Can they *reason*? nor, Can they *talk*? but, Can they *suffer*?'⁴⁶ The difficulty with this view was quite simply that it ill-suited the theological framework within which I wanted to work. Not surprisingly perhaps, the selection of sentiency appeared arbitrary, as Frey's paper, 'What has sentiency to do with the possession of rights?' indicated.⁴⁷ What this criterion was searching for was some way in which the theological sense of community with animals could be expressed. To put it bluntly, I wanted to find some way in which the spiritual capacities of animals could be recognized as giving them a status beyond that of cabbages and greenfly. While I now take my leave of sentiency as by itself a sufficient criterion for theos-rights, it should, however, be clear that the capacity to experience pain is still implicit in my new three-fold definition of spirit, flesh and blood. Indeed I must take issue with Frey's statement that 'the implicit assumption that having mental experiences or mental states is valuable in its own right' which 'lies at the very basis of sentiency criterion' is 'by no means obviously true'.⁴⁸ Now clearly it is not 'obviously true' in the sense that it is demonstrable (although I would hope that Frey takes account of *my own* preference for it before he regards it as valueless). But it is theologically comprehensible to say the least, and in historical terms it needs to be remembered that it is the denial of 'mental experiences' to animals, and therefore rationality, that has led to their lack of moral status. For some secular philosophers the relative appeal of the value of 'mental experiences' may not be great, but for Christians this has been an issue, if not *the* issue, which lies at the heart of their theological, and therefore moral, rejection of the status of animals. To be in a relationship with God is a good which doubtless all created things (perhaps even stones) possess, but to be a *responding subject* in relationship with God, with all that that entails, including spiritual perception and self-consciousness, is undoubtedly a greater (though not unmixed) good. This I accept is not '*obviously* true' even if one believes that God is the meaning and purpose of creation and therefore the meaning and purpose of one's individual life, but it is at least a rational, even plausible argument. A similar point must be advanced against Frey's insistence that pain is not intrinsically evil.⁴⁹ Doubtless, pain can be viewed in a variety of ways, but from a theological perspective, pain and suffering and death are evils *overcome* in the passion and resurrection of Christ. Sentiency as a criterion for rights is not in this way entirely theologically unfounded, and although I now see that it needs to be superseded by a more rounded theological criterion, it is worth remembering that Christian hope has always been for a world where God 'will wipe away every tear from their eyes, and death shall be no more, neither shall there be mourning nor crying nor pain any more'.[50]

My theological definition of rights in terms of Spirit-filled individuals composed of flesh and blood has some correspondence with Tom Regan's recently advanced 'subject-of-a-life criterion'. Regan argues that individuals are subjects-of-a-life if

> they have beliefs and desires; perception, memory, and a sense of the future, including their own future; and emotional life together with feelings of pleasure and pain; preference and welfare interests; the ability to initiate action in pursuit of their desires and goals; a psychophysical identity over time; and an individual welfare in the sense that their experiential life fares well or ill for them, logically independently of their utility for others and logically independently of their being the object of anyone else's interests.[51]

Regan does not argue that only these beings can be subjects of inherent value and therefore only beings with rights can claim our moral attention. Practically, rights are possessed by humans and by animals who are 'mentally normal mammals of a year or more'.[52] Regan's work is a massive intellectual edifice and I cannot begin to do justice to the depth and subtlety of his position here, except to indicate some points of convergence and divergence.

We diverge at the point where Regan's system makes no use of the concept of God as the upholder and sustainer of value. We diverge at the point where, according to Regan's view, being a subject-of-a-life is itself a sufficient criterion for the possession of rights. According to the theological view I have just outlined, what sustains subjective individuals as holders of rights is the objective right of God in creation. I do indeed posit, like Regan, features of special value to God in his creation, and certainly many of the characteristics he outlines will obviously be possessed by Spirit-filled individuals, but where we differ is in our insistence that these features can only be ultimately justified by reference to God's own right as sovereign Creator. In sum: theos-rights are concerned with the defence of God-given spiritual capacities exhibited within his creation and realized through his covenant relationship with them, and not with any capacities which may be claimed by the creature itself in defence of its own status. And yet there are also important convergences. Regan and I are agreed that in our differing perspectives we can properly perceive subjects of inherent value in creation. Moreover, we are agreed that the concept of rights centres on those beings which have inherent value, though Regan accepts that some beings which are possibly 'rightless' may also be subjects of inherent value. Finally, Regan and I are agreed that the language of rights is indispensable for animals since it indicates an objective moral claim upon us. In sum: theos-rights value Spirit-filled individuals because God especially values them whereas, for Regan, individuals which are 'subjects-of-a-life' have inherent value and therefore objective rights.

The basic question, however, has yet to be confronted. Even if we accept that vegetable life cannot claim to fulfil the criterion of Spirit-filled life, where precisely, if at all, is the line to be drawn in the animal kingdom? There seem to be two major options. One we may call the 'inclusive view' and the other the 'exclusive view'.

The inclusive view holds that *all* classes of animal, over and above insects, have theos-rights. It argues that within the animal kingdom any making of distinctions between say mammals and fish is inherently problematic. At the very best we are dealing with a continuum of life where no clear biological lines can be drawn. It supports its view with the evidence, for example, of the Medway Committee, which concluded that 'all vertebrate animals (i.e. mammals, birds, reptiles, amphibians and fish) should be regarded as *equally* capable of suffering to some degree or another, without distinction between "warm-blooded" and "cold-blooded" members'.[53] The inclusive view therefore adopts the widest possible definition of spiritual life to include almost any being which is self-conscious, capable of self-determining movement, and possibly or even potentially open to the experience of pain, however momentarily. Did not the saints, they may argue, also show concern for the least among the animal kingdom like reptiles and snakes, and after all did not St Anthony reputedly preach to the fishes?

The exclusive view holds that only animals which come clearly within the definition of 'Spirit-filled, breathing beings composed of flesh and blood' have theos-rights. It argues that rights can only properly and clearly be extended to those animals *known* to possess spiritually analogous lives to those of humans. However complex the lives of fish, we cannot easily determine whether they are subjects of a spiritual life, whereas with mammals we can be as certain as possible. This view argues that to confuse *known* cases with *doubtful* cases weakens the overall force of the argument for theos-rights. Regan makes the point that knowing where to draw the line about consciousness is in some ways analogous to questions about 'how tall one has to be to be tall, or how old one must be to be old'. While there 'is no precise height or exact age one must be to be tall or old . . . there are clear cases nonetheless'.[54] In the same way, while there may be a continuum of consciousness and of spiritual possibility, it is still possible to judge a clear case from a doubtful one, or to be more precise, a clearer case from a more doubtful one.

Both views have their difficulties. The danger with the first is that it gives so much benefit of the doubt to the doubtful that it may obscure the moral standing of the almost-certain. The second view carries with it the danger of leaving potentially, or even actually, Spirit-filled beings with little moral protection. Frey lost no opportunity, for example, in castigating those like myself who once held sentiency as the sole basis for rights, as licensing the tyranny of sentients over non-sentients.[55] How then are we to draw the line? How exclusive or inclusive dare we be?

In determining a question which may affect the lives, if not the sufferings, of millions of species, we do well to be cautious. My preference, however, is for the exclusive view. To the anticipated charge of 'mammalocentricity' instead of 'anthropocentricity', the defence must be that mammals so clearly live Spirit-filled lives which are analogous to human beings, that it is plainly inconsistent to deny them a fundamentally similar status. This is, for all its difficulties, the more clearly biblical view and one that is most consonant with the meaning of the Genesis narrative. 'O Lord, thou preservest man and beast'[56] suggests a line of priority which deserves to be taken seriously. To the other anticipated charge that 'mammalocentricity' is nothing less than crude anthropomorphism of our closest relatives (in evolutionary terms), we may reply with Konrad Lorenz that 'The similarity [between mammals and humans] is not only functional but historical, and it would be an actual fallacy not to humanise'.[57] Besides, from a theological perspective, this 'humanizing' has some (albeit limited) justification. If it is true that humans are most capable of spiritual freedom and therefore of spiritual communion, it follows that those species most clearly related to us also share something of the spiritual life of which we are capable. This argument must however be utilized with great care. We must not rush from affirmation to negation. We know so little about the lives of fish, insects or microbes, that it is vital that we do not presume too much about their spiritual capacities, if any. Our unknowing cannot and must not be turned into denial.

We may then only endorse our exclusivist view on the strict understanding that while we make a special case for Spirit-filled individuals as bearers of theos-rights, we hold equally that all living beings are subjects of value. To the charge that we make them valueless by our emphasis upon the rights of others, we rather insist that all created life has some claim upon us and that respect for life—including slugs, snails, and earthworms, remains a clear duty. Because, guided by biblical tradition and reason, we regard mammalian and bird life as especially valuable as bearers of Spirit-filled life, that in no way detracts from the fundamental value of all other creatures. And what is more, we must always be open to the possibility that we are wrong. It could well be that the Spirit has yet to teach us things about God's creation that will surprise and amaze us. It may be that the Spirit has found homes that we have not yet discovered or resting places in what are to us the most unlikely of species. Since we are dealing here with the movement of God's Spirit we do well to be humble. Even if we judge on the basis of knowledge, we do well to realize the partiality and fragmented nature of all human knowing. It could be that there will come a time when our view is thought to be as ludicrously narrow as the previous anthropocentric ones we have criticized. These considerations press upon us the need for caution, and I for one am not at all confident that we have yet anything like the measure of the Spirit in God's mysterious creation. And yet we are also called to the work of spiritual discernment; we cannot allow the possibility of failing to grasp what we do see, for the sake of the more that may yet be revealed to us.

In short: doubtless there is something beautiful about flowers and magnificent about the intricacy of insects. Doubtless trees too have some dignity and standing before God. Perhaps there is spiritual power in the earth and all its attendant life. We cannot doubt that in some way God's Spirit touches everything created. And yet the glory of created life must not blind us to the reality of individuals filled with the gift of the Spirit. To recognize and celebrate God's right in these creatures can only be possible because the Spirit is right there with all creation, indeed incessantly moving it forward to possibilities beyond itself.

(e) Stewardship not rights

It is not surprising that some Christians, uneasy with talk of animal rights, should press the case for the language of stewardship. Not only is it, they claim, more biblical but also more 'appropriate'. Alastair S. Gunn makes three substantive points in this vein. In the first place, animal rights are impractical. 'It must be stressed that *no* forms of human life—hunter/gatherer, pastoralist, agricultural, industrial are possible without harming the interests of animals'. 'How can we be justified', Gunn argues, 'in infringing their rights?'[58] The argument seems to be that because the adoption of animal rights challenges centuries of conventional practice, then it must surely be impracticable. Such a view simply begs the moral question. It presupposes that the kind of society in which human beings have lived in the past can be the only kind of society possible for the future. 'There is little point in talking of animals' rights unless it is typically our duty to respect them', argues Gunn.[59] But if the argument is sound, we might equally apply it to human rights. What is the point of speaking of human rights, in say warfare, since they are so typically disregarded? Indeed what is the point of international law regulating human conduct in warfare since the 'rules' of war are so frequently broken?[60] Since all human societies have to a greater or lesser extent infringed human rights, indeed there is not one human right we can recall that has not been so infringed, how can we be justified in speaking of human rights? What Gunn elaborately misses is that we need to speak of human and animal rights precisely *because* they are so 'typically' overridden, and precisely *because* without doing so we would have no adequate means of raising the question of injustice to either humans or animals. The fact that we regularly infringe rights provides us with no philosophical or theological ground for refusing to admit their existence.

Gunn's second point is that the concept of stewardship more adequately answers the question: 'How should a superior being treat inferior beings?' Since the 'world as conceived here manifestly is not a society of equals' talk of animal rights 'seems inappropriate'.[61] But the model to which Gunn is working here is one of reciprocal political rights, not that of God's rights in creation. From a theological perspective, what is the function of a steward but to safeguard what God has given and to value what God values? Now, I accept that God may not value *equally* all that is given in creation, but arguably the whole point about stewardship is that the stewards should value what God has given as highly as they value themselves. To be placed in a relationship of special care and special protection is hardly a licence for tyranny or even what Gunn calls 'benevolent despotism'.[62] If we fail to grasp the necessarily sacrificial nature of lordship as revealed in Christ, we shall hardly begin to make good stewards, even of those beings we regard as 'inferior'.

The third point brings us to the heart of the problem. The steward's job according to Gunn is neither to 'maximise utility, nor to protect rights'. The steward's duty is to pursue the Creator's plan. But this plan 'is certainly not designed to reduce [animal] suffering or to protect rights'. Stewards may then 'puzzle' about the evil in creation, but they 'will certainly not be able to evaluate the divine plan on the basis of utility or rights, but may rather conclude that *nature* is a Hobbesian state, where the terms *right* and *wrong*, *just* and *unjust*, have no proper application'.[63] Now the truth is out. Whatever may be the Creator's will for his creation can only properly be deduced from the state of nature as it now is, however Hobbesian it may appear. But since this state of nature (as Gunn construes it) has no place for moral distinctions it is ludicrous to think that animals have rights, or presumably that they can be wronged or treated unjustly. But why stop at animals, we may argue? Why not include the whole species of human beings as well? If nature, which is (we are assured) the true demonstration of the Creator's will for his creatures, shows no concern for animal suffering, why should we be concerned for human suffering either? Indeed if God is not concerned in any temporal or ultimate way to 'reduce suffering' in animals, why should we suppose that human suffering is any barrier to him? If moral terms have 'no proper application' in the field of human–animal relations, why, we must ask, should we be so presumptuous as to suppose that they do in the arena of human–human relations?

Readers may think that we have simply knocked down some Aunt Sallies, but in fact Gunn advances his arguments with all seriousness. Put crudely: Gunn's notion of stewardship involves making the best of a bad job. Creation is a bad job—'these systems are less than perfect'.[64] But God is not actually working through his human 'viceregents' to restore creation, to right wrongs, or to redeem suffering. The role of the steward in all accounts which take 'the world as it is' as the moral model inevitably ends up justifying the status quo.

Stewardship is actually essential to theos-rights and vice versa. Human beings are to be stewards of God's right in creation, that is, they are to co-operate with the Spirit in actualizing his right reign of peace and justice. What is given is God's, and God's right will reverse all wrongs. Now, it is true that 'wickedness flourisheth' and that at the present time no form of life seems possible without injury and wrong, but one of the characteristics of stewards is that they keep faith with the one who gives. 'Faith', argues Hebrews, 'is the giving substance to the things which are hoped for, the discerning of things which are not seen'.[65] In this sense our dominion is eschatologically orientated. The work that is done is performed towards the end of ultimate redemption. Quite how this will all come to be is a matter about which we can be legitimately agnostic and questioning. If we are to 'till and keep' creation it is not, as Gunn unfortunately suggests, because of 'the absent ruler', but precisely because God keeps faith with us and will never ultimately let us go. The point is strikingly expressed in one of the visions of St Julian of Norwich:

> He showed me a little thing, the quantity of an hazel-nut, in the palm of my hand; and it was round as a ball. I looked upon with

eye of my understanding, and thought: *What may this be*? And it was answered generally thus: *It is all that is made*. I marvelled how it might last, for methought it might suddenly have fallen to nought for little[ness]. And I was answered in my understanding: *It lasteth, and ever shall [last], for that God loveth it*. And so All-thing hath the Being by the love of God.

In this Little Thing I saw three properties. The first is that God made it, the second is that God loveth it, the third, that God keepeth it.[66]

Perhaps God's 'keeping' or stewardship may sometimes appear absent because his deputies are so slow to work with his Spirit and get down to business. 'I cannot think it extravagant to imagine', writes Alexander Pope, 'that mankind are no less, in proportion accountable for the ill-use of their dominion over creatures of the lower rank of beings, than for the exercise of tyranny over their own species'.[67] Stewardship undoubtedly involves making tough decisions, taking power and responsibility. Because it involves this, it necessarily requires discrimination and discernment, for whatever else is true, God's will is not self-evident. Christians, like Gunn, sometimes appear to opt for the 'softer' language of stewardship because they think it rescues them from the 'hard' language of rights. But they fail to see that 'keeping' God's right in creation is a hard thing involving many challenges. In short: To be a steward is to know God's right in the creation entrusted to him.

(f) Rights resolve no conflicts

Even if we accept that animals which are Spirit-filled have analogous rights to human beings, the question must surely be raised: How do we settle the inevitable conflicts that occur between animal and human rights? Rights theory might be said to multiply conflicts without supplying the means whereby they can be resolved. It seems to me that this argument could be conceded, partially at least. Increasing the number of right-holders in the world does surely increase the likelihood of moral conflicts. And if this be a weakness, then rights theory has simply to accept it. But two important qualifications should be added. The first is that moral conflicts can serve a moral purpose. When I am faced with a conflict of rights, I am brought face to face with the fact that I must choose and that I have responsibility to both parties concerned. Working out how I am to square one kind of responsibility with another is never easy and in a whole range of situations the given interests of both parties may appear equally strong. But from the rights standpoint, the surely significant fact is that by so doing I am accepting that animals have a fundamentally analogous claim upon me. In other words, rights language poses in a sharp and heightened form a serious obligation which I might otherwise overlook. Now, I may decide that there is a higher right and that the rights of animals should be overridden. But at least in so doing I have acknowledged, if the decision is taken conscientiously, that there is a claim to be entertained. All this is gain. Rights language serves a vital function of focusing moral obligation and insisting upon proper moral justification, even if the animal's right in question is finally overridden.

Secondly, if the tendency to create moral conflicts is a characteristic of rights theory, then at the very least we have to say that this is a weakness (if it really be so) which is inherent in almost all moral theory. Even if I accept, for example, that I have some duties to animals, it is not difficult to envisage a range of situations in which my duty to animals and my duty, say, to my wife and family, may conflict. Even if I accept only some minimalist obligation to animals, for example to save them from wanton injury, I am still not precluded from the possibility of conflicting obligations. It seems impossible to envisage any moral theory that can dispel all moral conflict, or indeed suggest answers in each and every conceivable situation as to how such conflict should be resolved. Perhaps there may be one way as far as animals are concerned. If we take the view of scholastic Catholicism, which has held that animals have to all intents and purposes no moral standing and that whatever we do to them, arguably even downright acts of cruelty, are not moral actions in any recognizable sense, then surely we could in this way avoid all moral conflicts. Few theologians today would want to go so far as this. Some, perhaps most, would surely say that moral conflict is inevitable so long as the person or species concerned has any kind of moral status. Here is the rub. To devise a moral theory that does not allow even for the possibility of conflict between one party and another is simply to deny that one or either party has moral standing. The attempt to dispel every possibility of moral conflict over the claims of animals means effectively that we deny that they have any claims which can be disputed. Those who are opposed to animal rights need to consider whether the argument against rights on the basis that they do not resolve conflicts is actually a weakness in rights theory or simply a failure to grasp that animals can have genuinely competing moral claims.

Some Christians, however, are predisposed to understand talk of rights only in absolute terms. To accept that an individual has a right to life means to them that it should never, absolutely never, be taken in whatever circumstances. Such a view is not infrequently indebted to a perception of moral obligation as divinely given law—a law which it is thought should not be trespassed on any occasion. Doubtless there is something to be said for such a robustly clear view of the moral imperative, and I am not sure for myself whether some human or animal rights cannot be said to be absolute in some way. But it is not clear to me why rights must be considered absolute in order to qualify for the title. It is surely impossible to envisage any human right, considered absolute or otherwise, that has not in fact been overridden at one time or another. If there can only be absolute obligations if they are absolutely and universally obeyed, then we have to sadly conclude that there cannot be any. In practice, therefore, we are always inevitably speaking of rights which may be overridden if there is sufficient moral justification. All infringements of rights, animal or human, require good justification. Where such justification cannot be had, the act of infringement is an act of immorality, or put theologically, a sin against God.

It will be questioned whether we have given a sufficient account of how we should actually resolve conflicts between animal and human rights. We shall return to this issue in the next chapter, when considering the use to which we put animals in, for example, farming and research.

(g) Only God can defend his rights

This argument can be subtle. It can mean, firstly, that God's own work must be completed in his own good way and in his good time; that human efforts to bring about the Kingdom are simply premature and doomed to disappointment. Secondly, it can mean that God has no need of human accomplices. If we are really speaking of divine work, only unaided divinity can bring it to completion.

Both arguments in their own way go to the heart of the Christian doctrine of God as Trinity: Father, Son and Holy Spirit. A variant of the first argument is found in Karl Barth. On the one hand, he sees the force of the prior command in Genesis to live in peace with creation but, on the other, he judges that vegetarianism represents 'a wanton anticipation of . . . the new aeon for which we hope'.[68] It is not that vegetarianism is judged to be devoid of a moral or theological basis, indeed quite the reverse. Universal peace and living non-violently is God's will for the world to come, but not just yet. The moral questions surrounding vegetarianism will be discussed in the next chapter. For our purpose here, what is striking in Barth's argument is the way in which he postpones to the end of time any possibility of creaturely redemption. So keen is he to defend divine sovereignty that he will not allow any form of human co-operation with the Holy Spirit. God alone has all the prerogatives; humans have none.

But it must be protested that this view, if held with any consistency, inevitably weakens the moral resolve in all cases of human behaviour, whether the issues concern animals or human beings. How do we make sense of the urgency of so many of the ethical demands of Jesus if in fact moral decisions can be relegated to the end of time? 'The hour is coming and now is'[69] is one of those hauntingly recurring phrases in St John's Gospel, pointing both to the eschatological realization of all hope as well as the need for urgent action in the present time. Of course there is no getting away from it: Christian hopes are eschatologically orientated. Peace and justice are *goals* for creation, but there is no suggestion in Barth as regards *human* peace and justice that we are not right to pursue these goals now. Why then the reticence, we may ask, about non-human creatures? The sense one gets in Barth is that the issue is too vast and too demanding for appropriate human response. 'Consistent apostles of the protection of animals' are charged with not facing the world as God intended it to be: 'in virtue of which the big fish does not greet the little fish but eats it'.[70]

The weakness in Barth's position is that the arguably most trinitarian theologian of our age is simply not trinitarian enough.

Many have commented on the lack of a developed pneumatology in Barth which makes it difficult for us to see a connection between the present and the future worlds. The world of creation is viewed as a strangely static place where the Spirit of God sparingly moves on the face of the waters and seems to interact with non-human creation hardly at all. To be fair, the non-human will according to Barth be redeemed, but there is crucially no correspondence between their present suffering and the God who will act in the future. This caveat leaves human moral action in a vacuum as regards the non-human creation. Barth confronts us with a crossroads in our theology. Either we are to see God working out his purpose of redemption in creation and willing human co-operation in the process, or the non-human creation must be seen as otiose from the standpoint of its Creator.

This is not to resist the central point in the second argument, that God alone can bring order out of chaos and that redemption is properly a divine work. But it does not follow that because God in the end does not need human accomplices that they are not welcome disciples. As Christians see it there is a priority in moral action: God calls and we follow. It is his Spirit that moves us, energizes us and heals us. But we are not passive receivers of the Spirit: he 'works for good' with all who love God. This trinitarian picture frees us from the deistic view in which creation is largely irrelevant to God on the one hand, and from the pantheistic view in which creatures have no room to be themselves on the other. In Christ, God humbles himself to be with us, to work within us and within all creation. God is not a dictator who brutalizes his creation, but according to Jesus, the one who comes among us to serve. To *oppose* human moral response to God's work in redemption is sadly only to create another ugly dualism after years in which Christianity has sought to free itself of others— whether they be the dualism of mind and body or the separation of man from creation. We rend asunder what God has brought together.

To the objection then that only God can vindicate his right and restore creation, the Christian should give a loud 'amen'. The whole case for theos-rights depends precisely upon God being able to deliver what he promises. But it does not follow that as God's appointed deputies or trustees or stewards, we can simply sit back and wait. There is surely a case for waiting, but only to give ourselves time for reflection, discernment and further openness to his Spirit. Openness to the Spirit is meant after all to be a precurser to a greater, conscientious, Spirit-filled life. Doubtless God's time-scale is not ours, and we might wish it otherwise. At the very least we cannot rule out the possibility that God will use our frail offerings of obedience to further his glorious kingdom.

Theologically Qualified Rights

The argument that Christians should continue to utilize rights language and extend its use to animals needs to be subject to three qualifications. The first is that Christians should not claim that rights theory is the *only* theory of moral obligation. To the objection that rights theory may in some ways be deficient or inadequate, we have to reply that no one theory can possibly do justice to the complete range of themes and insights from within the Christian tradition. If this sounds like something less than a complete endorsement of rights, then it needs to be considered whether any moral theory, either of divine command or human duty, can claim to be the only possible one from a theological perspective. What we are characterizing in Christian moral theory is nothing less than the will of God. Divine will is undubitably complex, even subtle and possibly developing. When we opt for the language of theos-rights, we do it with necessary reserve and caution, not because this theory is necessarily more difficult than any other, but because *all* moral theory is theologically problematic. Whenever we move from any straightforward identification of God's will with a particular imperative in a specific situation to the work of characterization, that is, to characterizing and systematizing God's will in general terms, then we are faced with the continual danger of over-simplification. Of course God's will can be simple, but it can also be remarkably mysterious. Even Karl Barth, that robust defender of divine commands, accepts that it is not an easy task for Christian ethics to tell us what God's will is. By our intellect and language we are always, through characterization, *approximating* God's will for his creation. Though theos-rights may be the best way of characterizing the divine imperative, it does not follow that we must hold that such theory is in every way adequate or that in God's good time some new form of theo-moral characterization may not better it. Doubtless our own moral reasoning, however inspired, is like the rest of creaturely life itself, in need of redemption.

The second qualification is that rights language cannot claim to be comprehensive. I mean by this that it cannot exclude other forms of moral language and insight. Talk of generosity, respect, duty, sacrifice and mercy as well as rights is essential. It may be that animal rightists have so stressed the importance of rights as a concept that they have neglected talk of compassion and respect. It may be, but for Christians my hope is that we can take such language for granted. Earlier in Chapter One, for example, we found it important to defend the notion of respect for creation in general. One function of rights language is to provide checks and markers *en route* to living a less exploitative way of life with other creatures. This is surely a valuable function, but by itself does not provide a wholistic or sufficiently positive interpretation of the divine imperative. In other words, Christian ethics is not simply about preventing the worst but promoting the good. For the elaboration, definition and pursuit of the good with animals we require more terms than rights language can provide. It may be in some situations that we should accord animals more than that which rights theory may strictly give them, and err, if we do, on the generous side. For generosity is surely an important notion and rights language must be careful not to limit it even if we cannot persuade ourselves that it has the status of a declared 'ought'. To those who feel that we should not just respect the rights of say, sparrows, but actually seek loving, caring relationships with them, the rights view offers no obstacle. To those who feel called to especially heroic acts of mercy and self-sacrifice towards particular kinds of animals, the rights view again advances no objection. There will always be people, inspired by the life of Christ and the many saints, who feel moved to morally heroic, sacrificial acts. But, of course, it is not to these people that rights language is normally directed. In short: in fighting for the positive good of animals and humans, Christians will need to utilize a varied vocabulary. All that is claimed here is that rights language should be part of the necessary armoury.

Thirdly, we need to reiterate that the rights of which we speak are properly and solely God's rights. He alone wills that givenness of life which makes them possible; he alone charges man with the stewardship of them; and he alone can in the end properly guarantee them. One conclusion follows from this: as our knowledge of God increases by the power of the Spirit, so may our knowledge of the nature of his will and therefore our understanding of his rights. Some theologians regard rights terminology as far too static a way of describing God's relationship with what is, after all, a dynamic and open creation. But theosrights are not necessarily as static as may be their secular counterparts. The possibility of change is inherent in the fact that our understanding of God develops, whether for better or worse. It may be that God's Spirit has much more to show us about the nature and variety of valuable beings in his universe. Again it may be that God's Spirit will move us to a new understanding of our place in the universe such as to make previous controversies about individual salvation in the Reformation period appear trivial by comparison. It may be or may not be. In either case it is our responsibility to recognize God's rights in creation and to champion them.

The Significance of Theos-Rights

The question may not unreasonably be posed: What then is the overwhelming advantage of rights theory which justifies it in spite of these serious qualifications? The answer may be obvious. Rights language insists that we envisage the claims of animals in analogous terms to those of other, human, beings. This is why Frey and Gunn hesitate or reject animal rights: they deny that the claims of other Spirit-filled breathing beings can be in any real sense analogous to human claims. In the issue of animal rights, perhaps more than any other, Christians confront the limitations of their own scholastic history. Scholasticism has for centuries regarded animals as 'things'. The consequence is unsurprising: animals have been treated as things. For all the intellectual sophistication of the arguments against animal rights, one quite practical consideration is frequently dominant. *To accept that animals have rights must involve accepting that they should be treated differently from the way most of them are treated at present.* Explicitly acknowledging that animals have rights involves accepting that they have a fundamental moral status. If they have no such status, they cannot make claims; and if they have no claims, they can have no rights. Perhaps in the light of their tradition, it is easier for Christians to see the historic significance of the debate about rights than many of their secular contemporaries. Those who deny rights to the non-human do well to ponder the history of what rightlessness has meant for animals; if the opposing arguments do not convince, it is invariably because they do not want to accept that most animals are treated unjustly.

Here is the rub. To grant animal rights is to accept that they can be wronged. According to theos-rights what we do to animals is not simply a matter of taste or convenience or philanthropy. When we speak of animal rights we conceptualize what is objectively owed to animals as a matter of justice by virtue of their Creator's right. Animals can be wronged because their Creator can be wronged in his creation. Some philosophers are still adamant that it is possible to provide a theoretical framework for the better treatment of animals without recourse to the notion of rights.[71] It may be possible in this way to provide for something better, but how much remains historically open. Perhaps through utilitarian calculation it may be possible to prevent some of the worst possible from happening to animals, but will their status be fundamentally changed thereby? Language and history are against those who want the better treatment of animals and who also want to deny the legitimacy of the language of rights. For how can we reverse centuries of scholastic tradition if we still accept the cornerstone of that tradition, namely that all but humans are morally rightless? If the foregoing appears to invoke the dubious need for penitence in formulating ethical theory, it can only be replied that repentance is a cardinal duty for Christians. If calculation of the consequences is to be allowed some say in moral assessments, then we have to accept that Christians have good reason for looking at what their own theology has created and, in the light of this, theologizing afresh.

But apart from this obvious practical need to reverse centuries of neglect, theos-rights makes sense of a whole range of crucial theological insights—three in particular. The first is the sheer givenness of created reality. Unless God is really indifferent to creation, those beings whose lives are filled with his Spirit have special value and therefore require special protection. The second is the need to witness to the electing power of God in his covenant relationship. Man and animals form a moral community, not only because of their common origin, but because God elects them within a special relationship with himself. Catholic scholasticism has denied the possibility of a moral community with brutes. 'Nothing irrational can be the object of the Christian virtue of neighbourly love, charity', writes Bernard Häring. 'Nothing irrational,' he tells us, 'is capable of the beautifying friendship with God'.[72] What scholasticism here neglects or disputes, theos-rights assumes. Because men and brutes are elected by God, we form one covenanted community of Spirit-filled beings before him. Thirdly, the perspective of theos-rights gives meaning to the long tradition of rating man's God-like powers in creation. According to theos-rights, humans must exercise power, but only towards God's end. The unique significance of man in this respect consists in his capacity to perceive God's will and to actualize it within his own life. Man is 'to commit himself to the divine task', argues Edward Carpenter, 'of lifting up creation, redeeming those orders of which he forms part, and directing them towards their end'.[73]

Those who deny theos-rights to animals need to show how it is that they can give sufficient reality to these insights without participating in the moral neglect of the non-human which still characterizes continuing elements within the Christian tradition.

6 Ways of Liberation (I)

Registering a Problem

In our urbanized communities it might now be possible for some people to grow up without actually seeing a live animal, let alone witnessing an act of cruelty or neglect. If a good number of Christians react rather unbelievingly to the suggestion that our ill-treatment of animals is a major moral problem, then it could be in part a simple result of 'not seeing is not believing'. The irony is that although a whole range of public spectacles involving wantonness towards animals have disappeared from view, we actually utilize more animals today than ever before. In the two major areas of farming and experimentation alone, approximately a hundred billion animals are killed in the world every year. Use of experimental animals in the United States is conventionally estimated in the region of seventy to a hundred and twenty million. World-wide the total is probably somewhere around five hundred million.[1] When it comes to farming, in the United Kingdom alone there are approximately forty-five million laying hens in intensive conditions,[2] and in the United States this figure probably exceeds a billion at least. These figures, even if exaggerated, indicate a scale of animal usage hitherto unknown in the history of humankind. We eat, ride, shoot, fish, wear, trap, hunt, farm and experiment upon billions of animals world-wide every year. Even if we only grant animals some minimal moral status, it could be seriously claimed that in terms of pain, suffering and deprivation alone, the treatment of the non-human ranks among the most important moral issues confronting the human species. To include animals among the class of right-holders in a world where they are almost universally disregarded is surely a bold act of faith. Not surprisingly Henry S. Salt, one of the pioneers of the animal rights movement in the nineteenth century, entitled his autobiographies respectively, *Fifty Years Among the Savages*, and twenty years on, *Seventy Years Among the Savages*.[3]

So difficult indeed is it to envisage a better world for animals, that when presented as a moral issue the current situation invariably provokes one of two reactions: despair or zeal. Even among Christians moral despair about animals is rife. To admit that much of what we now do to animals is frankly tyrannous, and to suppose that humans can surmount the fundamental changes of attitude and lifestyle required to counter it, invokes incredulity. If we cannot prevent war, greed, cruelty, stupidity and deceit among our own species, what chance have we of behaving any better to the non-human? 'We must accept the world as it is', counsels the resigned conscience. To prosecute the cause of animal rights in a world of animal wrongs is to pursue a fancy or, more poignantly, to elect oneself a hero. In short: the moral reformation of humankind presupposed by taking animal rights seriously is beyond our reach.

The second reaction of moral zeal may not be as common, but has always had a foothold among a tormented minority. Moreover it is probably on the increase. If the despairing attitude accepts the world as it is, the zealous is determined to change it at all costs. If saving animals requires a hating attitude to humanity, the zealous will take that attitude on board. 'In my view they [vivisectors] should all *die*, in the same way the animals die that are at their mercy,' as one spokesman for the Animal Liberation Front recently put it. 'They should all have the same treatment.'[4] The alleviation of animal suffering becomes a goal to be pursued even at the cost of murder and terrorism. 'Violence is the only language some of these people understand,' says Ronnie Lee.[5] The morally zealous will also accept personal costs like social isolation and ridicule. They will scorn the 'middle ground' of compromise and accommodation in *every* instance. Those who work practically for 'realistic' reforms will be classed as 'traitors' to the cause. In brief: the zealous commit themselves to the cause of animals at any human cost, including murder, intolerance and self-righteousness.

Some may complain that these are caricatures. I have met both sorts of people, however, and in some ways understand both reactions. The first, for all its apparent complacency, is often more deeply concerned about the plight of animals than might at first appear. He or she, especially if Christian, is simply appalled at the prospect of Utopianism in moral affairs and distrusts grandiose schemes for human self-improvement. The second, despite all the nauseating aspects of self-righteousness, is often a deeply sensitive human being driven to sheer anger at indifference to suffering and misery in the non-human world. Those who object to the growing tide of militancy among the zealous frequently ignore the difficulties of achieving discussion of unfavoured causes. I can supply one example. At a press reception prior to a well-attended meeting in London as part of a campaign against the export of live food animals, I inquired of an agricultural correspondent from a leading newspaper whether he would report the meeting. He said that he would not. I indicated the obvious popular support for the cause and the various arguments against the trade. He indicated little interest. 'What must we do then to get coverage in your paper?' I remonstrated. He replied, 'Go to the House of Commons and pour a bucket of blood over the sitting members.' It is easy to knock the press, but it is equally easy to understand why some people are driven to activity in support of a cause which they know will be reported in newspapers.

Theological Moralizing

Christians need to bring to the discussion about animal rights two theological insights. The first is that all human beings are sinners. 'All have sinned and fall short of the glory of God,' writes St Paul.[6] None of us can be justified by our works in the sight of God. Man's alienation from God and lostness in the world are the perennial themes of Christian preaching. Even the Son of Man appears to accept his own part in the fallenness of the world. 'Why do you call me good?' he asks. 'No one is good except God alone'.[7] This perspective, while recognizing real degrees of goodness and the possibility of human merit, accepts at the outset that there is no pure land. No human being can live free of evil. In consequence, self-righteousness is not only wrong but inappropriate. One of the main thrusts of the ethical teaching of Jesus seems directed against those who are cocksure of their own moral standing. Moral reformation, if it is to be pursued, must begin with ourselves. Such considerations mean simply that zealous campaigning, self-righteous postures and methods of blatant intimidation must be eschewed. To pursue even good ends by any means risks the increase of moral evil in the world. There is, of course, a dilemma here for all moral campaigners, whether for human or animal causes. To have moral insight at all frequently requires unusual perceptions; to sustain it frequently requires unusual emotions. Very few can conduct moral warfare without bitterness, acrimony, jealousy or hatred. There is no easy way through all this. Perhaps all crusading causes necessarily involve conflict and with it the inevitable dangers of self-justification, exaggeration and mistrust. J. S. Mill once wrote that 'Every great movement must experience three stages: ridicule, discussion, adoption';[8] I wish I could persuade myself that it was all so straightforward. At the very least, animal campaigners would do well to endorse George Bernard Shaw's verdict that those who exploit animals are simply like the rest of us. 'Custom will reconcile people to any atrocity; and fashion will drive them to acquire any custom.' Again, 'Far from enjoying it, they [in particular people who experiment on animals] have simply overcome their natural repugnance and become indifferent to it, as men become indifferent enough to anything they do often enough.'[9] At best, animal rightists will acknowledge our common guilt before God. A clean conscience is surely a figment of the imagination or, as Schweitzer describes it, 'an invention of the devil'.[10]

The second insight is that with God all things are possible. Doubtless there is a fine line between endorsing every kind of human Utopianism on the one hand and believing that with God's Spirit all things can be made new, on the other. Moral visions, however, are characteristic of theology. In some sense all theology is visionary. As Isaiah found out, to have a vision of the holiness of God is to know oneself a sinner. 'Woe is me!' he cries.

> I am lost,
> for I am a man of unclean lips
> and I dwell among a people of unclean lips;
> yet with these eyes I have seen the King, the Lord of Hosts.[11]

At its best the Christian tradition has articulated vision which has sustained moral effort throughout centuries of history. Morality may depend upon theology in the way in which human will relies upon the imagination. If our moral theorizing is not to be reduced to utilitarian calculations and accommodating pragmatism, then we need some fundamental vision of how the world should be and how we are to play a part in achieving it. Of course there is some kind of balance to be struck here between, as Ward calls it, 'Scylla and Charybdis, between a loss of vision and idealism and an intolerant and repressive rule-worship'.[12]

This needs to be held with the realization that the Holy Spirit is ever before us, moving creation forward, however mysteriously, to the realization of God's hope for us and his world. We can certainly betray God by fantasy and wishful thinking, but we can equally betray him by cutting our own moral notions to serve our own short-term interests. I like the line from Plato, who compares philosophers in a democratic state to those who 'wrangle over notions of right in the minds of men who have never beheld Justice itself'.[13]

Vision and Humility

If these insights are to be taken seriously then Christians need to commit themselves to the work of animal liberation with vision and humility.

Firstly, vision. The goal is nothing less than the establishing of God's right in creation, and the liberation of non-human creation from the hand of tyranny. Isaiah again has just the right vision to feed our imagination and kindle our will.

> Then the wolf shall live with the sheep,
> and the leopard lie down with the kid;
> the calf and the young lion shall grow up together,
> and a little child shall lead them;
> the cow and the bear shall be friends,
> and their young shall lie down together.
> The lion shall eat straw like cattle;
> the infant shall play over the hole of the cobra,
> and the young child dance over the viper's nest.
> They shall not hurt or destroy all in my holy mountain;
> for as the waters fill the sea,
> so shall the land be filled with the knowledge of the Lord.[14]

This is surely a daunting prospect, describing as it does both cosmic redemption and universal peace. Cynics may deride the very possibility, but I do not think Christians are free to do so. It needs to be held together with the realization that God's hope for creation is not simply presented before it as a future state, but a realizable possibility through the Holy Spirit. The groaning and travailing of creation awaits the inspired sons of God. In this way we can see that the God who demands is also the God who enables, or put more theologically, that what is given by God the Father is reconciled by God the Son and being redeemed by God the Spirit.

Secondly, humility. Christians do well to stop and pause before the mysterious workings of such a God. But having seen the vision, the task is to co-operate with its completion. Man is set within creation with the almost impossible commission to make peace, respect life and affirm God as the centre and goal of all existence. But because God's right will ultimately vanquish all wrong, man's almost impossible task is made possible by the very power which sustains him. Therefore, all conscientious openness to the Spirit and every attempt, however trivial, to disengage ourselves from violence has spiritual meaning and purpose. No effort, however small, is lost within the divine economy.

But the question may be posed: How far do we take all this? The answer is obvious: As far as we are enabled by the Spirit. The creation waits with eager longing for the revealing of the sons of God. And who are these? They are, simply put, Spirit-led individuals who will make possible a new order of existence; who will show by their life the possibility of newness of life. Quite practically the task required of us is to recognize God's rights in his creation, rights for animals to be themselves as God intends: to live; to be free; and to live without suffering, distress and injury. Doubtless the vision cannot be realized at once. What God's time scale is we do not know. We can only trust and hope, taking one step at a time. In what follows, I propose a plan of progressive disengagement from exploitation. Not all stages will be immediately possible. Some may appear more visionary than others; some more pragmatic than others. From where each of us stands, we see differently. What is overridingly important is that we all move as far as is possible. We have no alternative but to trust that the Spirit will do the rest.

Liberation from Wanton Injury

It will not be possible under each heading to treat every possible aspect of our use of animals, but I hope to assess the main areas and by so doing present a composite picture of the basic forms of exploitation. By 'injury' I mean all activity which causes pain, suffering, harm, distress, deprivation and death to any Spirit-filled living creature as detailed in Chapter Five.[15] By 'wanton' I include all those activities (and implicitly attitudes) which fall below the standard of moral justification which applies in analogous cases of human use and treatment. Put simply: wanton actions are those devoid of moral justification like 'need', 'defence', 'survival' or even 'benefit'. Wanton injury to animals includes their use for sport, recreation, pleasure and entertainment, as well as their ill-treatment through neglect, lack of care and downright cruelty. 'Cruelty' is an inexact term to describe wantonness. Some actions, for example, may cause pain or harm to animals without being cruel in the sense that an individual deliberately or consciously chooses to inflict pain. Again cruelty mainly concerns the infliction of suffering, but it needs to be remembered that animals suffer deprivations and distress which, while sometimes painful, may not always be so. Generally the use of the term cruelty should be eschewed in animal discussions as too narrow or inexact. I shall use the term *in this section only* in the widest sense, including all manner of deprivation and harms whether or not there is any deliberate intention so to do.

Liberation from wantonness would undoubtedly involve opposition to (*inter alia*) hunting and coursing; bull-fighting, bear-baiting and cock-fighting; the use of performing animals in circuses, wildfowling (shooting birds for sport) and the injurious use of animals in the production of cinematic and television films. These practices cannot be morally justified for five reasons in particular.

The first is that such wantonness betokens a moral meanness of life. Every act of making animals suffer harm, pain or deprivation for our pleasure or entertainment is a practical sign of our ungenerosity to God. It shows that we have not begun even in a minimal way to grasp divine benevolence. Humphry Primatt, writing in 1834, was one of the first to champion this insight and develop it in systematic form.

We may pretend to what RELIGION we please, but Cruelty is ATHEISM. We may make our boast of CHRISTIANITY; but Cruelty is INFIDELITY. We may trust to our ORTHODOXY; but Cruelty is the worst of HERESIES. The

Religion of Jesus Christ originated in the MERCY of GOD; and it was the gracious design of it to promote Peace to every creature upon Earth, and to create a spirit of universal Benevolence or *Goodwill* IN men.[16]

Christians without mercy, then, have failed to grasp the gospel of Jesus Christ. 'For, indeed, a Cruel Christian is a Monster of Ingratitude, a Scandal to his Profession, and beareth the name of Christ in vain: and in vain will he plead the mercies of GOD in Christ Jesus, when he appeareth before the GOD of universal nature'.[17] In this sense, to lack mercy is to betray God and also our own humanity. Aquinas almost got it right. Cruelty should be condemned not because it *sometimes* dehumanizes us, but because it *necessarily* does so.

Secondly, wantonness constitutes a practical rejection of the inherent value of creation. Those who defend hunting in particular frequently point to the other 'values', such as human pleasure, which their practice provides. Indeed St Francis de Sales, unlike his namesake, listed the hunting of animals among those 'innocent recreations' which we 'may always make good use of'.[18] We may suppose that St Francis simply did not know enough about the nature of animal suffering to include animals within his field of concern. For on any utilitarian calculation, the claims of the animals must have priority because they have so much more to lose. Human pleasure may be judged a 'value', even a 'good', but to let this override the claim of animals to live without suffering is strikingly disproportionate. It is not without irony that the argument from human pleasure should be used by Christians, since for many centuries pleasure was regarded as a sign of the moral unworthiness, if not downright immorality, of a proposed course of action. Textbooks like those of St Francis de Sales abound in condemnation of earthly pleasure as barriers to spiritual growth and refinement.[19] Henry Vaughan specifically castigates the 'silly snares of pleasure' that dominate a fallen world.[20]

The third reason why wantonness should be opposed is because it repudiates our moral covenant with animals. Quite simply, if there is to be no moral content to our relationship with animals such as even to prevent wanton treatment of them, it can hardly be claimed that we exist by God's decree in close spiritual proximity. It is God who elects man and beast into fellowship and unity, and it is we who repudiate this unity by acts of gratuitous destruction. Slowly but surely Christian Churches have begun to grasp this. The Society of Friends in a prophetic resolution in 1795 opposed the practices of hunting and shooting. 'Let our leisure be employed in serving our neighbour, and not in distressing, for our amusement, the creatures of God'.[21] The reasons for this resolution were only partly concerned with animals, but it still represented a significant opposition at a time when animal sports were immensely popular. In 1817, the House of Bishops of the Episcopal Church became the first governing body of an American denomination to condemn 'cruelty to the brute creation' and, by implication, hunting.[22] But it was not until 1970 that the National Assembly of the Church of England opposed hunting and coursing as 'cruel, unjustifiable and degrading' and resolved that Christian people should 'make plain their opposition to activities of this sort and their determination to do all in their power to secure their speedy abolition'.[23] What does our covenant with animals mean if we are not to prevent their needless destruction?

Fourthly, and inevitably, to act wantonly to animals is to deny their moral status. Rickaby, who regarded animals as 'things in our regard',[24] specifically alludes to the right to kill them for pleasure. Despite their enormous popularity and continuing appeal, animal sports implicitly support the view that the non-human are 'there for our enjoyment'. What we do to them is not a moral matter in itself, because it is presumed that they are not moral subjects. In the end we have to say that if a being cannot make a claim upon us of sufficient seriousness to merit desisting from wantonness, then that being must be presumed to have no moral standing. According to the theos-rights view even insects can make something like this claim (whether we have eventually to override their claims or not) even though they do not possess rights as we have described them. When pressed, hunters and shooters defend their practice by admitting, as Thorstein Veblen indicates, 'of other motives . . . besides the impulses of exploit and ferocity'.

Sportsmen . . . are more or less in the habit of assigning a love of nature, the need of recreation and the like, as the incentives for their favourite pastime . . . These ostensible needs could be

107

more readily and fully satisfied without the accompaniment of a systematic effort to take the life of those creatures that make up an essential feature of that 'nature' that is beloved by the sportsman. It is, indeed, the most noticeable effect of the sportsman's activity to keep nature in a state of chronic desolation by killing off all the living things whose destruction he can encompass.[25]

These words were written in 1899. And yet the moral confusion continues. It is best expressed by the sportsmen themselves as in the current motto of the Wildfowlers' Association of Great Britain: 'For Conservation and Shooting'. Now it cannot be doubted that sportsmen do indeed conserve nature, and especially those birds and animals they wish to hunt or shoot. In particular pheasants in plenty and even foxes are sometimes preserved for hunting.[26] The argument for controlling 'pest' populations is therefore shown to be disingenuous to say the least.

The fifth and final argument is to my mind the strongest. It is simply that wantonness violates God's right in creation. To breed and rear creatures for gratuitous destruction is not simply human perversity but a reversal of divine purpose. Animals are not made simply for human use and pleasure but for God's glory. God's right endues all Spirit-filled creatures with rights. We may argue about the details of animal rights, even perhaps dispute some of the situations where we hold animals to have analogous and competing rights, but this much is gospel: wantonness cannot coexist with generosity. The rights view upholds the generosity of God and in so doing, defends the rights of animals to live free of needless misery. The germ of this position was advocated centuries ago by St Thomas More. The Utopians of More's imagining conceived themselves not as 'masters' but 'stewards' of God's creation. Only humane farming was allowed in Utopia. Animal sacrifice was anathematized and hunting forbidden. Utopians 'do not believe that the divine clemency delights in bloodshed and slaughter, seeing that it has imparted life to animate creatures that they might enjoy life'.[27]

But having concluded that wanton injury to animals is immoral, we should still avoid the language of condemnation. Even at this point, surely the clearest from an animal rightists' perspective, we do well to recognize that few are entirely free from wantonness in any form. Condemning attitudes can become habit-forming and induce a censorious disposition. 'Some people enjoy a good moral condemnation the way others enjoy a good dinner.'[28] What Christian animal rightists should want to do is to liberate their fellow humans from their addiction to killing. This does not mean that legislation to prevent animals from wanton injury should be eschewed. On the contrary, legislation is urgently required to prevent the worst possible happening. In this respect, it is entirely without moral principle or foundation that the Wildlife and Countryside Act of 1981 should exempt from its protection clauses those animals it classes as 'ground game' (hares and rabbits).[29] The only moral difference between these animals and the others, such as bats, which the Act protects, is that by definition most 'ground game' are subjects of sport. Legislation needs to reflect our growing sense of the inherent value of all Spirit-filled creatures and not just those animals who are deemed to have some rarity value. From the standpoint of theos-rights, it makes some difference but not much whether it is the very last tiger, or one of many thousands, that is gratuitously killed.

Nevertheless, it needs to be appreciated that legislation can only take us so far. Isaiah hoped that the people of God would learn to 'beat their swords into ploughshares, and their spears into pruning hooks' and that they would not 'learn war any more'.[30] The goal of theos-rights is that humans will respect God's right and live in peace with creation. The moral agenda is therefore formidable. We must encourage those who wantonly injure animals to find less violent recreations. Those who hunt live animals to exhaustion should be encouraged to turn to drag hunting; those who shoot live birds should be encouraged to find 'clay' alternatives, and those who enjoy bull-fighting should be encouraged to take up sport with willing human participants. If these suggestions sound naive, we can only point to the reality of moral conversion. 'Every people, no matter how civilized, must have the chance to yell for blood,' argues the sociologist Max Lerner.[31] But the truth is that we have moral choice, we can resist, and in all these cases we lose nothing significant thereby.

Jeremiah envisaged a time when the Lord would write his commandments into our hearts to ensure compliance with divine law. In this way we would be freed from our hardness of heart.

Humane education and encouragement are essential, not only for the sake of the animals, but for humans themselves. Animal rightists need to show by precept and example how it is possible to live at peace with creation. 'Moral education, as I understand it, is not about inculcating obedience to law or cultivating self-virtue, it is rather about finding within us an ever-increasing sense of the worth of creation'.[32]

Liberation from Institutionalized Suffering

It is important to begin by distinguishing between pain and suffering. Pain is a 'specific physical sensation' whereas suffering, as John Hick points out, 'is a mental state which may be as complex as human life itself'.[33] While pain may be, and frequently is, an element in suffering, it is not necessarily so. In speaking of animal suffering we reject years of Cartesian history. To affirm that animals can experience not only pain, but also suffering, is to reject decisively the idea that animals are only 'things in our regard' as Rickaby postulated.[34] To accept that animals suffer is to acknowledge that they have a mental life: they experience fear, foreboding, anxiety, stress, discomfort, boredom and so on, and that all these reactions differ only in degree from those which are experienced by human beings. Animals 'bring subjectivity into our world', as Tom Regan explained at a recent conference.[35] It follows that animals suffer not only harms but also deprivations.[36] We cause animals to suffer not only by inflicting regular or semi-regular pain, but also by depriving them of some aspect or condition of their natural life without ameliorating compensation. We need to nail once and for all the notion that animals can suffer deprivations without violation of their rights because 'they haven't known anything better'. It is what animals already know of their life as mentally alive and experiencing creatures that makes deprivation as morally objectionable to them as it is for human beings.

When we use the words 'institutionalized suffering' we think primarily of those activities which involve habitual or regular use of animals and which in turn involve employment, trade or business. Institutionalized use is marked by the taking of creatures as means-to-human-ends. Animals in farming, research and trapping are viewed primarily not in terms of their own value but in terms of human utility. The 'meta-economic value' of animals, as E. F. Schumacher observes, is partially or wholly disregarded.[37] Animals become in relation to us 'commodities' to be bought and sold: 'tools' for scientific research or 'units of production' in intensive farming. We shall now explore three areas where theos-rights pose radical challenges to these practices.

(a) Intensive farming

It is well known that during the last thirty years or more, farmers have been under increasing pressure to tailor traditional farming methods to the needs of 'cost-effective' production. This has meant in practice a dramatic increase in the number of animals used, a tendency to specialize in one form of production and, more usually than not, systems of close confinement. 'The design of systems has thus moved out of the hands of the traditional stockmen and into the hands of engineers and technicians, men of great skill and ingenuity but usually with little knowledge of animals, and in particular animal behaviour'.[38] Farming animals intensively has become the norm.

> Within the systems of extreme confinement in Britain we now have *inter alia* around forty-five million laying-hens kept in crowded battery-cages, unable to spread even one wing and standing permanently on sloping wire-mesh; around half a million sows kept in narrow stalls in which they are unable to turn round, standing on open-grid flooring or on an unbedded floor of concrete; and some tens of thousands of young calves, destined for the 'white-veal' market, kept in slatted-floored crates, unable to turn round, unable to lie down freely, or even freely groom themselves. All these animals may be in darkened buildings as an antidote to restlessness, aggressiveness or the abnormal behaviour to which such conditions give rise. Some of the mutilations carried out on farm animals, such as the tail-docking of pigs and the de-beaking of chickens, are used for the same purpose.[39]

'Of course these systems of extreme confinement are to be abhorred,' argues Archbishop Runcie. 'As a practical pig-farmer I have found it possible to keep my pigs in conditions which respect their natural sphere of existence,' he adds.[40] But *why* is intensive farming abhorrent? One obvious answer is to point to the suffer-

111

ing inherent in these systems. And yet the difficulty in proving that animals suffer through deprivation of their natural life is formidable. If suffering is defined at the outset not in terms of deprivations but continuous painful stimuli, then it is impossible to *prove* suffering in ways that are acceptable to sceptical farmers or scientists. Another answer is to posit that animals are 'unhappy' in such environments. Again the task of establishing criteria and measurements in this area is overwhelmingly difficult. For many years the RSPCA financed scientific research into the 'preferences' of battery hens only to find (as some of us warned at the beginning) that such research was almost entirely incapable of establishing such preferences or even finding clear criteria by which such 'preferences' could be measured.[41]

It seems to me that the only satisfactory basis on which we can oppose systems of close confinement is by recourse to the argument drawn from theos-rights. To put it at its most basic: animals have a God-given right to be animals. The natural life of a Spirit-filled creature is a gift from God. When we take over the life of an animal to the extent of distorting its natural life for no other purpose than our own gain, we fall into sin. There is no clearer blasphemy before God than the perversion of his creatures. To the question: Why is it wrong to deny chickens the rudimentary requirements of their natural life, such as freedom of movement or association?, there is therefore only one satisfactory answer: Since an animal's natural life is a gift from God, it follows that God's right is violated when the natural life of his creatures is perverted. Those who in contrast opt for the 'welfarist' approach to intensive farming are inevitably involved in speculating how far such and such an animal may or may not suffer in what are plainly unnatural conditions. But unless animals are judged to have some right to their natural life, from what standpoint can we judge 'abnormalities', 'mutilations' or 'adjustments'? The de-beaked hen in a battery cage is more than a moral crime, it is a living sign of our failure to recognize the blessing of God in creation.

What makes this situation all the more lamentable is the realization that the use to which animals are put in intensive farming 'goes far beyond even the most generous interpretation of need'.[42] Whether we need to kill animals for food will be discussed in Chapter Seven. But it will be obvious that humans can live healthy, stimulating and rewarding lives without 'white-veal', pâté de foie gras, or the ever-increasing quantities of cheap eggs. The truth is that we can afford to be much more generous to farm animals than is frequently the case today.

What then must be done? The first and most obvious require-ment is that we should press for the enforcement of minimum standards in farming. Writing in 1834, Humphry Primatt defended the 'undoubted right' of animals 'intrusted in our care' to 'FOOD, REST and TENDER USAGE'.[43] Securing even these minimal rights in an age of intensive farming would be a colossal enterprise. The food given to animals in these conditions is frequently deficient, as in the case of the iron-deficient diet given to calves to make their flesh whiter. Rest without appro-priate bedding and freedom of movement is similarly deprived. Tender usage presupposes the old-fashioned role of farmers as stockmen rather than operators of huge intensive plants. The application of technology to farming has made the plight of farm animals infinitely worse since the time of the early pioneers in animal welfare. The *Animals and Ethics* Report proposed 'basic guidelines' which should have the force of law. These include: 'freedom to perform natural physical movement'; 'facilities for comfort activities' such as rest, sleep and body-care; 'provision of food and water to maintain full health' and 'minimal spatial and territorial requirements'.[44] The present situation in the United Kingdom, where farmers are virtually free to treat animals as they wish save for certain safeguards against excessive suffering and downright cruelty, and where the voluntary codes are so voluntary that farmers do not even need to have read them, is a situation ripe for regulating legislation.

The second need is for the exercise of consumer choice. Many farmers, even those who dislike intensive systems, justify their practices on the grounds that the public prefer cheap food in spite of the obvious cost to farm animals. This *may* be so. But have we put it to the test? The recent experiments by some leading supermarket stores which allow consumers to choose between battery-produced eggs and free-range eggs have shown that some, even many, consumers prefer to pay more when they know what they are buying. Animal rightists must encourage super-markets to give the consumer a choice. Let us have food counters selling non-intensively farmed meat with accurate labelling information and then, and only then, will we be able to test consumer demand. The idea has potentially great appeal. The Bishop of Dudley recently wrote of how Christians 'need to go shopping with God' because 'what Christians do with the things of the world and the way they live their everyday lives are expressions of their faith'.[45] All that animal rightists need to ask is that we give non-Christians as well as Christians an opportunity to exercise their moral choice.

The third need is for Churches to reflect in their own collective actions the sensitivity they not infrequently hope for in others. The Church Commissioners, for example, own and lease over 160,000 acres of farming land. While it is true that the Commissioners do ask tenants 'not to permit any livestock for the time being on any part of the holding to be treated in such a manner as to be caused unnecessary pain or unnecessary distress',[46] this condition goes no further than existing British law which prohibits the infliction of 'unnecessary' suffering. Under present legislation animals can be subject to intensive farming and are so on Church-owned land. It is anomalous that the Church of England should allow on its land farming practices which many senior ecclesiastics oppose and which one bishop recently likened to 'Auschwitz' for animals.[47] It is sad to see the Church wrong-footed in a debate to which it has so much to contribute. Even individuals like myself who are indebted to the Church Commissioners (for they help to provide my stipend) would be happier if their generosity to clergy were matched by a similarly generous attitude to the non-human creation. It would certainly be a gesture, and no empty one for the farm animals concerned, if the Commissioners felt able to proscribe by contract some of the worst features of intensive farming on the land they hold in trust for the wider Christian community.

(b) Painful experimentation

The range and variety of the use of animals in experimentation is enormous. At almost every level of scientific investigation there is some recourse to the 'animal model'. Coming to grips with the sheer diversity of use on one hand, and the ramifications of sustaining this use which involves the breeding, selling and captivity of millions of animals world-wide on the other, is a daunting business. Animals are used in product testing, behavioural research, for instructional purposes, *in vivo* tests for the pharmaceutical industry, in emergency medicine, in long-term medical research and in biological research. In product testing alone, animals are used to test the safety of a staggeringly wide range of products including: oven-cleaners, hair-sprays, skin-fresheners, anti-perspirants, nail polish, lubricants, dyes, fire-extinguisher substances, deodorants, facial make-up, floor-cleaners and brake fluids.[48] We scarcely appreciate how the world in which we live is affected at almost every level by the use of animals in scientific inquiry, from psychological theories of dependence developed by subjecting animals to various forms of emotional deprivation on the one hand, to the utilization of animals in crash tests to 'analyse the adequacy of seat belts, helmets and shoulder harnesses' on the other.[49]

Reviewing my earlier work, Hugh Montefiore criticized me for failing to sufficiently consider the benefits of animal research.[50] In this section therefore I want to get to grips with this central issue: Can the ends justify the means?

Perhaps the most radical attack on the institution of animal experimentation was made in a little known essay written in 1947 by C. S. Lewis. Lewis, never a person of moral compromise, does not mince his words:

> Once the old Christian idea of a total difference in kind between man and beast has been abandoned, then *no argument for experiments on animals can be found which is not also an argument for experiments on inferior men.* If we cut up beasts simply because they cannot prevent us and because we are backing up our own side in the struggle for existence, it is only logical to cut up imbeciles, criminals, enemies or capitalists for the same reason. Indeed, experiments on men have already begun. We all hear that Nazi scientists have done them. We all suspect that our own scientists may begin to do so, in secret, at any moment.[51]

Lewis' argument may appear contentious in at least two ways. In the first place, is it true that Christian doctrine maintains a '*total* difference *in kind*' between man and animals? We have seen how precisely the opposite should be the case; that the biblical material requires us to view man and animals as subjects of common creation bound together in the same covenant relationship. The difference 'in kind' must surely relate to the moral obligations present in humankind which are absent in animals, and which elsewhere Lewis defends as the major difference between humans and non-humans.[52] In the second place, the notion that 'no argument . . . can be found' for experimentation on animals which does not also justify experimentation on humans will strike many as absurd. Is it not precisely the moral difference between animals and humans which justifies their respectively different treatments? Anyone who does not already oppose animal experimentation will surely regard these lines as anti-vivisectionist propaganda. And yet could it be that Lewis was right?

On 15 May 1941, Dr Sigmund Rasher, who was the Nazi Medical Officer of the Luftwaffe, wrote to Himmler concerning his experiments on the psychological and physiological troubles involved in high-altitude flights:

> I have noticed with regret that no experiments on *human* material has yet been introduced here, because the tests are very dangerous and no volunteers have offered their services. For this reason I ask in all seriousness: Is there any possibility of obtaining from you two or three professional criminals to be placed at our disposal? These tests, in the course of which the 'guinea-pigs' may die, would be carried out under supervision. *They are absolutely indispensable to research* into high-altitude flying *and cannot be carried out, as has been so far attempted, on monkeys*, whose reactions are completely different.[53]

Notice how it was the apparent failure of experiments on animals which led directly to the request for human subjects. A request, incidentally, that Himmler was 'delighted' to comply with.[54] But, it may be protested, it is wholly wrong to compare the Nazi scientists of yesterday with the humane, morally scrupulous animal researchers of today. After all, the Nazis *were* Nazis, they only represented an aberrant, if morally shocking, episode in the history of experimental science. But is this true?

'I sometimes felt sorry for the logs of wood. I wondered, is it right to do such things to them?'[55] The speaker is Naoji Uezono, leader of the vivisection team of the 731st Japanese regiment during the Second World War. The 'logs of wood' (*maruta*) were some three thousand Chinese, Russian, Mongol and American prisoners of war. These human prisoners were subjected to 'injection of plague, cholera, typhus and other germs, the freezing of limbs, the infecting of syphilis [and] the prolonged exposure to X-rays'.[56] If people wonder why details of these experiments are not so well known as their Nazi counterparts, the answer is even more grotesque. An arrangement was made whereby the vivisection team would be granted immunity from prosecution, if the useful results of their researches were handed over to the Americans. The 'freezing experiments were so thorough that the team leader became the world authority on the science of human adaptability to [the] environment'.[57] Dr Edwin Hill, a US Army scientist, said in 1947 that the important information 'could not be obtained in our laboratories because of scruples attached to human experimentation'.[58]

But, it may be objected, these experiments happened during 'wartime'. We agree that awful, sometimes terrible, things happen in war. But is 'human material', as Dr Rasher puts it, safe during 'peacetime'? Was Lewis wrong when he argued that humans could find what they regard as 'inferior' humans to experiment upon, once the logic of using animals becomes widespread?

During the last twenty years or more, scientists working in the area of human genetics have developed *in vitro* techniques of human fertilization. This has given the opportunity for experimental work on embryos, and at the present moment it is possible for scientists to create embryonic 'material' for the sole purpose of research. The majority of the Warnock Committee in the United Kingdom recommended that 'Legislation should provide that research may be carried out on any embryo resulting from *in vitro* fertilization, whatever its provenance, *up to the end of the fourteenth day after fertilization* . . .'[59] These experiments, under the legislation proposed, would be formally legalized and experimenters licensed for their work. The majority of the Committee did not regard an embryo 'as a person, or even as a potential person'.[60] Experimentation could be justified because respect for the embryo 'cannot be absolute, and may be weighed against the benefits arising from research'.[61]

What then is the moral status of the embryo? The Committee argued that it should have a 'special status' and that 'it should be afforded some protection in law'.[62] But this protection is *not* that which extends to other adult humans; so long as it is 'spare' it can still be used and destroyed for research purposes. In short: the embryo is a 'sub-human'; it fares a little better than the animals, but only a little. Its practical status is hardly distinguishable from the 'inferior' humans of which Lewis wrote.

It must be remembered that these developments have taken place against the institutionalized, routinized use of millions of animals for experimentation every year in the world today. In the United Kingdom the number of animals so used has grown from less than a thousand in 1876, when the first Act legalizing animal experimentation was passed, to annual figures in the region of three to four million. Figures for the United States, as we have seen, range from around seventy to a hundred and twenty million. Animals as a matter of course have been subject, and still are subject, to burning, scalding, starving, mutilating, depriving and in almost every other way, harmful experiments. It must be very difficult for anti-vivisectionists not to have a sense of *déjà vu* when listening to debates about the use of embryos in experimentation. The talk of licensing, essential controls, advisory committees and inspectors all have a familiar ring. The battle was lost for animals when, after years of such discussion, two Royal Commissions, and despite royal and archiepiscopal patronage of the anti-vivisection cause, amended legislation in the end allowed the infliction of 'severe pain'.[63]

It may be protested that the foregoing amounts to scare tactics which obscure the important distinctions that should be made between the cases of humans, embryos and animals. But the distinctions that may be drawn in this area seem to work for animals rather than against them. Unlike embryos (although we cannot be certain at present) animals are sentient. Like embryos, but not some adult human beings, animals cannot give or withold their consent to procedures inflicted upon them. Where are the morally relevant distinctions which justify experimentation upon primates (in for example outrageous head-injury experiments) but which cannot justify experimentation upon embryos or even adult humans?

What characterizes *all* these experiments, whether on criminals, prisoners of war, embryos or animals, is that they are defended on the basis of benefit. Dr Rasher was sincerely convinced that research on criminals was 'absolutely indispensable' in order to increase understanding of the problems involved in high-altitude flying. The Warnock Committee was convinced (surely no less sincerely) that respect for the embryo must be 'weighed against the benefits arising out of research'. And many experimenters are no less convinced today (and equally sincerely) that experimentation on animals is essential. Even a distinguished scientist like W. D. M. Paton can justify '*nicotine* injections into monkeys with brain electrodes' because 'these experiments showed that nicotine produces a state of brain arousal resembling normal arousal more closely than does that produced by caffeine or amphetamine' and are therefore 'important for understanding the smoking habit'.[64]

Some people, even those who seek reform of animal experimentation, still justify some experimentation on the basis of benefit. 'If one, or even a dozen animals had to suffer experiments in order to save thousands, I would think it right and in accordance with equal consideration of interests that they should do so', argues Peter Singer. 'This, at any rate, is the answer a utilitarian must give,' he adds.[65] But even if utilitarianism is a satisfactory moral philosophy (which some of us would doubt), it fails to grapple with the fact that it is always possible to justify experimentation on the grounds of utility, if only for the reason that nothing can be *proved* to be useless. It is simply impossible to deny the utility of experiments on humans, sub-humans or animals. Like Lewis, I simply find myself unable to find any justification for experiments on animals which do not also justify experiments on humans, 'sub' or otherwise. 'Once you grant the ethics of the vivisectionists', argued George Bernard Shaw, 'you not only sanction the experiment on the human subject, but make it a first duty of the vivisector'.[66]

Some may still regard this Lewis/Shaw argument as propaganda. But its logic is accepted even by those who publicly deride any notion of animal rights. Raymond Frey, that dedicated opponent of rights theory, has sadly to conclude that 'we cannot, with the appeal to benefit, justify (painful) animal experiments without justifying (painful) human experiments'.[67] Frey accepts this even though he justifies experimentation on animals. Again: 'The case for anti-vivisectionism, I think, is far stronger than most people allow', he writes.[68] Alas, Frey does not seem to regard it as sufficiently strong to oppose experiments on animals *or* humans.

Now, I do not believe that the vivisectors of animals and embryos of today, any more than the vivisectors of criminals and prisoners of yesterday, are particularly awful or terrible people. Those who are so eager to demonstrate their abhorrence of animal experimentation that they accuse the whole system of 'greed, cruelty, ambition, incompetence, vanity . . . sadism, insanity' are wide of the mark.[69] There is reason for thinking that *some* experimenters are sadistically inclined or at least grotesquely callous. This is shown, I think beyond doubt, by the recently stolen film, produced by the experimenters themselves in the United States, which pictures researchers laughing at the suffering of severely brain-injured primates.[70] But by and large it is wrong to accuse scientists of sadism. Doubtless sadists exist in every profession and perhaps all humans are prone to sadistic impulses in some way. Self-righteousness, however, is not a satisfactory response to collective sinfulness (or indeed to any form of sinfulness) and it is hard to believe that anyone is morally innocent when it comes to the exploitation of animals.

But why precisely then do we hold animal experimentation to be sinful? The straightforward answer is that the philosophy which justifies it inevitably justifies other evils. Once our moral thinking becomes dominated by crude utilitarian calculations, then there is no right, value or good that cannot be bargained away, animal or human. Some will find this a hard judgement. Doubtless there is some case for utilitarian calculations in moral thinking. There are times when it seems right to calculate the consequences in a relatively straightforward way. And there are some Christians who, however scrupulous with their use of animals, feel strongly the pull of appeals to benefit. But even if we accept that some albeit limited experimentation was justified in particular and special circumstances, could we accept the *institutionalization* of this practice? Antony Flew made the point some years ago when discussing the practice of torture. He writes as one who holds that the torture of suspects may be justifiable if the benefits seem overwhelming. But he also makes the point that even if torture might be justifiable in very limited circumstances, it can never be acceptable as 'an institutional legal or social practice'.[71] In other words, to make an institution of torture would still be wrong from what he calls the 'deontological' as well as the 'consequentialist' approaches.

There was a time after *Animal Rights* when I held for a while that some form of experimentation might be justified. It seemed to me inevitable that some appeals to benefit have moral claim upon us. But the intervening years have also confirmed my earlier view that the institutionalization of experimentation presents us with nothing less than the massive subjugation of millions of animal lives who are bred, sold, confined and used on the presupposition that they have *only* utilitarian value. 'Evil' is the only appropriate moral category I can find which expresses the enormity of the immorality that this involves. If we do not often use such 'calmly stern language' it is perhaps, as Lewis indicates, that 'the other side has in fact won'.[72] To oppose such a widespread, highly organized and well-represented institution as that of experimental science is indeed a bold step, and even within the animal movement there are those who would prefer not to confront the issue directly. But in such an area where millions of animal lives are at stake it would be wrong to turn away from the moral vision that the acceptance of animal rights demands of us. As Lewis crisply reminds us, even our vision of our own humanity is at stake:

> And though cruelty even to beasts is an important matter, [the vivisectors'] victory is symptomatic of matters more important still. The victory of vivisection marks a great advance in the triumph of ruthless, non-moral utilitarianism over the old world of ethical law; a triumph in which we, as well as animals, are already the victims, and of which Dachau and Hiroshima mark the more recent achievements. In justifying cruelty to animals we put ourselves also on the animal level. We choose the jungle and must abide by our choice.[73]

What then must we do? If our moral vision requires us to turn away from the institution of animal experimentation, in which direction should we move? Of the many ways of liberation, four seem especially appropriate.

The first is *legislation*. Ideally I would like to see applied to animals subjects the provision of the Declaration of Helsinki, adopted by the World Medical Assembly of 1964, which held that 'the interest of science and society should never take precedence over considerations related to the well-being of the subject' in experimentation.[74] In other words, we need legislation forbidding the use of animals as experimental material. Until that day, we must work *progressively* for reform. One way is to highlight those areas of experimentation which even some researchers would like to see diminished or proscribed. These include: the use of animals for product testing, tests of obvious brutality such as the Draize test or the LD50 test, experiments which involve severe pain, the reuse of animals which have recovered from anaesthesia, or experiments on certain species of animal such as primates. In addition, the conditions under which animals are kept prior to experimentation frequently leaves much to be desired. Acceptance of the minimal guidelines for animals kept in captivity advocated by the *Animals and Ethics* Report would be a major breakthrough. In the United States opposition to 'pound seizure' where unwanted animals are automatically transferred to laboratories is growing but urgently needs the support of legislation.[75] In a whole host of ways, the plight of laboratory animals needs to be kept on the legislative agenda. If more inspectors, increased animal welfare representation on advisory and ethical committees and further systems of licensing will actually bring more scrutiny and control then they should be welcomed. Since the issues involved in animal experimentation concern the whole community and not just the experimental scientists themselves, it is only right that all interested sections of the community should have some voice. Legislative proposals, even if unsuccessful, help to focus the mind wonderfully by encouraging discussion and debate of otherwise neglected issues.

The second is *dialogue*. There are some experimenters who are simply not interested in dialogue about the morality of experimentation. Conversely, there are also some animal rightists incapable of dialogue. But not all experimenters or animal rightists are of this sort. Indeed my experience has been that there are a number of scientists deeply troubled about experimental techniques and some animal rightists who are willing to grapple with the complexities which the issue involves. This dialogue needs our urgent support. I vividly remember attending a conference on alternatives to the use of animals some years ago and finding myself in discussion with a laboratory technician working in the field of cancer research. We discussed the rights and wrongs of experimentation at some length. Some years later, I found to my amazement that this same person had given up her job, exposed the conditions under which animals had been kept in her laboratories and become a leading light in the anti-vivisection movement. Of course one chance meeting and spirited discussion was not by itself the cause of moral conversion, but dialogue always contains with it the possibility of change—on both sides, of course. The more both sides move away from stereotyped pictures of each other, either of sadistic scientists with hands dripping with blood on the one hand, or of sentimental anti-vivisectionists who have no knowledge of the facts on the other, the better it will be for human tolerance as well as the cause of animal rights.

The third is *alternatives*. Already in Britain the government has given a small amount to funding specific research devoted to developing alternatives to animals. The majority of the work, however, is financed by public charities including the Dr Hadwen Trust for Humane Research, the Lawson-Tait and Humane Research Trust, the Lord Dowding Fund for Humane Research and FRAME (The Fund for Replacement of Animals in Medical Experiments). All these bodies should be supported and their admirable work encouraged. Even the Research Defence Society helped sponsor an important publication on *Alternatives to Animal Experiments* which, while defending the need for research involving animals, offers a useful compendium of viable alternatives.[76] That anti-vivisectionists have spent so much of their money trying to develop alternatives to animals should give the lie once and for all to the notion that opposing animal experiments involves opposition to all forms of experimental science. Scientists need to be encouraged through voluntary self-restriction, as Catherine Roberts indicates, to avoid animal use.[77] Through dialogue and the utilization of alternatives, the moral consciousness of scientists can be raised. But in the end, as Brigid Brophy observes, 'necessity will mother invention'.[78] We would be in an entirely different situation today if the consensus among scientists in previous years had opposed animal experimentation in principle and therefore made the development of alternatives an urgent necessity.

The fourth is *choice*. It is frequently argued, especially by pharmaceutical companies, that public concern for safety demands animal tests. But the truth is as the *Animals and Ethics* Report concludes: 'Commercial competition leads firms to market new products differing only minutely in formula from the old, but because of the change in formula they require testing on animals'.[79] There is a whole variety of substances known to be safe and a whole range of products including cosmetics and toiletries which can be produced that do not require testing on animals. Again let the matter be put to proper consumer choice. Let us have in our departmental stores those cosmetics developed with the aid of animal tests and those products by, say, Beauty Without Cruelty. So long as the items are accurately labelled and marked, let us see if it is true that consumers will only buy animal-tested products. If competition is to be the justifying criterion for animal tests, let us have a little consumer competition to gauge the truth of the manufacturers' claims. As a rule we far too easily accept the view of manufacturing industry about what the public wants. Animal rightists should invite multinationals to spend just a small part of their annual turnover on the production of goods which require no animal testing and let the consumer choose.

Yet it would be wrong to suppose that industries which finance animal tests or even the scientists themselves should bear the full weight of responsibility. The questions posed by the *Animals and Ethics* Report deserve a hearing:

> Basic to the question of the validity of experiments is the type of society man actually wants and the cost to himself of achieving it. Do we as a society, for example, really want research to be continued into such devastating ways of killing our fellows as those involved in biological weapons of warfare? Are there any ills we are prepared to bear rather than resort to experiments on animals? Are we, for example, through blind obedience to 'technological progress' continuing to create problems that perpetuate the necessity for animal experimentation, or are we actively creating a society in which the necessity for experiments on animals will be drastically reduced?[80]

One *Christian* answer to these questions has yet to be heard. It is that, deeply conscious of our divinely given stewardship over creation and our special bond of covenant with animals in particular, we should elect to bear for ourselves whatever ills may flow from not experimenting on animals rather than be supporting an institution which perpetuates tyranny. This may be a hard option for many, but it is as arguably a Christian response as many of the others which claim that appellation. If it is the *good* shepherd as opposed to the hireling who actually lays down his life for the sheep, perhaps the *good* steward is the one who desists from any path of injury in deference to the prior right of God in creation.

(c) Fur-trapping

We come face to face with institutionalized suffering in the food we eat, the products we buy and also the clothes we wear. At first sight the case for the trapping of fur animals for adornment purposes will appear the weakest of all. How can adornment articles like fur coats possibly justify the sustained suffering that fur-bearing animals have to endure? If there is some dispute about the suffering of farm animals, there can be none when it comes to trapping. Almost all the methods involved are *inherently* painful.[81] And yet fur-trapping has not lacked its defenders, and Christian apologists too. A recent statement issued by the Anglican and Roman Catholic Bishops in Northern Canada expressed their 'solidarity with the aboriginal peoples of the North who are engaged in a struggle to save fur-trapping as a way of life'.[82] Their arguments appear to be threefold. The first is that trapping 'is a way of life deeply rooted in the cultural traditions of aboriginal societies in the Canadian North'.[83] The second is that sudden declines in trade, as when the European Economic Community placed a ban on the importation of baby seal skins, cause the 'loss of economic self-sufficiency' and with it 'a sense of hopelessness' and even a 'suicide rate in native communities . . . more than six times the national average'.[84] The third argument is that trappers are environmentally responsible: 'The aboriginal harvesting process entails the responsible stewardship of creation' because they practise 'conservation in their annual harvesting each year'.[85]

The first argument is question-begging. The issue is not of course whether a particular way of life depends upon fur-trapping but whether fur-trapping can be justified from the outset. The second argument also begs this point. It is not difficult to understand why bishops as 'pastoral leaders' should be concerned for the welfare of the peoples they apparently represent.

Unemployment, a sense of hopelessness and suicidal tendencies are matters of concern to pastors especially. But the Christian concern demonstrated by these bishops does not appear to extend to fur-bearing animals at all. They clearly do not see it as part of their responsibility to the Christian gospel to ask whether ways of life which necessarily involve suffering to other forms of life are in fact worth defending in the first place. Since it is well known that Christian missionaries all over the world have disrupted the natural life of indigenous peoples, we may fail to see how it is that defending the 'social and cultural values' of traditional life is now to be regarded as a self-evident Christian concern. Of course the bishops may reply that they are simply trying to pay back indigenous culture something of what imposed Christian culture once took from them. 'The anti-fur campaign', argue the bishops, 'violates the dignity of aboriginal peoples and some of their deeply felt cultural and spiritual traditions'.[86] One cannot help wondering whether some sense of guilt is being rationalized here for all the previous disruption that Christian missionaries have caused.

To the third argument, that trappers are also conservationists and thus obeying the Christian doctrine of stewardship, two replies are appropriate. The first is that conservation, far from being a religious duty, may be little more than enlightened self-interest for the trappers concerned if their way of life depends upon it. The second is that in stewardship thus defined we have no specific responsibilities to the individual animals concerned, save that of not making them extinct as a species. Stewardship clearly does not encompass issues such as the right of suffering creatures to be relieved of their suffering or more directly the justifiability of trade which necessitates such suffering. This point is surely the most disturbing from the standpoint of theos-rights. Wild fur-bearing animals are simply assumed to be renewable for humans to 'harvest' (their word). Issues of suffering can be put to one side, if it can be shown that some human interest, represented by a way of life people wish to lead, is at stake. As an exercise in moral theology it is partisan to say the least. To argue that suffering animals count for little is one thing. To argue that the welfare of animals should be absolutely subordinated to human needs is another. But it is altogether

126

lamentable that suffering animals should count for nothing save that of being a renewable human resource.

And yet it may be argued that humans have a right to their culture and their way of life. What would we be, it may be questioned, without our land and history and ways of life? In general, culture is valuable. But it is also the case that there can be evil cultures, or at least cherished traditions which perpetuate injustice or tyranny. The Greeks, for example, despite all their outstanding contributions to learning did not appear to recognize the immorality of slavery. There can be elements within every culture that are simply not worth defending, not only slavery but also infanticide and human sacrifice. At the very least the case must be made that trading in animals is a morally acceptable, as well as a culturally essential, element within that which we are concerned to preserve. In short: human traditions and ways of life may be generally worth defending, but not at any cost and certainly not when they depend upon the suffering of thousands, if not millions, of wild animals every year.

What then must we do? In the first place we must address the cultural claim by seeing how far human lives, as distinct from preferences, are actually at stake in the moral issue. 'In one twelve-month period', according to the RSPCA, 'when 38.2 million wild animals were killed for their fur, a substantial proportion were caught in traps in the USA where only 2% of trappers are professional'.[87] From a practical point of view there is a distinction between what is genuinely indigenous and what are indigenous skills exploited for our benefit. My own view is that no human lives will or need be lost by the rundown of the fur-trapping industry. Dollars may be lost, of course. Some individuals may have to face some difficult questions about where they should live and how they are to be employed. *Perhaps* the human population, and therefore the ecclesiastical congregations of the North, will diminish over a period of time. But from the perspective of theos-rights these will be acceptable costs if the result is the reduction of suffering to millions of animals. No moral options are cost free. The pastoral task, and incidentally I can think of no better people than bishops to lead the way, is to help people desist from a cultural life which however otherwise laudable can only be achieved at the expense of pain and suffering to other creatures. Moreover, this policy may restore, where possible, the genuinely indigenous form of life which has been prevented by our own gain. It remains an open question how far the exploitation of crimes by indigenous cultures is in fact the result of our exploitation of them for commercial profit.

The second response is to underline the gravity of our consumer choice. Our choice to wear fur is made quite literally at the cost of a number of animals that have died in agony. The claims by the 'Ecology Section' of the International Fur Trade Federation that among other things 'acrylic fibres, which are often used in the production of fake fur, are highly inflammable and therefore constitute a fire risk', or that 'the use of the chemical industry makes heavy use of irreplaceable mineral resources for the production of fibres for synthetic fur' are signs of an industry clutching at any straw in the face of growing unpopularity.[88] The campaign against fur-wearing led by the RSPCA in 1985 resulted in a significant number of high-street stores abandoning their retail trade in fur. Consumers who effectively organize themselves can change the frequently volatile fashions in dress and adornment.

The third response is the development of effective international trading restrictions. The bishops were able to testify in their statement to the effect of the recent EEC ban on baby seal skins which resulted in the devastation of 'the market for all seal products'.[89] Restrictive legislation will not of course meet every situation, but since business is at the heart of the trade in furs, consumer demand and import controls can destroy markets as well as create them. Our hope for the indigenous peoples of the North is that they may live in peace with wild animals (as arguably many of them once did) but, if they cannot, perhaps it is better that the animals be left free to live according to *their own* way of life.

7 Ways of Liberation (II)

Despite the heavy judgements made in the foregoing, many would now accept that wantonness or the causing of suffering to animals requires serious moral justification. That so many think this way is in no small measure due to our Christian forebears active in the RSPCA and to what has been called the 'moral feat' of the Society in changing attitudes.[1] And yet despite their principal objectives of 'promot[ing] kindness and prevent[ing] ... cruelty',[2] the RSPCA has increasingly found it necessary to go beyond a simple concern with animal cruelty as such. The Society's current policies oppose a wide range of practices which *may* cause stress or which *may* diminish the quality of an animal's life, or practices like dissection in school biology lessons, which can 'readily lead to desensitization and a lessening of respect for life'. The Society is against non-veterinary mutilations of animals, such as tail-docking and ear-cropping; the selective breeding of animals which 'produces changes in bodily form and/or function'; the sale of puppies and kittens in pet shops; the killing of lobsters, crabs and crayfish by the usual methods; the giving of live animals as prizes and the keeping of animals in schools where 'adequate provision cannot be made for their physical and mental well-being'.[3]

This extension of welfare concern is both inevitable and logical. But it also represents a significant change in moral perspective. The debate about animals is now not simply about whether we should kill needlessly or cause suffering but also about the way we should manage animals in general and how we should respect their God-given lives.

Liberation from Oppressive Control

Some Christians are still apt to interpret human dominion over animals as a licence to control them in every situation. While it cannot be denied that Christian teaching gives humans the responsibility of controlling and managing the earth, there are two vital qualifications. The first is that this power must be exercised *under God*. The second is that our manipulation of creation must be in conformity with God's own moral design for the cosmos. Correctly perceived, therefore, humans have no absolute rights. Any 'right' we claim for humans is derived from, dependent on, and must be morally grounded in the will of God. The challenge in this section is to spell out the distinction between moral and immoral management.

(a) Captive animals

The concern here is with the captivity of *wild* animals. Are wild animals best left alone? Can we justify the keeping of them in zoological gardens or safari parks? We need to begin by understanding the harm done to wild animals by captivity. To deny liberty to a wild animal involves the diminishing of that animal's life. It is an inherent characteristic of wild things to be free. We may reasonably suppose that in almost all cases the denial of this inherent characteristic involves stress, frustration, anxiety and even aggression. One recent work on the 'failure' of British animal collections, by two people with a lifetime's experience, claims that 'many animals remain neglected and live in conditions ranging from poor to what can only be described as absolutely inhumane'.[4] As if the denial of liberty was not enough by itself, many environmental conditions for animals are unsuitable, restricting and boring. Ironically it is the lack of 'normal' stress in the caged environment that helps compound the deprivation. The RSPCA is opposed to 'any degree of confinement likely to cause distress or suffering' and specifically to the 'capture, transportation and acclimatisation of animals' inevitable in the zoo trade.[5]

But quite apart from these humanitarian concerns, there is a theological issue which is frequently overlooked. It is that animals have some right to be free. Not only does Genesis envisage the giving of land as a common possession of man and animals, but also divine 'blessing' is designed to give creatures freedom to be themselves. 'Listen my people,' says the Lord in rejecting blood sacrifices:

> all the beasts of the forest are mine
> and the cattle in thousands on my hills.
> I know every bird on those hills,
> the teeming life of the fields is my care.[6]

In other words, God rejoices in the life of free animals he has made. He does not need them to be offered in sacrifice because they are already his and within his care. There is of course something cursed as well as blessed about the wild creation that lives around us. But wildness is not synonymous with being cursed. Indeed the wildness of nature has its own particular praise to offer:

> all mountains and hills;
> all fruit-trees and all cedars;
> wild beasts and cattle,
> creeping things and winged birds . . .
> O praise the Lord.[7]

The taming, manipulating and subduing of nature is not self-evidently a Christian pursuit. The precise opposite can be claimed: it could be our responsibility to respect what God has given and let it be.

Potential justifications for keeping wild animals captive are threefold: entertainment, education and conservation. The first is surely the weakest. The harm done to animals cannot be justified, even in utilitarian terms, by whatever entertainment value such parks may possess. But, of course, it is seldom the seemingly altruistic desire to entertain and amuse that is at stake—it is the desire for profit. One worrying feature of the proliferation of zoos in Britain consists in their increasing commercialization. 'For many zoo operators', argue Bill Jordan and Stefan Ormrod, 'the wild animals are simply goods placed on display in exchange for hard cash'.[8] *All* zoos, however high-minded their intentions, also hope to entertain, give pleasure or provide recreation. But to entertain at the animals' expense only compounds the wrong done to them. Are sources of entertainment so scarce, we may ask, that they can be justified even at the cost of animal misery?

The second justification, namely education, takes us a little further, but only a little. For what precisely have humans to learn about wild animals when they are deprived of their liberty? Many of the inmates of our zoos are not 'normal' specimens in the sense that we may view them interacting in their usual environments or with their chosen companions. It is sometimes argued that there can be no substitute for 'seeing the real thing', and that children especially are given an impression of animals that is often positive and admiring. But is there something 'positive' about seeing caged or confined animals? Is it not at least possible to argue that what children in particular 'see' in zoos is damaging to a sense of the dignity of animals? In point of fact, *few* zoos run educational programmes that are worth the name beyond that of 'spot this sort of animal' and 'spot this other sort'.[9] Any educational aspect of zoos is frequently secondary to the desire to make money, to entertain or to win prestige for the individual zoo owner. A recent Government inquiry into dolphinariums in Britain commissioned the views of unaligned educationalists who concluded that 'the unnatural, anthropomorphic exhibition of animals as performers may be merely showing the majority who witness the displays . . . that the animals' existence is legitimated only by their ability to meet the demands for human entertainment'. Far from being useful, those consulted concluded that such displays were *'anti-educational'*.[10]

The fourth justification concerning conservation is frequently the most seductive. Surely it is right to make some animals captive, perhaps only for a short time, if the species can be returned to the wild? In point of fact, very few zoos indeed are involved in conservation of this kind, and for obvious reasons. Captivity can very easily make animals the kind of creatures that are not returnable to the wild; prolonged captivity can induce neurosis, impotence, aggression or death. But let us accept that there may be some situations where the enforced capture, transport and captivity of some animals may conceivably lead to their successful transplantation in other regions. Is not the relative deprivation of some animals justifiable in the light of the ultimate goal of conservation?

What this argument assumes is that the rights of some individual animals should be subordinated to those of the species concerned. In other words, for the good of the species, some individuals within it may legitimately suffer deprivation or harm or both. Indeed some conservationists like Aldo Leopold hold that 'a thing is right when it tends to preserve the integrity, stability, and beauty of the biotic community'.[11] Such a view, as Tom Regan indicates, might be labelled 'environmental fascism'. It implies that 'the individual may be sacrificed for the greater biotic good',[12] and if the rights of animals can be thus traded away, what prospect might there be for human beings? This is not to suppose that the rights of animals or humans are absolute. It is only to deny that it is morally satisfactory to subordinate the rights of an individual to those of the species as a matter of course. We may sometimes be justified in infringing the rights of an individual animal where there is a clear and direct situation of conflict between respective right-holders or where such infringement is necessary for the greater good of the *individual* animal concerned. But we treat animals and humans unjustly if we proceed on the assumption that their rights can normally be sacrificed to the interests of others.

But of course conservationists frequently argue that the plight of endangered species is not a 'normal' situation and that extraordinary measures are required to save threatened species. The argument again is not as strong as it looks.

In most if not almost all situations, animals are threatened with extinction because their rights are not respected in the first place. Humans destroy their habitats, hunt them mercilessly and trade in their dead bodies. Endangered species are simply one more symptom of our failure to grasp the claims of animals as individual beings. 'Were we to show proper respect for the rights of the individuals who make up the biotic community,' asks Regan, 'would not the *community* be preserved?'[13] In short: when we press wild animals into captivity, even for the otherwise righteous aim of preserving endangered species, we do those captive individuals a harm that cannot be outweighed by the potential benefit that may accrue to the species concerned. Those who are concerned to let animals be, should first set their sights on preserving the habitats where animals already live.

(b) Companion animals

Some may think it a mistake to include the use of domestic pets under the heading of 'oppressive control'. If we are to include animals within a covenant relationship with man then it may be argued that some form of companion relationship with them is only right and inevitable. If humans are to form truly symbiotic relationships with animals then some give and take as illustrated by domestication is only natural. And surely, it may be protested, many companion animals receive as much, if not more, than they give to their human owners. It is true that for many centuries humans have lived an interdependent existence with animals, often including some species within their household fellowship. Doubtless some of the reasons for this were practical, some economical and some stemmed from notions of fellow-feeling.

There is no parallel, however, to the modern, almost universal, practice of keeping other species for purposes of companionship. Literally millions of animals are kept in the world today for human company and enjoyment. This practice is seldom questioned and even many 'animal lovers' appear to support and encourage it. Yet the effects of maintaining high populations of domestic animals are frequently deleterious to their welfare. Here are four neglected aspects:

(i) Trade. It is frequently overlooked that the trade in pets involves the breeding, selling and buying of living creatures as little more than enjoyment commodities. Pet shops and street markets are there to make money and the welfare aspect is almost always secondary. The trade in exotic animals such as tortoises, reptiles, birds and monkeys can cause great suffering. Research by the RSPCA showed that 'the mortality rate of tortoises is between 80%–90% during the first year in captivity'.[14] How is it possible to respect the dignity and freedom of animals' lives if they can be bred, bought and sold with as few legal restrictions as cabbages?

(ii) Abuse. It is sometimes argued that since in most cases humans have to pay for their chosen companions, it must follow that they will respect and care for their acquisitions. The evidence is largely against this. Prosecuted cases of cruelty brought by the RSPCA against pet owners are at an all-time high. Literally thousands of animals are subject to wantonness, neglect, ill-treatment and nothing less than savagery every year. In addition, the Society annually destroys thousands of unwanted family pets. It is a grim irony that the one Society most active in the general field of animal welfare should have to spend a good slice of its time and income actually destroying perfectly healthy animals. To this needs to be added a range of non-veterinary mutilations demanded by pet owners including: tail-docking, ear-cropping, de-barking and de-clawing. Moreover the selective breeding of animals which involves 'changes in bodily form and/or function' is entirely legal; and the entering of dogs and cats into commercial shows provides impetus for further innovation, frequently at the expense of the animals concerned.

(iii) Control.   The abolition of the dog licence in Britain demonstrates Government reluctance to operate any control of dog populations. As the *Animals and Ethics* Report indicates, 'there is a lack of any overall control of pet populations' and 'no adequate statistics are kept which would enable the recording of the number and variety of such animals'.[15] Lack of control invariably works *against* the interests of animals, since it encourages over-breeding with the predictable results of abandonment, neglect or premature destruction. JACOPIS (the Joint Advisory Committee on Pets in Society) has repeatedly pressed the case for dog wardens organized on a national basis to deal with the 'estimated 500,000 stray dogs in the UK'[16] but has met with little success, though some authorities have begun to implement local schemes.

(iv) Food.   Sustaining millions of pet animals arguably involves a less than serious stewardship of world food resources. But from the animals' point of view, it is only possible to feed millions of largely carnivorous pets by destroying other species like kangaroos, whales, horses and rabbits. Apparently it is possible for dogs to live on a vegetarian diet with no health disadvantages, but it is not so with cats.[17] If we really have the welfare of animals at heart, here is a good reason for not encouraging an ever-increasing pet population. In short: every carnivorous pet is fed at the expense of another animal's life.

Taking into account these factors, it is not difficult to see how high pet populations encourage the view that animals are throwaway consumer items. The animal movement has yet to come to grips with the need for the serious reduction in the number of companion animals for the sake of the animals themselves. Fundamental steps need to be taken to reintroduce licensing, to limit commercial breeding, to prevent the sale of puppies and kittens in pet shops (as is already RSPCA policy), to implement dog-warden schemes, to outlaw non-veterinary mutilations, to prevent selective breeding, and to provide for population control through free neutering services. It may be that Britain is a nation of 'animal lovers', rather than simply a nation of 'animal keepers', but in either case, animal rightists must press for the recognition of responsibility towards those we love or keep on our own terms.

The question may be raised: Is pet-keeping immoral in itself? Very few in the animal movement seem prepared to tackle this question head on, and yet it is an issue that merits serious discussion. My answer at the present moment is to reply that *some forms* of pet-keeping may well be immoral, and for these reasons. In the first place, I take the view of Schweitzer that whenever we force animals into our service or company, we take on a quite specific responsibility.[18] Quite simply we make the animal dependent upon us for every important facet of its life, including food, exercise, mental and emotional environment, and companionship (or lack of it). We tie ourselves to animals in a quite specific way and with corresponding obligations. I am very doubtful whether most pet owners realize the extent of these obligations. Buying pets for children, while often well-intentioned, betokens a grotesque parody of responsible steward-ship. Taking care of animals is an adult responsibility. Many children are barely capable of taking responsibility for them-selves, let alone for a living creature entirely in their control. Unless adults are prepared to rigorously supervise a child's keeping of animals, then it is better for the animal, and perhaps the child itself, that it finds an alternative playmate.

Secondly, it is possible to do real harm to pet animals through oversight, ignorance or insensitivity. The RSPCA rightly draws our attention to 'the inadequate standards for cages which appear to be commonly accepted for many birds and mammals',[19] but how many pet owners seriously consider the social and environ-mental needs of their animals? Almost all exotic animals cannot be kept in Britain without environmental deprivation or loss. Many animals need social companionship, as in the case of birds like budgerigars, which are frequently kept alone in relatively small cages. Domestication can so easily distort the remaining natural and instinctive life of animals. Neutering must sadly be accepted as essential to prevent more unwanted animals, but we should be clear that this is inevitably at some cost to the indi-vidual animal, which presumably lives closer to its natural instincts and is therefore denied something important to its animality. The British Small Animal Veterinary Association argues that a neutered dog can be 'markedly less aggressive . . . less inclined to stray' and 'less jealous of his own territory'. In particular 'he becomes more responsive to training and a greater joy to the owner'.[20] But this is surely just the point. Neutering, I repeat, is essential, but that the animal loses something of itself in becoming more malleable to its owner is difficult to dispute.

Thirdly, pet-keeping can so easily accentuate or even create a false view of animals. In a paper published by the Pet Food Manufacturer's Association, Richard Ryder argued that pets can 'satisfy our psychological needs in a number of ways, some not especially selfish but others extremely so'. In particular:

> they give us physical tactile comfort, they flatter us and make us feel important, they help us to drop our social façades and to be ourselves, they give us a feeling of companionship and security, especially at night, they can boost our egos as extensions of ourselves or as compensations for our weaknesses. We can gain satisfaction from showing off our pets to others, they increase our self-confidence by submitting to our authority and sometimes, alas, they relieve our hostilities by acting as our scapegoats—they pander to the tyrant in us by becoming our slaves.

'Above all', concludes Ryder, 'pets allow us to love and to be loved—the experience of feeling loved and needed is the greatest psychological service which they give to us'.[21] I am not at all sure that allowing animals to become emotional supports for human beings sufficiently allows for their dignity. It would certainly be wrong to exclude the non-human from the sphere of human loving. But what kind of love is it that is predominantly expressed through the keeping of animals as pets? 'We need to distinguish', I wrote in 1976, 'between a kind of love which respects animals for what they are and allows them to pursue their own lives according to their own natural instincts, and another selfish form of love which seeks to condition animal lives in accordance with our own human desires'.[22] Perhaps this doctrine is too harsh, since all loving is in practice a subtle blend of altruism and self-seeking. But where the interests of animals are entirely subordinated to human emotional needs, we need to beware that we are not involved in a self-deceiving tyranny.

The fourth and last reservation is theological. It is that the Creator has some right to see that the creation he has made has some corresponding right to be what he intends it to be. On the theistic view of animals, they are not simply made for human pleasure; they cannot be refashioned like human artefacts or remade like toys in a factory. If God has the right to see that his creation is treated with respect, it must be considered whether animals do not have some right to be animals, whatever compelling human need is at stake. This is not to depart from the biblical insight that mutual dependence as implied in the covenant concept is God's will for humans and other species. Ryder rightly warns us against the idea that inter-species relationships are unnatural or cranky. But it has to be questioned whether this symbiotic relationship can properly exist except on the basis that humans respect the natural life of animals. Where this is not possible, we must try to find ways of compensating animals for their loss. In short: the more humans use animals, the greater the responsibility entailed.

(c) Culling and control

Philosophers like Mary Midgley are adamant that the need to control animal populations poses the clearest moral conflict between animals and humans. 'There are cases where competition between people and other species is unavoidable and drastic,' she writes. 'Crop pests of all kinds—not just insects, but rodents, birds, even deer, baboons and elephants—*must* be killed, if only by starvation, by people who mean to survive'.[23] Indeed the argument for control appears so clear cut that few animal rightists seem to question it seriously.

Let us begin then by envisaging two situations in which we can realistically suppose that the rights of animals should take second place to those of human beings. The first is that of self-defence. Where an individual animal poses a clear threat to the life and well-being of an individual human being, then it should follow that the threatened individual has a proper recourse to defence. Such situations may be quite rare. Most human beings do not live in those parts of the world where wild animals roam around seeking humans to molest or devour. But I do not wish to evade the possible dilemma. When there is a *direct* choice between the life of an individual human and an individual animal, we may rightly choose to save the human agent. The right of self-defence against animals is simply an extension of the similar right we hold in the case of a human being when faced with an attack by another human being. It does not follow of course that we may go to *any* lengths to defend ourselves and that the attacker forfeits all rights by his intending aggression. We may reasonably use sufficient force to repel the attack (which may incidentally involve the death of the attacker) but surely no more. We have no subsequent right to inflict torture should the attacker still be conscious, or to engage in retaliatory mutilations.

The second situation, by extension, is where animals constitute a direct threat to the growing of food which is essential to human survival. Successful agriculture demands a more or less controlled environment, which necessitates in turn the destruction of competing life forms. Many of these may be insects, such as locusts, with the potential to wreak devastation. But it is difficult to dispute Midgley's contention that there are also situations in which mammals also compete with us. Because food is essential to survival it is difficult to resist the need to kill in this situation. Again this does not mean that farmers are entitled to control competing animals with *any* means at their disposal or to wage war on animal life without clear evidence that competition will seriously, even substantially, damage their farming interest.

As I see it, these two situations concern, more or less directly, the chances of human survival. Much more problematic, however, is the claim to control animals where the human interest involved appears to turn on questions of 'nuisance', 'convenience' or 'efficient management'. In *all* cases of proposed control of animal populations we need to bear four particular considerations in mind.

The first is that many farmers and growers are apt to utilize justifications for control where none really exist. In some, but only some, situations do animals constitute a real and direct threat to growing crops. We must not allow the legitimate justification that applies in some limited situations to be extended indiscriminately. Every case for control needs to be scrutinized. It is difficult to avoid the conclusion that in some situations 'reaching for the gun' has become an habitual response.

The second is that attempts at control may frequently be short-lived in their effectiveness. Ecological evidence indicates that animals control themselves in accordance with the food and environment available.[24] This means that numbers can only be affected in some situations by *repeated* culling exercises which have no chance of lasting success. Hundreds, if not thousands, of rabbits, squirrels and birds are shot by farmers each year who find that the effort has to be repeated within a short period of time. The same is true of the control of pigeons by local authorities. One sometimes wonders whether the time and money involved in killing pigeons would not be better spent by simply cleaning the defaced buildings every year. With pigeons, and possibly other species, there are important preventative measures which should be employed before the habitual recourse to the net, gun or poison bottle.

The third is that organized control, as distinct from those rare situations of self-defence, can only be acceptable if it is truly humane. One example may illustrate the difficulty. It *appears* humane to kill seal pups by a blow to the head and in this way render them unconscious. It may appear unaesthetic but theoretically it sounds a humane procedure which causes death instantaneously. In fact, however, RSPCA research showed that *repeated* blows to the head were required to render seal pups unconscious and that arguably some were skinned while still alive. What *theoretically* sounds like a humane procedure was only possible in *ideal* conditions, for example: when the aim was direct (not always easy when one is standing on snow and ice), when the seal's head was motionless, and moreover when it was not also trying to defend itself by burying its head beneath its shoulders, or when its mother was not also sheltering the pup.[25] The moral challenge has to be that where humane methods of control are not available, we should desist from killing. The RSPCA specifically opposes the use of snares and 'any trap which causes suffering', as well as poisons such as strychnine which are invariably inhumane.[26]

The fourth point is that however convenient we may find it to categorize animals such as rabbits, squirrels or rats as 'pests' or 'vermin', such appellations are without biological foundation. We simply deride those animals whom we think pose some 'threat' to us, whether that threat is little more than a nuisance or an irritation. I remember being informed by one person who was justifying his decision to shoot starlings in our neighbourhood, that he was only going to kill 'feral starlings'. 'The fact that these species ... are so regarded', argues the *Animals and Ethics* Report, 'does not in any way imply that they have a higher threshold of pain than other species'.[27] In the case of seals it was possible to mobilize support for restrictive regulation, but we need to remember that many other species which may not look cuddly and attractive are nevertheless just as capable of being harmed and hurt.

To these considerations must be added a strong theological proviso: the earth as envisaged in Genesis is a *common* gift to both humans and animals. We cannot take on board the all-too-familiar argument that whenever animals pose any kind of nuisance to us we have absolute rights of destruction. 'It is *we* that steal their land for cattle, and for roads, and industry,' argues Stephen Clark, 'and then complain that they come poaching.'[28] The theos-rights of animals can mean little if they are not to be allowed some room to be, to live and to multiply. Humans have no rights to push all other kinds of species off the land as though it was solely our property, especially when 'better husbandry of *our* food and less destruction of their natural landscape might leave enough for all'.[29] We have to ask ourselves whether God's right is served by the ever-increasing numbers of human beings that every day lay *exclusive* claim to more and more of this *common* earth. Our lack of regard for the rights of animals means in practice that we reverse the design of Genesis: we misappropriate a common gift. The RSPCA, in a far-sighted policy, opposes 'in principle' the 'taking of or killing of wild animals' and urges that they 'receive a far greater degree of protection under the law'.[30] Giving practical effect to this principle remains a daunting theological and moral task.

Liberation from Primary Products of Slaughter

As we have seen, the biblical tradition appears to give us two contrasting insights concerning the morality of eating meat. On one hand, men as well as animals are commanded to be vegetarian. 'I give you all plants that bear seed everywhere on earth, and every tree bearing fruit which yields seed: they shall be yours for food.'[31] This command is reinforced by the messianic prophecies which specifically envisage a world at peace where 'They shall not hurt, nor destroy in all my holy mountain'.[32] On the other hand, after the Fall and the Flood God commands a new relationship with us whereby 'Every creature that lives and moves shall be food for you; I give you them all, as once I gave you all green plants.'[33] This 'necessary evil', as it is described by Anthony Phillips,[34] has been justified throughout much of Christian history partly—we may suppose—because the Prince of Peace was himself not a thorough-going vegetarian. He possibly ate meat and certainly ate fish.

And yet are these two traditions incompatible? The second command carried with it a puzzling condition—'But you must not eat the flesh with the life, which is the blood, still in it.'[35] 'The Hebrews recognised', comments Phillips, 'that death occurred through loss of breath or blood, and since God was responsible for creation, both must belong to him.'[36] Thus even within this permissive tradition, human beings are not given an entirely free hand. They do not have absolute rights over the lives of animals. Even the animal about to be eaten does not belong to its intending consumer. In this way the Priestly tradition, while accepting the necessity of killing, refuses to accept that humans can appropriate the life of an animal. In short: according to the permissive tradition, the fact that man kills is a necessary consequence of sin but the act of killing itself must not misappropriate the Creator's gift.

A Christian case for avoiding meat can therefore claim to have two justifications, even within the biblical tradition which apparently sanctions it. The first is that killing is a morally significant matter. While justifiable in principle, it can only be practically justified where there is real need for human nourishment. Christian vegetarians do not have to claim that it is always and absolutely wrong to kill in order to eat. It could well be that there were, and are, some situations in which meat-eating was and is essential in order to survive. Geographical considerations alone make it difficult to envisage life in Palestine at the time of Christ without some primitive fishing industry. But the crucial point is that where we are *free to do otherwise* the killing of Spirit-filled individuals requires moral justification. It *may* be justifiable, but only when human nourishment clearly requires it, and even then it remains an inevitable consequence of sin. Karl Barth to his credit gives full weight to this point. What we do to animals in killing them is 'very close to homicide'; that it can be justified is never 'self-evident' and slaughter must never become a 'normal element' in our thinking.[37]

The second point is that misappropriation occurs when humans do not recognize that the life of an animal belongs to God, not to them. Here it seems to me that Christian vegetarianism is well founded. For while it may have been possible in the past to rear animals with personal care and consideration for their well-being and to dispatch them with the humble and scrupulous recognition that their life should only be taken in times of necessity, such conditions are abnormal today. In the institutionalized and mass destruction of billions of farm animals every year, we see more clearly than anywhere else the predominant philosophy of animals as 'things' in our regard. In increasing secular societies, farm animals have become merely ends-to-human-means.

Thus even within the permissive tradition that sometimes accepts the need to kill for food, there is still ample justification for vegetarianism, whether based on calculation of animal or human interests. Here are four currently canvassed arguments:

(i) *Humane slaughter is frequently a contradiction in terms.* It is ironical that the religious communities that keep literally to the biblical notion of draining blood prior to slaughter (without prior stunning) arguably practise the most inhumane method of slaughter. This at least is the view of the British Government's Farm Animal Welfare Council, which concluded that animals which have their throat cut while still conscious can suffer an agonizing period of fourteen to thirty-five seconds before complete unconsciousness.[38] Despite the thoroughness of the Report, the Jewish and Muslim communities in Britain have still resisted the practice of stunning prior to slaughter. Some Jews, to be fair, find *all* slaughter abhorrent and in obedience to what they regard as the primary biblical command have founded the International Jewish Vegetarian Society.[39] It would certainly not be possible to absolve Gentile methods of slaughter from inhumanity. The conveyor-belt method of destruction for poultry, where birds are stunned prior to throat-slitting, can cause prolonged suffering if the technology is faulty and even the captive bolt system utilized for cattle and sheep crucially depends for its effectiveness upon the skill of the operator. Those who prefer to avoid sanctioning animal suffering would do well to live independently of the primary products of slaughter. It is said of St Richard of Wyche that 'when he saw poultry or young animals being conveyed to his kitchen [he never ate meat himself] he would say half-sadly, half-humorously, "Poor, innocent little creatures: if you were reasoning beings and could speak you would curse us. For we are the cause of your death, and what have you done to deserve it?" '[40] The fact is that almost all slaughter is achieved at *some* cost in terms of animal suffering.

(ii) *Most meat is the product of intensive systems of farming.* While it is true that not all meat comes from intensively farmed animals, individuals who want to free themselves from all such systems would need to exclude many primary products from their diet, including pork, veal and chicken. The only way of guaranteeing freedom from factory farmed produce is by not eating primary animal products and some by-products too. Karl Barth, it appears, endorsed vegetarianism as a 'protest' against the excesses of farming.[41] Even if our concern is solely for the suffering that animals have to undergo in the process of farming, vegetarianism can be well justified as a practical gesture of conscientious objection.

(iii) *'Live more simply so that all of us may simply live.'* This is the motto of the Lifestyle Movement, which suggests that individuals eat 'less grain-fed meat', reduce their meat consumption or become vegetarians. The welfare of animals is only part of the Lifestyle concern, which extends to 'avoid[ing] wasteful use of resources and show[ing] care for the environment'.[42] Personal asceticism is therefore recommended as a gesture towards a fairer, more caring world. The line from Edmund Burke is commended: 'Nobody made a greater mistake than he who did nothing because he could only do a little.'[43] Simplicity of diet has strong monastic support of course: 'Except the sick who are very weak', maintains the Rule of St Benedict, 'let all abstain entirely from the flesh of four-footed animals.'[44]

(iv) *'One man's meat is another man/woman/child's hunger.'* The slogan is part of the 'Enough' campaign, with its aim of reducing meat consumption. The Campaign highlights the waste of resources involved in feeding grain to animals. 'Every minute 18 children die from starvation, yet 40% of the world's grain is fed to animals for meat.'[45] Vegetarianism for a trial period is advocated to 'help the hungry, improve the environment' and 'stop untold animal suffering'.[46] Vegetarianism is also commended on health grounds, and it is true that research into the diet of vegans in particular showed some significant health advantages.[47]

Without wishing to disparage these arguments, it seems to me that the strongest argument for leaving flesh foods to one side is of a different sort. It begins by taking seriously the notion that the life of an animal does not belong to human beings but to God. What the biblical narratives are expressing is that nothing less than God's right is involved in the business of killing for food. While under situations of clear necessity, given the sinful world as it is, meat-eating may sometimes be justified, it cannot be uniformly accepted as such. In other words, our mistake in interpreting Genesis has been to suppose that one exception can establish a permanent rule. Since God's world is a changing and dynamic creation we have to be open to the possibility of moral change. This means quite simply that what was once thought to be right can subsequently be thought to be wrong and vice versa. What precisely may have been the moral freedom of our fore-bears is not easy to determine. In many instances we do not know enough about our past to make clear, unequivocal judgements. But one thing of which we can be relatively certain is that for most people living today in Western society, dependence upon primary animal products is not essential to fullness of life.

In 1926 Dean Inge, in an otherwise perceptive essay on the 'Rights of Animals', argued that we could not give up flesh, because 'we must eat something'.[48] What Inge obviously did not appreciate, as many are only now beginning to grasp, is that we do not need to kill for food in order to eat well or to sustain healthy lives. Once this *has* been realized, it is difficult intellectually to find a route back. For if luxury rather than necessity can justify killing, where will it all end? 'Honourable men may honourably disagree about some details of human treatment of the non-human,' argues Stephen Clark, 'but vegetarianism is now as necessary a pledge of moral devotion as was the refusal of emperor-worship in the early Church.' Eating animals, says Clark, is 'gluttony'. 'Those who still eat flesh when they could do otherwise have no claim to be serious moralists.'[49] Clark's final comment goes further than I would want to go. Given the confusing interrelationship of light and darkness, blessing and curse, it is difficult to hold out for any truths so self-evident that people who fail to see them are somehow morally culpable. That said, Clark's conclusion has real force and its power has yet to be sufficiently appreciated by fellow Christians. Far from seeing the possibility of widespread vegetarianism as a threat to Old Testament norms, Christians should rather welcome the fact that the Spirit is enabling us to make decisions so that we may more properly conform to the original Genesis picture of living in peace with creation.

The Christian argument for vegetarianism then is simple: since animals belong to God, have value to God and live for God, then their needless destruction is sinful. In short: animals have some right to their life, all circumstances being equal. That it has taken Christians so long to grasp this need not worry us. There were doubtless good reasons, partly theological, partly cultural and partly economic, why Christians in the past have found vegetarianism unfeasible. We do well not to judge too hastily, if at all. We cannot relive others' lives, or think their thoughts, or enter their consciences. But what we can be sure about is that living without what Clark calls 'avoidable ill'[50] has a strong moral claim upon us now.

Some will surely question the limits of the vegetarian world here envisaged. Will large-scale vegetarianism work in practice? Can animal farming really be turned to the growing of crops, grains, nuts and lentils? Will a vegetarian world not mean fewer farm animals? These are questions to which we do not have sufficient answers. I confess that I am agnostic, surely legitimately, about the possibility of a world-transforming vegetarianism. But clairvoyance is not an essential prerequisite of the vegetarian option, and what the future may hold, and its consequences, cannot easily be determined from any perspective. What I think is important to hold on to is the notion that the God who provides moral opportunities is the same God who enables the world, slowly but surely, to respond to them. From a theological perspective no moral endeavour is wasted so long as it coheres with God's purpose for his cosmos.

Liberation from By-Products of Slaughter

Some vegetarians press their case to the exclusion of all by-products of the slaughter-house, including not only dairy produce but also the wearing of leather shoes or woollen clothes. They argue that it is not sufficient to be a 'vegetarian' in the general sense (one who abstains from meat), or a lacto-vegetarian (one who abstains from fish, flesh and fowl), but that one should become a vegan (one who abstains from all meat and dairy produce completely). Not without justification, they point to the exploitation of animals for the dairy, as well as the meat, industry. 'The modern dairy cow leads a hell of a life', according to the *New Scientist*. 'Each year, hopefully, she produces a calf which means that for nine months of the year she is pregnant. And for nine months of each year she is milked twice a day. For six months she is both pregnant and lactating.'[51] In addition, the frequent separation of the calf from its mother within a period of days after its birth is a less than joyful experience. Indeed the Brambell Committee reported that this practice 'undoubtedly inflicts anguish on both', since cattle are 'highly intelligent' and the 'attachment between the calf and the mother is particularly strong'.[52] Egg production, too, is not immune from criticism, since it invariably involves the slaughter of male birds and unproductive hens which are deemed surplus to requirements.

Given present farming practice, the case against dairy produce, appears strong. But unlike meat-eating the issue is surely less direct. It *can* be possible to produce milk from non-intensively farmed goats or cattle, and it *can* be possible to obtain eggs from free-range hens without slaughtering their male partners. But it is sadly a sign of how endemic our exploitation of animals has become that almost everywhere even that possibly legitimate use of animals has been turned into abuse.

How practicable is the vegan world, where only plant foods are grown and few animals are utilized directly in farming? 'No-one—whether nutritionist, physician, sociologist or layman—can rebut the veganic argument in any important respect', argues Jon Wynne-Tyson. And yet, despite his eloquent advocacy of veganism, even he admits of limitations. 'I am not yet a fully practising vegan,' he writes, 'although I would like to be.' The reason? 'The pressures on most of us not to go the whole way are tremendous and, in many a family, sadly divisive.'[53] The fact is that it is amazingly difficult to free ourselves completely from the by-products of slaughter—and remain a member of ordinary society at least. A plausible case can be made for boycotting Australian wool in the light of the barbaric practices employed in the Australian wool industry,[54] but even if we decide to wear plastic shoes (if we can find them) rather than leather ones, we still face the difficulty that many man-made substances are tested for their toxicity on animals. Even licking postage stamps may be problematic since most glues have their origin in the offal that results from the slaughter house. In short: although the 'logic' of the vegan case may be 'absolute', its practical ramifications are currently beyond most of us.

That does not mean, of course, that we should not go on *trying* to reduce our dependence upon all kinds of animal products. The production of animal-free Beauty Without Cruelty cosmetics is a striking example of how individual initiative and business acumen can provide us with a most welcome choice.[55] There are important signs that some business concerns are going out of their way to market toiletries with 'no animal testing' labels. In a whole host of ways active, conscientious consumers can make their wishes known and press for different kinds of products. All moves in this direction towards the non-utilization of animal products need to be strenuously supported by those concerned for animal rights.

But at the same time we need to dispel the myth of absolute consistency or 'pure land' theology. 'Western society is so bound up with the use and abuse of animals in so many fields of human endeavour', I argued recently, 'that it is impossible for anyone to claim that they are not party, directly or indirectly, to this exploitation either through the products they buy, the food they eat, or the taxes they pay.'[56] Vegans are right to prick the consciences of those like me in the animal movement who find some recourse to animal by-products inevitable, but they can mislead us if they claim some absolutely pure land which only they inhabit. Self-righteousness can be a killer not only of moral sense but also of moral encouragement.

Living in Peace

We return in this way to our opening remarks concerning the need for humility as well as vision. What we need is *progressive* disengagement from our inhumanity to animals. The urgent and essential task is to invite, encourage, support and welcome those who want to take some steps along the road to a more peaceful world with the non-human creation. We do not *all* have to agree upon the most vital steps, or indeed the most practical ones.

What is important is that we all move some way on, if only by one step at a time, however falteringly. To my mind every pheasant which is left to live rather than shot is a gain. If that is all the humanity one hunter can muster at least we have saved one creature. If we can encourage one researcher to save one mouse, at least that is one mouse saved. If we can persuade an intensive farmer to refrain from de-beaking one hen then at least some small burden of suffering is lessened in the world. The enemy of progress is the view that everything must be changed before some real gains can be secured. Some may disagree with the major contours as well as the details of the vision I have outlined. Some may argue that such and such a judgement is too hard or such and such an option is too soft. There can be areas of genuine disagreement even among those who are committed to a new world of animal rights. But what is essential for this new world to emerge is the sense that each of us can change our individual worlds, however slightly, to live more peaceably with our non-human neighbours.

'I could not but feel with a sympathy full of regret all the pain that I saw around me, not only that of men, but that of the whole creation,' wrote Schweitzer in a telling passage in his autobiography. 'From this community of suffering, I have never tried to withdraw myself.' He concluded: 'It seemed to me a matter of course that we should all take our share of the burden of suffering which lies upon the world.'[57] The vision of Christ-like lordship over the non-human is practically costly. Our moral choices inevitably entail sacrifice and pain. In this way we anticipate, if not actually realize, the future joy of all God's creatures.

Appendix: Church Statements on Animals 1956–86

General Assembly of the Presbyterian Church in Ireland, 1956

The General Assembly, recognising the welfare of animals and their just treatment as an essential part of Christian responsibility, urge members of the Church to be active in this sphere of service, and commend to their support the work of the Societies for the Prevention of Cruelty to Animals throughout Ireland. They recommend that this matter be kept before congregations, Sunday Schools and organisations of the Church through instruction and intercession, particularly during Animal Welfare Week, at the beginning of May, or on any other convenient Sabbath in each year.

(Cited in C. W. Hume, *The Status of Animals in the Christian Religion*, London: Universities Federation for Animal Welfare, 1957, p. 58).

Lambeth Conference, 1968

The Conference urges all Christians, in obedience to the doctrine of creation, to take all possible action to ensure man's responsible steward-ship over nature; in particular in his relationship with animals and with regard to the conservation of the soil, and the prevention of the pollution of air, soil and ocean.

(*Lambeth Conference 1968: Resolutions and Reports*, London and New York: SPCK and Seabury Press, 1968, resolution no. 6, p. 30).

Cardinal Heenan, Roman Catholic Archbishop of Westminster, 1970

When I was young I often heard quoted a piece of Christian philosophy which was taken as self-evidently true. It was the proposition that animals have no rights. This, of course, is true only in one sense. They are not human persons and therefore they have no rights, so to speak, in their own right. But they have very positive rights because they are

God's creatures. If we have to speak with absolute accuracy we must say that God has the right to have all his creatures treated with proper respect.

Nobody should therefore carelessly repeat the old saying that animals have no rights. This could easily lead to wanton cruelty. I speak of wanton cruelty because only the perverted are guilty of deliberate cruelty to animals or, indeed, to children. The difficulty is that many people do not realise the extent to which cruelty to animals is practised as a matter of business ... It was once pointed out to me that the catechism had no question about cruelty to animals. This was true but in giving lessons on Christian doctrine teachers now include the subject of cruelty to animals. The best and most experienced teachers do not, of course, talk of cruelty to animals. They talk of kindness to animals. Christians have a duty not only to refrain from doing harm but also to do positive good.

(Foreword to Ambrose Agius, *God's Animals*, London: Catholic Study Circle for Animal Welfare, 1970, p. 2).

National Assembly of the Church of England, 1970

That the Church Assembly is of the opinion that the practices of hare-coursing, deer-hunting, and otter-hunting are cruel, unjustifiable and degrading, and urges Christian people in the light of their Christian profession and responsibility to make plain their opposition to activities of this sort and their determination to do all in their power to secure their speedy abolition.

(Cited in *Man in His Living Environment*, Report of a Working Party of the Board for Social Responsibility of the Church of England, London: CIO, 1970, pp. 24/5).

Man and Nature Report, 1975

The Old Testament envisaged an end-time when man would live in perfect harmony with the other creatures, and this may have been conceived as the restoration of a 'golden age' at the beginning of time, before man's fall into sin. For everything that God had made he judged to be good. Although it cannot be denied that man is very much at the centre of biblical teaching on creation, this teaching does not hold that nature has been created simply for man's sake. It exists for God's glory, that is to say, it has a meaning and worth beyond its meaning and worth as seen from the point of view of human utility. It is in this sense that we can say that it has an intrinsic value. To imagine that God has created the whole universe solely for man's use and pleasure is a mark of folly. The wise man will be able to read lessons for human behaviour from his observation of nature. Although in the New Testament there enters a note of apocalyptic pessimism, it remains true that the world as God's

151

creation is in essence good. This natural world is not corrupt in itself (as Gnostics and some others held) but is in bondage to the powers of darkness, from whose grasp it can be delivered. God has a redeeming purpose for the whole creation, for nature as well as man. This, we would claim, is the teaching of the mainstream of biblical thought.

(From *Man and Nature*, edited by Hugh Montefiore, foreword by Lord Ramsey, London: Collins, 1975, pp. 67–8. This Report by Anglican theologians was commissioned by the then Archbishop of Canterbury, Michael Ramsey, in 1971).

Archbishop of Canterbury (Dr Donald Coggan), 1977

I am happy to follow the lead given to the Church some 150 years ago by the London vicar who called the meeting in 1824 which led to the Society's foundation and who was subsequently its Secretary for a number of years. There have always been and still are many Churchmen, both lay and ordained, who have seen it as part of their Christian profession to work for animal welfare. I want to offer my support to the RSPCA because without their constant vigilance and the devoted work of their Officers and Inspectors the level of unnecessary animal suffering in this country would be so much higher. Animals, as part of God's creation, have rights which must be respected. It behoves us always to be sensitive to their needs and to the reality of their pain.

(Presidential message to the Annual General Meeting of the RSPCA, reprinted in *RSPCA Today*, No. 22, July 1977, p. 1).

General Synod of the Church of England, 1977

That this Synod

(i) applauds the action taken by nearly 70 national and local animal welfare societies in this centenary year of the (un-amended) Cruelty to Animals Act 1876, in promoting and supporting Animal Welfare Year 1976–77;

(ii) welcomes the declared Animal Welfare Year objective, viz.: 'to prevent cruelty to animal life by the promotion of humane behaviour so as to reduce pain, fear and stress inflicted upon animals by mankind whether relating to pet animals, wild animals, animals used in laboratory experiments, farm animals, performing animals or any other form of animal life'; and

(iii) urges members of the Church of England and all others concerned for the due rights of sentient creatures in God's world to have a regard to this objective; to make more widely known the plight of many animals and birds today; and to take all possible steps:

(a) to make life more tolerable for those creatures, and
(b) to safeguard species threatened with extinction, and

(c) generally to prevent ignorance, neglect, cruelty, degradation and commercial exploitation so far as animals are concerned.

(*General Synod Report of Proceedings November 1977*, vol. XII, No. 3, London: CIO, 1977, p. 10).

Church and Nation Report of the Church of Scotland, 1978

The theological ground for a Christian approach to animal welfare is in the Biblical doctrine of Creation. The unity of creation is affirmed as a corollary of the Oneness of God. Man is one with all things animate and inanimate, being composed of the same elements 'dust of the earth', but he has been given also a unique character and role in the scheme of things in that he bears the image of God and has been given a delegated permission to exercise authority over the creation including the animals. That all seems simple and ideal, but the Bible makes it clear that a complicating and perverse state of affairs overlies this basic pattern, the essence of which is a fouling-up of relationships. Man, left to his own devices, is inclined to get his relationships wrong, whether it be in regard to God, his fellow-man or his fellow-creatures. In his relationship to the animals man misuses his authority in the direction of exploitation and cruelty. Nevertheless, he regains his true relationship as a responsible steward to the creation to the degree that he becomes 'renewed in his mind' in regard to that particular relationship (Romans 12.2).

Humane concern in the matter of animals must therefore be welcomed and fostered by the Church.

(From the Report 'Church and Nation' made to the General Assembly of the Church of Scotland, 1978).

Methodist Conference, 1980

It is true to observable fact that some of the ways in which we treat animals regard them as expendable and wholly subservient to presumed human needs. Some judgements on the situation as it now is can be made with confidence.

(a) Unnecessary or unjustifiable experimentation, as on the effect of cosmetics; the use of numbers of animals in an experiment far in excess of a reasonable control and check number; excessive duplication of experiments in different laboratories; the use of animals when valid results could be secured from tissue cultures; are all to be condemned.
(b) Those aspects of the practices of intensive factory farming which do not consider the welfare of the animals involved are to be condemned.
(c) Patently cruel sports, such as stag hunting and hare coursing, are to be condemned, not only for the suffering imposed on the animal but also the effect on the human participant.

153

(d) The extinction or drastic reduction of animal species by over-hunting is to be condemned.

(e) The preservation of species through the conservation of appropriate natural habitats is to be welcomed.

(f) In all his dealings with the creatures who share creation with him, the proper function of the Christian man or woman is to serve as a steward under God.

('A Methodist Statement on the Treatment of Animals', adopted by the Methodist Conference, London, 1980, p. 3).

Animals and Ethics Report, 1980

Certain basic guidelines should govern the welfare of animals under the direct control of man. No husbandry method should deny the environmental requirements of the basic behavioural needs of these animals. These needs will include the following;

—freedom to perform natural physical movement
—association with other animals, where appropriate of their own kind
—facilities for comfort activities, e.g. rest, sleep and body care
—provision of food and water to maintain full health
—ability to perform daily routines of natural activities
—opportunities for the activities of exploration and play, especially for young animals
—satisfaction of minimal spatial and territorial requirements including a visual field and personal space.

Deviations from these principles should be avoided as far as possible, but where such deviations are absolutely unavoidable efforts should be made where possible to compensate the animal environmentally.

(Edward Carpenter and Others, *Animals and Ethics*, London: Watkins, 1980, pp. 16–17. This Report was produced by an ecumenical working party of theologians and biologists convened by the Dean of Westminster).

Archbishop of Canterbury (Dr Robert Runcie), 1981

I am very conscious of a contemporary unease felt by many serious-minded and responsible people at the dangers inherent in an uncontrolled application of technology to man's relationship with his environment, not least *vis-à-vis* animals. The simple fact is that there has now been thrust into the hands of fallible man a dimension of manipulative control over his environment hitherto without parallel. This unease is shared by Christian people since it is integral to our Christian faith that this world is God's world and that man is a trustee and steward of God's creation who must render up an account for his stewardship. He must therefore exercise his 'dominion' in conformity with God's will and purposes, not only in relation to himself but to the whole area of created life. Man is not an absolute owner of the earth which he inhabits . . .

Many have written to me on the subject of hens in battery cages and veal calves in crates. Of course these systems of extreme confinement are to be abhorred, and it is encouraging to see that research on alternative livestock systems, such as straw yards for veal calves and the more extensive systems for laying hens, are already yielding results which promise an end to the more restrictive systems. As a practical pig farmer I have found it possible to keep my pigs in conditions which respect their natural sphere of existence. I derive pleasure from seeing their response to this more humane treatment and am sure that other stockmen feel the same towards their animals in similar circumstances . . .

('Statement by the Archbishop of Canterbury On Animal Welfare Matters', London: Lambeth Palace, January 1981, pp. 1–2).

Society of Friends London Yearly Meeting, 1981

Our stewardship of the world does not allow us to exercise an absolute right over animals. All animals should be treated as if they have rights and as if they suffer pain and stress similar to human experience and differing only in degree. We have a duty to consider the consequences of our influence on the environment and its effects on animals, taking great care to reduce the harmful effects. Some activities, like killing for sport and aspects of trapping or hunting, which involve cruelty in a slow death, are indefensible and we need to urge those who engage in these activities to reconsider their position.

We have been told of basic guidelines for the care of animals on farms, as pets and in zoos, and we urge Friends to study these guidelines and press for their acceptance in all circumstances of animal care.

We have heard of the serious concern of many Friends over the use of animals in experiments and we recognise the need to limit and control these experiments to those which are absolutely essential for the welfare of animals and people.

(Minute of the Session on Animal Welfare, extract in Chris Lawson, *Some Quaker Thoughts on Animal Welfare*, London: Quaker Social Responsibility and Education, 1985, p. 4).

Pope John Paul II, 1982

St Francis is before us also as an example of unalterable meekness and sincere love with regard to irrational beings who make up part of creation. In him re-echoes that harmony that is illustrated with the striking words of the first pages of the Bible: 'God placed man in the garden of Eden to cultivate it and care for it' (Gen 2.15), and he 'brought' the animals 'to man to see what he would name them' (Gen 2.19).

In St Francis we glimpse almost an anticipation of that peace proposed by Sacred Scripture, when 'the wolf shall dwell with the lamb, and the leopard shall lie down with the kid, and the calf and the lion shall graze together, and a child shall lead them' (Is 11.6).

He looked upon creation with the eyes of one who could recognise in it the marvellous work of the hand of God. His voice, his glance, his solicitous care, not only towards men, but also towards animals and nature in general, are a faithful echo of the love with which God in the beginning pronounced his 'fiat' which had brought them into existence. How can we not feel vibrating in the Canticle of the Creatures something of the transcendent joy of God the Creator, of whom it is written that 'he saw everything that he had made, and behold it was very good' (Gen 1.31)? Do we perhaps not have here the explanation for the sweet name of 'brother' and 'sister' with which the Poverello addressed every created being?

We too are called to a similar attitude. Created in the image of God, we must make him present among creatures 'as intelligent and noble masters and guardians of nature' and 'not as heedless exploiters and destroyers' (cf. Encyclical *Redemptor Hominis*, 15).

(Message on 'Reconciliation' delivered at Assisi on 12 March, 1982. Reprinted in *L'Osservatore Romano*, 29 March, 1982, p. 9).

Archbishop of Canterbury (Dr Robert Runcie), 1982

I do recognise . . . that the use of animals in research is a use above all others, in which man faces conflicting responsibilities—that of not inflicting unnecessary harm on others, and that of working towards a reduction in suffering in both man and animals. Nevertheless I feel that there is a justifiable unease about the widespread duplication and repetition of animal experiments, especially in routine testing of pharmaceutical products, and abhorrence where this involves infliction of pain. Some experiments would appear to have little justification as, for example, those testing non-essential articles such as adornment articles (of which there are already sufficient for any essential purpose), and products such as tobacco which man continues to use in full consciousness of the hazards involved.

In the end a lack of regard for the life and well-being of an animal must bring with it a lowering of man's self respect, and it is integral to our Christian faith that this world is God's world and that man is a trustee and steward of God's creation who must render up an account for his stewardship. A prerequisite to any ethical justification of an animal experiment must therefore be whether the end to be realised is sufficiently significant to warrant such infliction of pain and stress as might be involved. I am not happy that the examples mentioned above meet this criterion.

('Statement by the Archbishop of Canterbury on Vivisection', London: Lambeth Palace, January 1982, p. 1).

Minister-General of the Society of St Francis (Brother Geoffrey, SSF), 1984

Francis had a wonderfully sensitive affinity with the animal world. One of the best known stories is of him quieting the birds while he was preaching and afterwards he preached to them. We think of the falcon that came every day to his window when he was at a hermitage to wake him, and countless are the stories about his relationship with animals whom he called his brothers and sisters. It would seem that the redeemed creation includes the animal world where they have an acceptable place and dignity and live together in unity rather than fighting and living off each other.

What a different picture of the animal world we see today. On the one hand animals have become pets. There is nothing wrong with befriending animals—the horse has been called the friend of man. But there is also a sentimentality about animals in which they become projections of their owners or compensations and this often takes away their independence and dignity as animals. Restaurants and beauty parlours for dogs is going a little far! We have circuses in which great jungle animals are made to be buffoons for our pleasure. In the realm of agriculture we have seen the ascent of the agribusinessman whose farms are primarily business enterprises and animals can be subjected to every kind of exploitation, indignity and suffering in the sacred cause of commercial profit. As we savour our succulent veal are we aware that an animal that is still young and tender has been sacrificed for our pleasure? Lastly, we see increasingly inhumane experiments being carried out on animals in the cause of science . . . Man has the power and the authority over the animal world, but as in other spheres of life he must exercise restraint and responsibility, and most of all curb his selfish greed. I am not myself a vegetarian, though I respect those who are of that persuasion. Through the Bible we find the people of God feasting on animals and offering them in sacrifice, even young calves and lambs. But we need to safeguard and ensure the rights of animals to a natural life before they are taken for our food—the rights of chickens to enjoy freedom and not life-long imprisonment in batteries, to take but one instance. We need to get our values right and not sell our souls to the god Money.

('The Minister-General's Letter' in *The Franciscan*, vol. XXVI, No. 1, January, 1984, pp. 2–3).

Archbishop of York (Dr John Habgood), 1986

In short, we are in a muddle about our relationship to other creatures. When I say 'we' I mean our civilization, a whole way of life which has achieved its present level of comfort and security by ruthless exploitation of the natural world. Few would want to return to the stage of civilization, still shared by millions of our fellow human beings, in which a crop failure, a plague of locusts, or an epidemic can spell utter disaster. We have had too many terrible reminders in recent months of how precarious human societies can be. But alongside this exploitation has grown a feeling for nature, which expresses itself in conservation programmes, in a delight in animals for their own sakes, in a sense of kinship with 'all creatures great and small', and in a nagging sense of guilt about what we do to them . . .

Our understanding of ourselves as part of an evolutionary process has also sharpened the issues. On the one hand we have been made aware that the gulf between human life and other forms of life is not as great as was once supposed. It is true that we are 'made in the image of God'. But the whole creation also reflects His glory. Human beings have unique possibilities of relationship with God. We can justifiably claim that evolution reaches its climax in this God-given awareness of the divine source and ground of the whole process. There is no reason to suppose, however, that this relationship with God is totally exclusive. Does God not delight in the other things He has made? And if He does, and if He has enabled us to see more clearly the links between them and us, how should we treat them? Paradoxically, though, the exploration of this relationship in an evolving world has also revealed the extent to which all living creatures exploit each other. Big fish eat little fish . . . and so on ad infinitum.

I do not pretend to be able to find a way through this muddle. I simply draw attention to it as one which our civilization is going to have to tackle, and in which Christians ought to play a more constructive role than has often been the case.

('Our Civilization's Muddled Relationship to Other Creatures' from the *York Diocesan Leaflet*, reprinted in the Bulletin of the Anglican Society for the Welfare of Animals, No. 27, Spring 1986, pp. 4–5).

Notes

Introduction

1 Joseph Rickaby, *Moral Philosophy*, vol. II (Longman 1901), p. 248. The whole section is reprinted in Tom Regan and Peter Singer (ed.), *Animal Rights and Human Obligations* (New Jersey: Prentice-Hall 1976), pp. 179–80. *ARHO* is an invaluable collection of relevant philosophical extracts for and against animal rights.

2 See, e.g., H. Davis, *Moral and Pastoral Theology*, vol. II (Sheed & Ward 1946), p. 258.

3 A. Linzey, *Animal Rights: A Christian Assessment* (SCM Press 1976), foreword.

4 D. L. Edwards, *Church Times*, 13 February 1976, p. 8.

5 *The Expository Times* (May 1976), p. 255.

6 Hubert SSF, *The Franciscan* (May 1977), pp. 107–8.

7 Maureen Vincent, *Catholic Herald*, 16 April 1976, p. 8.

8 H. Montefiore, *Theology* (January 1977), pp. 72–3. Stephen R. L. Clark kindly took up this issue with the bishop in a subsequent letter, *Theology* (July 1977), pp. 288–9.

9 W. D. Paton, *Crucible* (July/September 1976). See also my reply, *Crucible* (October/December 1976), pp. 185–6.

10 David Roderick, *The Tablet*, 22 May 1976, pp. 409–500.

11 T. Regan, 'An Examination and Defense of One Argument Concerning Animal Rights', *Inquiry* 22 (1979), pp. 189–219.

12 T. Regan, *The Case for Animal Rights* (Berkeley, California: University of California Press 1983). See esp. pp. 243–65.

13 R. G. Frey, 'What has Sentiency to do with the Possession of Rights?' in David Paterson and R. D. Ryder (ed.), *Animals' Rights—A Symposium* (Centaur Press 1979), pp. 106–11, and *idem*, *Interests and Rights: The Case Against Animals* (The Clarendon Press 1980), pp. 28–37. See also Frey, 'Interests and Animal Rights', *Philosophical Quarterly*, vol. 27, part 108 (1977), pp. 254–59 and T. Regan, 'Frey on Interests and Animal Rights', *Philosophical Quarterly*, vol. 27, part 109 (1977), pp. 335–37.

14 Paterson and Ryder, *Animals' Rights—A Symposium*, op. cit.

15 For an account of 'Animal Welfare Year' and the 'Putting Animals into Politics' campaign, see Clive Hollands, *Compassion is the Bugler: The Struggle for Animal Rights* (Macdonald 1979).

16 'An Invitation to Participate in World Animal Rights Year', letter from P. J. Hyde, International League for Animal Rights, 9 June 1978, p. 1.

17 Frey, *Interests and Rights*, op. cit., preface.

18 *General Synod Report of Proceedings November 1977*, vol. XII, no. 3 (CIO Publishing 1977), pp. 10f; my italics. The resolution was passed by 158 votes to one, though it would only be fair to point out that one journalist observed that many Synod members took the debate as an opportunity for an extended tea-break.

19 Coggan, *RSPCA Today*, no. 22 (July 1977), p. 1; my italics.

20 Runcie, 'Statement on Animal Welfare Matters', January 1981, p. 2 and 'Statement on Vivisection', January 1982.

21 A. Linzey, *The Status of Animals in the Christian Tradition* (Wood-brooke College 1985), p. 6.

22 See A. Linzey, *The Neglected Creature: The Doctrine of the Non-Human Creation and its Relationship with the Human in the Thought of Karl Barth* (unpublished PHD, London University 1986).

Chapter 1: Blessing and Curse

1 Psalm 146.1, in *The Psalms: A New Translation*, ET by J. Gelineau (Collins 1963), p. 249.

2 T. S. Eliot, *Murder in the Cathedral* (Faber & Faber 1935), p. 92.

3 Psalm 103.24, in Gelineau, op. cit., p. 179.

4 Eliot, op. cit., p. 93.

5 See, e.g., Psalms 96 and 98.

6 Psalm 148.9 and 10, in Gelineau, op. cit., p. 251.

7 Psalm 36.6, cited and discussed by Karl Barth in 'The Work of Creation', *Church Dogmatics* III/1, *The Doctrine of Creation* (T. & T. Clark 1958), p. 181.

8 Mark 1.13.

9 Wisdom of Solomon 11.24 (RSV).

10 Wisdom of Solomon 12.1 (RSV).

11 Job 41.1–11 (RSV).

12 Barth, op. cit., p. 170.

13 See J. Moltmann's exemplary discussion in *God in Creation: An Ecological Doctrine of Creation*, ET by Margaret Kohl (SCM Press 1985), pp. 276–96.

14 'They shall strike at your head, and you shall strike at their heel', Genesis 3.15 (NEB).

15 W. Cowper, 'The Winter Walk at Noon' in *Poetical Works*, ed. R. A. Willmott (Routledge & Sons 1854), p. 296.

16 W. Blake, 'Auguries of Innocence' in Peter Levi (ed.), *The Penguin Book of English Christian Verse* (Penguin Books 1984), p. 189.

17 See John Macquarrie, *Principles of Christian Theology* (SCM Press 1966), p. 202.

18 Genesis 4.9–13.

19 Genesis 6.6–7 (NEB).

20 Sitwell, 'Still Falls the Rain' in Levi, op. cit., p. 294.

21 Luther, *Luther's Works*, vol. II, ed. by Jaroslav Pelikan (St Louis: Concordia Publishing House 1960), p. 132.

22 Romans 8.20 (RSV), my italics, and Romans 8.21 (NEB).

23 e.g. Morna Hooker: '... most of us are embarrassed by the eschatological hope for a restoration of this world; we do not know how to deal with the idea that creation itself will be redeemed', *Pauline Pieces* (Epworth Press 1979), p. 89.

24 H. A. Williams, *Tensions: Necessary Conflicts in Life and Love* (Mitchell Beazley 1976), pp. 46–7. I am grateful to Williams for the idea of the ambiguity of creation, pp. 47f.

25 See Peter Kropotkin's classic work, *Mutual Aid: A Factor in Evolution*, foreword by H. L. Beales (Pelican Books 1939), esp. pp. 21–73; Stephen R. L. Clark, *The Nature of the Beast: Are Animals Moral?* (Oxford University Press 1982), pp. 55–66 and more recently Patrick Bateson, 'Co-operation', *Theology* (January 1986), pp. 5–10.

26 Eliot, op. cit., p. 93.

27 See A. Linzey, *The Neglected Creature: The Doctrine of the Non-Human Creation and its Relationship with the Human in the Thought of Karl Barth* (unpublished PHD), pp. 276–7.

28 Schweitzer, *Civilization and Ethics*, ET by C. T. Campion (A. & C. Black 1967), p. 215.

29 ibid, p. 221.

30 J. Woolman, *Journal 1720–1742*, Moulton ed., p. 28, cited in Chris Lawson, *Some Quaker Thoughts About Animal Welfare* (Quaker Social Responsibility and Education 1985), p. 1. I am grateful to Chris Lawson for bringing this and other Quaker references to my attention.

31 A. Linzey, 'Moral Education and Reverence for Life' in David Paterson (ed.), *Humane Education—A Symposium* (Humane Education Council 1981), pp. 117–25.

32 Thomas à Kempis, *Imitation of Christ*, extract in Jon Wynne-Tyson (ed.), *The Extended Circle: A Dictionary of Humane Thought* (Centaur Press 1985), p. 150.

33 See, e.g., Hugh Montefiore (ed.), *Man and Nature* (Collins 1975), p. 67. This is a report of a working party set up by Archbishop Ramsey in 1971.

34 R. Attfield, *The Ethics of Environmental Concern* (Basil Blackwell 1983), p. 34. Attfield errs on the generous side in my judgement, the list should be longer. For while some theologians like Augustine rejected the view that creation was made specifically for man, they still held an instrumentalist view of animals.

35 For Barth's view, see Linzey, *The Neglected Creature*, esp. pp. 38–42 and 288–92. Although Barth is ambiguous, at one time he wrote, 'No doubt it is scriptural to say that the world was created for man's sake', *Credo*, ET by J. S. McNab (Hodder & Stoughton 1936), p. 33.

36 K. Thomas, *Man and the Natural World: Changing Attitudes in England 1500–1800* (Penguin Books 1984), p. 29.

37 Montefiore, *Man and Nature*, p. 67. The working party found itself

unable to oppose in principle acts of cruelty in, for example, hunting.

38   For the views of Voltaire, see the extract 'A Reply to Descartes' in T. Regan and P. Singer (ed.) *Animal Rights and Human Obligations* (New Jersey: Prentice-Hall 1976), pp. 67–8.

39   For St Basil, see Attfield, op. cit., p. 34; for St Chrysostom, see Donald Attwater, *St John Chrysostom* (Catholic Book Club 1960), pp. 59–60; for St Isaac, see Vladimir Lossky, *The Mystical Theology of the Eastern Church* (James Clarke 1957), p. 111.

40   For a popular account of the Society's history, see Anthony Brown, *Who Cares for Animals? 150 Years of the RSPCA* (Heinemann 1974); and for details of its religious benefactors, see esp. pp. 16–21.

41   A. Linzey, 'The Place of Animals in Creation—A Christian View' in Tom Regan (ed.), *Animal Sacrifices: Religious Perspectives on the Use of Animals in Science* (Philadelphia: Temple University Press 1986), pp. 115–48.

42   Woolman, *Journal*, cited in Lawson, op. cit., p. 2.

43   W. Hilton, *The Scale of Perfection*, ed., with an introduction, by Evelyn Underhill (Watkins 1923), p. 276.

44   Hosea 2.18 (NEB), my italics; see also Joel 2.21–3 and Ezekiel 34.24–31.

45   G. Fox, *Doctrinal Books*, vol. I (1831–1975 edn) p. 321, cited in Lawson, op. cit., p. 1.

46   Father Zossima's advice in F. Dostoyevsky, *The Brothers Karamazov*, ET David Magarshack (Penguin Books, 1958) vol. I, p. 375.

47   Cowper, op. cit., p. 300.

48   ibid.

49   F. D. Maurice, 'The Gift of Hearing' in *Sermons Preached in Country Churches* (Macmillan & Co. 1880), p. 14.

50   G. M. Hopkins, 'God's Grandeur' in *Poems and Prose*, ed., with an introduction by W. H. Gardner (Penguin Books 1953), p. 27.

51   W. Wordsworth, 'Lines composed a few miles above Tintern Abbey, on revisiting the Banks of the Wye during a Tour, July 13, 1798' in W. E. Williams (ed.), *Wordsworth* (Penguin Books 1943), pp. 38–9.

52   T. Merton, *Contemplation in a World of Action* (Allen & Unwin 1971), p. 164.

53   T. Merton, *Unlived Life: A Manifesto Against Factory Farming* (Campaigners Against Factory Farming 1966), cited in Wynne-Tyson, op. cit., p. 200.

Chapter 2: Dominion and Covenant

1   Aquinas, *Summa Contra Gentiles*, ET by the English Dominican Fathers (New York: Benzger Brothers 1928), Third Book, Part II,

Ch. CXII, extract in T. Regan and P. Singer (ed.), *Animal Rights and Human Obligations* (New Jersey: Prentice-Hall 1976), pp. 58–9.

2 J. C. McCarthy, *Problems of Theology*, 2 vols. (Browne and Nolan 1960), vol. II, *The Commandments*, p. 158.

3 Calvin, *Institutes of the Christian Religion*, ed. J. T. McNeill, ET F. L. Battles, The Library of Christian Classics, vol XX (SCM Press 1961) 1.16.6., p. 204.

4 Luther, *Luther's Works*, vol. II, ed. by Jaroslav Pelikan (St Louis: Concordia Publishing House 1958), pp. 132–3.

5 Barth, *Church Dogmatics* III/2, *The Doctrine of Creation*, Part Two ('The Creature') (T. & T. Clark 1960), p. 3.

6 Cited and discussed in James Gaffney, 'The Relevance of Animal Experimentation to Roman Catholic Ethical Methodology' in T. Regan (ed.) *Animal Sacrifices: Religious Perspectives on the Use of Animals in Science* (Philadelphia: Temple University Press 1986), p. 149 and pp. 159–60. 'It is scarcely surprising that nineteenth-century Catholic opposition to so seemingly innocuous a cause as that of animal protection (imported to the continent from Britain) was led by a pope for whom liberal slogans were part of the devil's idiom' (p. 160).

7 The term was coined by Richard Ryder in 1970 to denote discrimination based on species alone, as with sexism or racism. One cannot read some animal welfare papers without being struck by the preponderance of advertisements for spiritual philosophies of one kind or another.

8 P. Singer (ed.), *In Defence of Animals* (Basil Blackwell 1986), p. 3. See also Singer's 'Man's Dominion . . . a short history of speciesism', *Animal Liberation: A New Ethic for Our Treatment of Animals* (Jonathan Cape 1976), pp. 202–34, which gives a vastly oversimplified history of Christian influence.

9 R. D. Ryder, *Victims of Science: The Use of Animals in Research*, forewords by Richard Adams and Muriel, Lady Dowding (National Anti-Vivisection Society ²1983), p. 126.

10 M. Duffy, e.g. 'Briefly, the Bible, principally the Book of Genesis in the Old Testament, gives man, on God's authority, dominion over the other animals and the right to use them for his benefit,' *Men and Beasts: An Animal Rights Handbook* (Paladin Books 1984), p. 5. This highly summarized and popular view is almost certainly wrong as I try to show.

11 L. White Jr, 'The Historical Roots of our Ecological Crisis' in John Barr (ed.), *The Environmental Handbook*, pp. 3–16, reprinted from *Science*, 10 March 1967, pp. 1203–7. See Robin Attfield's *The Ethics of Environmental Concern* (Basil Blackwell 1983), pp. 20–34 for a discussion and critique.

12 A. Linzey, *Animal Rights: A Christian Assessment* (SCM Press 1976), esp. pp. 14–19, where I adopt the view of commentators concerning the common meaning of dominion.

13 M. Midgley, *Animals and Why They Matter: A journey around the species barrier* (Pelican Books 1983), p. 45.

14 For example, C. S. Lewis held that the development of animal experimentation marked 'a great advance in the triumph of ruthless, non-moral utilitarianism over the old world of ethical law; a triumph in which we, as well as animals, are already the victims, and of which Dachau and Hiroshima mark the more recent achievements', 'Vivisection' in *Undeceptions: Essays on Theology and Ethics*, ed. Walter Hooper (Geoffrey Bles 1954), p. 186. Reprinted in *First and Second Things: Essays on Theology and Ethics*, ed. Walter Hooper (Fount 1985), pp. 83–4.

15 See Attfield, op. cit., pp. 36f.

16 Stephen R. L. Clark, *The Moral Status of Animals* (The Clarendon Press 1977), p. 159. To be fair, Clark is here thinking of 'general agreement within the Church', but the way in which the question is posed and answered gives the unfortunate impression that we can never expect a developed theology of animals. However, I gladly acknowledge Clark's personal encouragement to complete a more openly theological work on animals.

17 Aquinas, *Summa Theologica*, ET by the English Dominican Fathers (Burns, Oates and Washbourne Ltd. 1922), Part One, QQ. LXXV–CII, p. 327.

18 R. Burns, 'To a mouse' in *Poetical Works* (London and New York: Frederick Warne & Co. 1892), p. 28.

19 Genesis 1.26–8. cf. David Cairns: 'My own conclusion is that "P" means by existence in God's image a personal responsible existence before God', *The Image of God in Man* (Fontana Books 1973), p. 32.

20 C. F. D. Moule, *Man and Nature in the New Testament: Some Reflections on Biblical Ecology* (Athlone Press 1964), p. 5.

21 J. A. Baker, 'Biblical Attitudes to Nature' in Hugh Montefiore (ed.), *Man and Nature* (Collins 1975), p. 93.

22 G. Wingren, *Creation and Law*, ET Ross Mackenzie (Oliver & Boyd 1961), p. 106.

23 Genesis 1.29 (NEB).

24 Baker, op. cit., p. 94.

25 Genesis 2.15 (NEB).

26 See Genesis 2.22–3.

27 Aquinas, *Summa Theologica*, op. cit., p. 328.

28 Aquinas, *Summa Contra Gentiles*, op. cit., extract in Regan and Singer (ed.), *Animal Rights and Human Obligations* (New Jersey: Prentice-Hall 1976), p. 56.

29 Attfield, op. cit., p. 26.

30 See A. Linzey, 'The Place of Animals in Creation—A Christian View' in Regan (ed.), *Animal Sacrifices*, pp. 137ff, and A. Linzey, *The Neglected Creature: The Doctrine of the Non-Human Creation and its Relationship with the Human in the Thought of Karl Barth* (unpublished PHD, London University 1986), esp. pp. 281–310.

31 Mark 10.42–5 (NEB).

32 Barth, *Church Dogmatics* III/1 (T. & T. Clark 1958), p. 42 (sectional summary).

33 Barth, III/4 (T. & T. Clark 1961), pp. 332–3. Barth does not overlook the fact that animals are included in the covenant (*CD* III/1, p. 180), but practically proceeds as though he had not noted the text.

34 The reference here is to the question of animal 'rationality', Barth, *CD* III/4, p. 348.

35 A. Schweitzer, *Civilization and Ethics*, ET C. T. Campion (Unwin Books 1961) p. 225; discussed in Barth, *CD* III/4, p. 349.

36 Genesis 9.8–11 (NEB), see also, e.g., Ezekiel 34.24–5.

37 Genesis 9.4. For commentary see Anthony Phillips, 'Respect for Life in the Old Testament', *King's Theological Review*, 6.2 (Autumn 1983), pp. 32–5.

38 Barth, *CD* III/2, p. 361.

39 Genesis 1.24–31.

40 Genesis 1.22; cf. 1.28.

41 Jeremiah 7.20 (NEB).

42 John 1.3–4 (NEB).

43 Colossians 1.16 (NEB).

44 1 Peter 3.20–2.

45 E. Irving, *Collected Writings*, vol. V, ed. G. Carlyle (Alexander Strahan 1865), pp. 295f. I am grateful to Colin Gunton for this reference. For an account of the contemporary significance of other aspects of Irving's thought, see Colin Gunton, 'The One, The Three and The Many', An Inaugural Lecture in the Chair of Christian Doctrine, published as a booklet (London: King's College, May 1985).

46 Exodus 23.5 (NEB).

47 Deuteronomy 25.4 (NEB).

48 Exodus 20.8–11 and 23.12.

49 David Bleich, commenting on these verses, makes clear that 'Judaism most certainly *does* posit an unequivocal prohibition against causing cruelty to animals', 'Judaism and Animal Experimentation' in Regan (ed.), *Animal Sacrifices*, p. 64. It is interesting that Jewish tradition posits a whole range of moral obligations towards animals which are not themselves a matter of law, ibid., pp. 84–9.

50 Jonah 4.11.

51 Proverbs 12.10 (NEB).

52 Bleich, op. cit., p. 63.

53 Maimonides, *Guide to the Perplexed*, Book III, Ch. 17; cited by Bleich, op. cit., pp. 74–5.

54 Bonaventure, *The Life of St Francis*, ET Ewert Cousins, The Classics of Western Spirituality (New York: Paulist Press 1978), pp. 254–5.

55 A. M. Allchin, *Wholeness and Transfiguration Illustrated in the Lives of St Francis of Assisi and St Seraphim of Sarov* (SLG Press 1974), p. 5.

56 See, e.g., the theology of St Maximus the Confessor, as described by

Vladimir Lossky, *The Mystical Theology of the Eastern Church* (James Clarke 1957), esp. pp. 111f.

57 Chrysostom, cited by John Attwater, *St John Chrysostom* (Catholic Book Club 1960), pp. 59–60.

58 R. Browning, 'Saul' in *Poems of Robert Browning* (London and New York: Oxford University Press 1911), p. 27.

59 Richard Griffiths refers to Genesis 9.1–7 as the 'basic text', and therefore begins his discussion of the biblical material with the assumption of the divine 'permission to kill and eat animals'. He may be right in accusing my earlier work of neglecting biblical material, but it has to be said that his method conveniently allows him to give insufficient attention to the Genesis narrative, which is, as Barth points out, critical to understanding the subsequent 'permission', *The Human Use of Animals* (Grove Books 1982), p. 6.

60 Genesis 9.2 (NEB).

61 Hosea 2.18–9 (NEB).

62 Isaiah 11.6–10 (NEB).

63 Ephesians 1.9–11 (NEB).

64 Athanasius, *Contra Gentes and De Incarnatione*, ed. and ET R. W. Thomson (The Clarendon Press 1971), p. 5. The Logos contains and encloses all being and 'gives life and protection to everything', p. 115.

65 H. Küng, *On Being a Christian*, ET Edward Quinn (Collins 1977), pp. 251–5; see A. Linzey, 'Is Anthropocentricity Christian?', *Theology* (January 1981), pp. 18–23 for a critique.

66 Teilhard de Chardin, *Hymn of the Universe*, ET Gerald Vann (Fontana Books 1970), pp. 24–5.

67 Barth, *CD* III/1, p. 18.

68 Robert South (1634–1716), extract in *A Lectionary of Christian Prose*, compiled by A. C. Bouquet (Peter Smith 1965), p. 30.

69 T. F. Torrance, *Divine and Contingent Order* (Oxford University Press 1981), p. 130; my italics.

70 F. D. Maurice, *Sermons Preached in Country Churches* (Macmillan & Co. 1880), pp. 345–7.

71 Lossky, op. cit., p. 111.

72 See, e.g., E. L. Mascall, *The Openness of Being: Natural Theology Today* (Darton, Longman and Todd 1971), pp. 257f.

73 For a recent discussion, see Tom Regan, *The Case for Animal Rights* (Berkeley, California: University of California Press 1983), esp. chapters 1 and 2.

74 See Linzey, *Animal Rights*, pp. 10–14.

75 W. A. Whitehouse, 'New Heavens and a New Earth' in *The Christian Hope*, Theological Collections no. 13 (SPCK 1970), and in *The Authority of Grace: Essays in Response to Karl Barth*, ed. Ann Loades (T. & T. Clark 1981), p. 205. I am indebted to Whitehouse for many points.

76 Whitehouse, op. cit., p. 210.

77 Ecclesiastes 3.19–20 (RSV).

78   K. Ward, *The Concept of God* (Basil Blackwell 1974), p. 223.
79   K. Ward, *Rational Theology and the Creativity of God* (Basil Blackwell 1982), p. 202.
80   J. Wesley, *Sermons on Several Occasions*, 3 vols., with biog. note by J. Beecham (Wesleyan Conference Office 1874), vol. II, pp. 281 and 282. The view concerning divine communication is found on p. 278.
81   A. Tennyson, 'In Memoriam' in *The Works* (Macmillan & Co. 1889), p. 261.

Chapter 3: Sacrifice and Peace

1   Genesis 8.20–2 (RSV).
2   F. Young, *The Use of Sacrificial Ideas in Greek Christian Writers from the New Testament to John Chrysostom*, Patristic Monograph Series, no. 5 (Philadelphia: The Philadelphia Patristic Foundation 1979), pp. 51, 54.
3   Isaiah 1.11–12 (RSV).
4   Young, op. cit., p. 60.
5   ibid., p. 67; for discussion of the moral criticisms see esp. pp. 57–66.
6   ibid., p. 69.
7   Mark 11.15–19 (RSV); cf. Matthew 21.12–17; Luke 19.45–8 and John 2.13–16.
8   Mark 12.28–34; cf. Matthew 22.34–40; Luke 10.25–8.
9   Al-Halfiz B. A. Masri claims that Islam channelled animal sacrifice into 'an institution of charity' whereby the sacrificed meat was given to the poor. This may be, but the system remains prevalent throughout Muslim countries. 'Animal Experimentation: The Muslim Viewpoint' in T. Regan (ed.), *Animal Sacrifices: Religious Perspectives on the Use of Animals in Science* (Philadelphia: Temple University Press 1986), p. 187.
10   Hebrews 9.12 (RSV).
11   See A. Linzey, 'The Place of Animals in Creation—A Christian View' in Regan (ed.), *Animal Sacrifices*, pp. 127ff.
12   E. Sitwell, 'Still Falls the Rain' in Peter Levi (ed.), *The Penguin Book of English Christian Verse* (Penguin Books 1984), p. 294.
13   Philippians 2.5–7 (RSV).
14   Romans 12.1–2 (RSV).
15   V. Hugo, 'The Relationship Between Man and the Animals' in *The Ark*, Journal of the Catholic Study Circle for Animal Welfare (August 1969), p. 116.
16   John Saward, *Perfect Fools: Folly for Christ's Sake in Catholic and Orthodox Spirituality* (Oxford University Press 1980), p. 84. For many of the legends concerning St Francis, see *The Little Flowers of St Francis, The Mirror of Perfection and St Bonaventure's Life of St*

Francis, intro. by H. McKay, Everyman's Library (Dent 1973), esp. pp. 289–96 and 350–8.

17 A. M. Farrer, 'Walking Sacraments' in *A Celebration of Faith* (Collins 1970), p. 111, cited in Saward, op. cit., p. 217.

18 *The Principles of the First Order SSF* (Hillfield: Dorset, SSF, 1984), pp. 1, 12.

19 See, e.g., the Minister-General's letter on animals in *The Franciscan* 26.1 (January 1984), pp. 2–3, a section of which is reproduced in 'Church Statements on Animals, 1956–86'; also Brother Ramon SSF, *A Hidden Fire: Exploring the Deeper Reaches of Prayer* (Marshall Paperbacks 1985), pp. 153f. on cosmic prayer.

20 David Marshall Lang, *Lives and Legends of the Gregorian Saints* (Mowbray 1976), p. 83.

21 St David, cited by Lang, ibid., p. 89.

22 See Eleanor Duckett, *The Wandering Saints* (Collins 1959). One of the many healings cited is that by St Kentigern of a robin which 'boys in malice had torn to pieces' (p. 89). For other examples, see Gilbert H. Doble, *The Saints of Cornwall*, Part 5, *Saints of Mid-Cornwall* (Dean and Chapter of Truro 1970).

23 St Catherine, cited from her biography, *Vita*, p. 72b, in Friedrich von Hügel, *The Mystical Element of Religion as Studied in St Catherine of Genoa and her Friends*, 2 vols. (J. M. Dent 1958), vol. I, p. 164.

24 'Prospectus of the SPCA', *RSPCA Records*, vol. II (1823–26), p. 198. Wilberforce, Martin and Broome were among the signatories of this first prospectus. I am grateful to the Society's librarian for a copy of this document.

25 Ezekiel 13.10 (RSV).

26 See Genesis 9.4. Anthony Phillips writes: 'Genesis 9:1–7 describes the world as no longer the idyllic place it was created to be: instead the animals live in fear of man who can legitimately kill them for food. For P, the end of vegetarianism is then a necessary evil though even here man is not given an entirely free hand: the blood of the animal must first be drained from it . . . The Hebrews recognized that death occurred through loss of breath or blood, and since God was responsible for creation, both must belong to him,' *Lower Than the Angels: Questions raised by Genesis 1–11*, foreword by Lord Blanch (Bible Reading Fellowship 1983), p. 48.

27 R. Attfield, *The Ethics of Environmental Concern* (Basil Blackwell 1983), p. 25

28 See, e.g., the discussion in Joachim Jeremias, 'Was the Last Supper a Passover Meal?', chapter 1 of *The Eucharistic Words of Jesus*, ET N. Perrin (SCM Press 1966), pp. 15–88.

29 Stephen R. L. Clark, *The Moral Status of Animals* (The Clarendon Press 1977), p. 196 on Matthew 11.18f.

30 See, G. L. Rudd, *Why Kill for Food?* (Vegetarian Society 1956), pp. 84–90 and Jon Wynne-Tyson, *Food for a Future* (Centaur Press 1979), pp. 133–5.

31 Isaiah 7.14–15 (CDV); see *Jesus Was a Vegetarian—Why Aren't You?* (Imlaystown, N.J.: The Edenite Society 1977).
32 J. A. Baker, 'Biblical Attitudes to Nature' in Hugh Montefiore (ed.), *Man and Nature* (Collins 1975), p. 105.
33 cf. Luke 13.15; 15.4; Matthew 12.11 and Luke 14.5.
34 Augustine, cited by Attfield, op. cit., pp. 29–30.
35 See Matthew 10.29 and Luke 12.6; Matthew 6.26 and Luke 12.24.
36 Matthew 6.28–9 and Luke 12.27.
37 Baker, op. cit., p. 105.
38 Attfield, op. cit., p. 29.
39 cf. Genesis 14.18; Hebrews 7.1–2, see J. J. Von Allmen, *Vocabulary of the Bible*, (Lutterworth Press 1958), p. 319.
40 Luke 1.79 (RSV).
41 Matthew 5.9 (RSV).
42 Colossians 1.20 (RSV).
43 Romans 12.18 (RSV).
44 D. Soper, *Tower Hill 12:30* (Epworth Press 1963), p. 91.
45 J. Habgood, *Church and Nation in a Secular Age* (Darton, Longman & Todd 1983), p. 75.
46 S. Hauerwas, *The Peaceable Kingdom: A Primer in Christian Ethics* (SCM Press 1984), p. xvii.
47 ibid., p. 103; his italics.
48 Romans 8.19 (RSV).
49 Brother Ramon, op. cit., p. 216.

Chapter 4: The Claims of Animals

1 A. W. Moss, *Valiant Crusade: The History of the Royal Society for the Prevention of Cruelty of Animals* (Cassell 1961), p. 13.
2 ibid.
3 Thomas Hardy, *Jude the Obscure* (1895), cited by Keith Thomas, *Man and the Natural World: Changing Attitudes in England 1500–1800* (Penguin Books 1984), p. 93. Hardy was strongly committed to animal welfare, as his novels and also his neglected poetry on this theme show, see especially 'The Puzzled Gamebirds', 'The Blinded Bird', 'A Sheep Fair', 'Bags of Meat' and 'The Lady in Furs', and in particular, 'Compassion: An Ode, In Celebration of the Centenary of the Royal Society for the Prevention of Cruelty to Animals', all in *The Complete Poems*, ed. James Gibson, The New Wessex Edition (Macmillan 1976).
4 *The Times*, 25 April 1800, cited in Moss, op. cit., p. 14.
5 ibid., p. 16f.
6 e.g., 'Even in 1959 an Inspector was savagely attacked at his own front door by a man whose wife earlier in the day had asked for her dog to be destroyed', ibid., p. 64.
7 J. Turner, *Reckoning with the Beast: Animals, Pain and Humanity in the Victorian Mind* (Baltimore and London: The Johns Hopkins

University Press 1980), p. 17. Turner's work is an exemplary historical study in many ways, but he is oddly constrained by his judgements that 'Victorian fondness for animals' was nothing but 'the sentimentalism of a mawkish age' (p. xi) and that Victorians, shocked by industrialization, turned to benevolence (xii and *passim*). I fail to understand the reasons for these reductionist tendencies which marr an otherwise exceptional book.

8   Lord Shaftesbury, 'Speech on the second reading of the Cruelty to Animals Bill, 26 May, 1876' extract in Jon Wynne-Tyson (ed.), *The Extended Circle: A Dictionary of Humane Thought* (Centaur Press 1986), p. 320.

9   Clapham Sect, cited in Turner, op. cit., p. 21.

10   These include: John Hildrop, *Free Thoughts upon the Brute Creation* (1742); Richard Dean, *An Essay on the Future Life of Brutes* (1767); Henry Crowe, *Zoophilos: or Considerations on the Moral Treatment of Inferior Animals* (1820); Humphry Primatt, *A Dissertation on the Duty of Mercy and the Sin of Cruelty to Brute Animals* (1834) and Joseph Hamilton, *Animal Futurity: A Plea for the Immortality of the Brutes* (1877). Despite their titles, many of these offer quite hard-headed assessments. Primatt's work is prophetic in many ways (see note 26 below) and Hamilton offers a valuable chapter on 'Reparation for Suffering' as an argument for animal afterlife (pp. 78–92).

11   Queen Victoria, cited in Moss, op. cit., p. 20. See also her abhorrence of 'this horrible, brutalising, *unchristian-like vivisection*', related in a letter to Sir William Harcourt in *Life of Sir William Harcourt* (original italics) cited in Jon Wynne-Tyson, op. cit., p. 386.

12   *RSPCA Minute Book*, no. 1, pp. 28, 40–1, cited in Turner, op. cit., p. 43. Turner claims that this declaration was passed 'to lay to rest the charge of "Pythagorean doctrines" ' and against '[Lewis] Gompertz's Jewishness', p. 154. Gompertz was the second secretary of the Society after Arthur Broome.

13   Lord Erskine, cited in Moss, op. cit., pp. 34–5.

14   ibid., p. 49.

15   ibid., p. 16.

16   H. Davis, *Moral and Pastoral Theology*, vol. II (Sheed & Ward 1946), p. 258.

17   For an account of the early parliamentary squabbles, see Moss, op. cit., pp. 11–19 and Turner, op. cit., pp. 15–38.

18   William E. Addis and Thomas Arnold (ed.), *A Catholic Dictionary* (Virtue & Co. ⁹1924), p. 31.

19   James Gaffney, in a significant paper, holds out some prospect of change: 'revisionism exists among Catholics, usually unorganized and often sentimental, but more and more, I think, reflectively conscientious. Given enlarging ecumenical experience, expanding sympathy with liberal ideologies, and increasing education in undogmatic ethical enquiry, I anticipate that Catholics' opinions

about the treatment of animals, in science and elsewhere, will be progressively less distinguishable from those of their neighbours', 'The Relevance of Animal Experimentation to Roman Catholic Ethical Methodology' in Tom Regan (ed.), *Animal Sacrifices: Religious Perspectives on the Use of Animals in Science* (Philadelphia: Temple University Press 1986), pp. 168–9. While welcoming almost any change, I shall be sorry if it comes via this . . . route of increasing revisionism rather than, say, through theological reflection upon the intrinsic value of creation, the evil character of pain or (dare we hope for it?) an appreciation that earlier work opposing rights was flawed in its negligence towards animals.

20 Colossians 1.16 (RSV); my italics.

21 Matthew Smith, *A Philosophical Discourse of the Nature of Rational and Irrational Souls* (1695) p. 21 and John Chishull, *Two Treatises* (1654), sig, A5; both cited in Thomas, op. cit., p. 33.

22 The list of theologians, according to Thomas (ibid., pp. 137–42), holding to animal souls or the possibility of afterlife include: Henry Moore, John Bradford, William Bowling, Richard Overton, Samuel Clarke, Charles Leigh, Ralph Josselin, Bishop Butler, William Whiston, John Lawrence, Matthew Henry, Adam Clarke, John Wesley, Augustus Toplady, J. G. Wood and Lord Shaftesbury.

23 Aquinas, *Summa Theologica*, ET by the Fathers of the English Dominican Province, 2nd revised edn. (Burns, Oates & Washborne, 1922), Part I, Q. 93, Art. 4, p. 289.

24 Thomas, op. cit., p. 43.

25 Fox, cited in William C. Braithwaite, *The Second Period of Quakerism* (1919) p. 270; cited in Thomas, ibid., p. 43.

26 H. Primatt, *A Dissertation on the Duty of Mercy and the Sin of Cruelty to Brute Animals* (T. Constable 1834), p. 65; last line is my italics.

27 'The statement that [animals] "have no souls" may mean that they have no moral responsibilities and are not immortal. But the absence of "soul" in that sense makes the infliction of pain upon them not easier but harder to justify. For it means that animals cannot deserve pain, nor profit morally by the discipline of pain, nor be recompensed by happiness in another life for suffering in this. Thus all the factors which render pain more tolerable or make it less totally evil in the case of human beings will be lacking in the beasts,' C. S. Lewis, 'Vivisection', first published as a pamphlet by the New England Anti-Vivisection Society (1947), and in Walter Hooper (ed.), *Undeceptions: Essays on Theology and Ethics* (Geoffrey Bles 1954), p. 183. (*First and Second Things* (Fount 1985), p. 80).

28 B. Brophy, 'The Rights of Animals', *The Sunday Times*, 10 October 1965; reprinted as a leaflet by the Animal Defence Society (London 1965), p. 8.

29 Thomas, op. cit., p. 48; pp. 121–36 and 166–91.

30 For a critique of our all-too-easy assumptions about nature 'red in tooth and claw', see Stephen R. L. Clark, *The Moral Status of*

Animals (Clarendon Press 1977), chapter 6 'The Imagination of War', pp. 110–32 and also *The Nature of the Beast: Are Animals Moral?* (Oxford University Press 1982), where he argues that while morality cannot be reduced to socio-biology, 'the ways of beasts may set us *good* examples' (p. 118); my italics.

31 H. A. Williams, *Tensions: Necessary Conflicts in Life and Love* (Mitchell Beazley 1976), p. 47.

32 B. Brophy, 'The Darwinist's Dilemma' in David Paterson and Richard D. Ryder (ed.), *Animals' Rights—A Symposium* (Centaur Press 1979), pp. 67f.

33 Origen, cited in Allan D. Galloway's *The Cosmic Christ* (Nisbet and Sons 1951), pp. 85, 93, and also reproduced in A. Linzey, *The Status of Animals in the Christian Tradition* (Woodbrooke College 1985), p. 10.

34 A. Elphinstone, *Freedom, Suffering and Love* (SCM Press 1976), p. 29; on the 'neutrality' of pain, see pp. 106f.

35 P. T. Geach, *Providence and Evil* (Cambridge University Press 1977), pp. 77, 79.

36 J. Plunkett, 'I see his blood upon the rose' in J. C. Squire (ed.), *Selections from Modern Poets* (Martin Secker ʼ1926), p. 363.

37 For a perceptive and sympathetic discussion, see H. Maurice Relton, *Studies in Christian Doctrine* (Macmillan 1960), pp. 61–91. He writes: 'In reading the history of early Christian doctrine we cannot fail to be struck with the remarkable reluctance on the part of Church teachers to ascribe anything so positive as feeling, still less sympathy and suffering, to God. They clung to the doctrine of the Impassibility of the Godhead with a tenacity which cannot but astonish us who study it in the light of the incarnation' (p. 78). The real issue in patripassianism, however, is not whether Christ suffers, or even whether God the Father suffers momentarily in Christ, but whether God *eternally* suffers. It *could* be that he does, and that all suffering everywhere is immediately transformed into joy. For myself, I do not see how God can eternally suffer and also at the same time offer us liberation from suffering which after all is the central hope of the gospel.

38 St John of the Cross, *The Complete Works*, ed. and ET by A. E. Peers, 3 vols in one ed. (Anthony Clarke, 1974), vol. II, part V, pp. 49, 48.

39 A view defended at length and with great subtlety by T. F. Torrance, *Divine and Contingent Order* (Oxford University Press 1981), pp. 122f and discussed in A. Linzey, *The Neglected Creature* (London University, 1986), pp. 295f.

40 Descartes, Letter to the Marquess of Newcastle (23 November 1646), in *Descartes: Philosophical Letters*, ed. and ET by Anthony Kenny (Clarendon Press 1970), and extract in T. Regan and P. Singer (ed.), *Animal Rights and Human Obligations* (New Jersey: Prentice-Hall 1977), pp. 63–64.

41 While Barth opposes the traditional view of 'the so-called soul'

based on the Greek model, he nevertheless develops a view of animal souls, or rather the lack of them, in terms strikingly similar to that of Descartes, e.g., 'Whether the beast is engaged in such self-knowledge or is even capable of it, I cannot know, because the beast cannot tell me anything about it,' *Church Dogmatics*, III/2, *The Doctrine of Creation*, ('The Creature') (T. and T. Clark 1960), pp. 374–5, and discussed in Linzey, *The Neglected Creature*, pp. 262f.

42 Descartes, Letter to the Marquess of Newcastle, in Regan and Singer, op. cit., p. 64.

43 Descartes, Letter to Henry Moore (5 February 1649), in Regan and Singer, op. cit., p. 65; my italics.

44 C. E. Raven, *The Creator Spirit* (Macmillan 1927), p. 120, cited and discussed in A. R. Kingston, 'Theodicy and Animal Welfare', *Theology* (November 1967), pp. 485f.

45 I. Trethowan, *An Essay in Christian Philosophy* (1954) p. 87; cited in Kingston, ibid., p. 487.

46 F. Van Steenbergen, *Hidden God* (Louvain 1966), p. 252; cited in Kingston, ibid., p. 486.

47 Kingston ibid., pp. 482, 487.

48 Edward Carpenter *et al.*, *Animals and Ethics* (Watkins 1980), p. 8. The working party was convened by the Dean of Westminster and included: Dr Michael Brambell, Prof. Kenneth Carpenter, Prof. Sydney Jennings and Prof. W. H. Thorpe.

49 ibid., p. 8; see also Marian Stamp Dawkins, *Animal Suffering: The Science of Animal Welfare* (London and New York: Chapman & Hall 1980).

50 H. D. Lewis, *The Self and Immortality* (Macmillan 1973), pp. 67–8. And yet Lewis goes on to *deny* (surely inconsistently) that 'we should speak of the *soul* of a dog' (p. 68; his italics). Perhaps this is an indication that, Cartesian habits of mind are not so easily overcome.

51 St Basil, *On the Holy Spirit*, chapter 15, 35–36, extract in Brother Kenneth CGA (ed.), *From the Fathers to the Churches* (Collins 1983), p. 319.

52 J. P. Mahaffy, *Descartes* (London 1901), p. 181; cited by Kingston, op. cit., p. 485.

53 Tertullian, *On Prayer*, chapter 29, extract in Brother Kenneth, op. cit., p. 262.

54 C. W. Hume, *The Status of Animals in the Christian Religion* (Universities Federation for Animal Welfare 1957), see pp. 26–35.

Chapter 5: The Theos-Rights of Animals

1 *Dictionary of Moral Theology*, ed. P. Palazzini, comp. F. Roberti, ET H. J. Yannone (Burns and Oates 1962), p. 73.

2   J. Foster, 'On Cruelty to Animals' in J. E. Ryland (ed.), *Critical Essays Contributed to the Eclectic Review* (Henry G. Bohn 1856), vol. 1, p. 440; his italics. I am grateful to Peter J. Wexler for this reference.

3   The International Society for Animal Rights (421 South State Street, Clarks Summit, Philadelphia 18411, USA) is now one of the major animal rights organizations.

4   Romans 9.20b–22 (RSV).

5   K. Barth, *Dogmatics in Outline*, ET G. T. Thomson (SCM Press, 1966), p. 54.

6   D. Bonhoeffer, *Ethics*, ed. Eberhard Bethge, ET N. H. Smith (SCM Press 1971), p. 127.

7   Even though his *Ethics* was not finished, there are few signs that Bonhoeffer saw the implications of his argument as they relate to animals. As a whole his work shares the same anthropocentric deficiency which characterizes almost all twentieth-century theology.

8   Bonhoeffer, op. cit., p. 127; my italics.

9   R. Griffiths, *The Human Use of Animals* (Grove Books 1982), p. 18.

10 T. Regan, *The Case for Animal Rights* (Berkeley, California: University of California Press, 1984).

11 *Charter of the Rights of the Family presented by the Holy See to all Persons, Institutions and Authorities concerned with the Mission of the Family in Today's World*, 22 October 1983 (Catholic Truth Society 1983). For a recent theological defence of human rights, see Jürgen Moltmann, *On Human Dignity* (SCM Press 1984).

12 *The Report of the Lambeth Conference 1978* (CIO Publishing 1978), p. 37. This Conference, unlike its predecessor in 1968, made no specific resolutions on animals save that of general support for conservation (ibid., p. 34). Keith Ward, in a preparatory paper, 'Changing Ethical Values: A Christian Assessment' in *Today's Church and Today's World: The Lambeth Conference 1978 Preparatory Articles* (CIO Publishing, 1978), p. 76, indicated, however, the need for a renewed sense of responsibility towards animal life because 'Christians have sometimes been callous'.

13 See R. G. Frey, *Interests and Rights: The Case Against Animals* (Clarendon Press 1980).

14 See the two extracts in the appendix, 'Church Resolutions on Animals'.

15 A. Agius, *God's Animals* (Catholic Study Circle for Animal Welfare 1970), p. 63.

16 H. Montefiore, *Hansard* (House of Lords 28 November 1985), p. 1018.

17 ibid.

18 ibid.

19 The question is discussed in Tom Regan, 'An Examination and

Defense of One Argument Concerning Animal Rights', *Inquiry* 22 (1979), pp. 196f.

20 The 'Scientific Procedures on Living Animals' Bill (1985) updates the 1876 Cruelty to Animals Act in the UK, which first legalized painful experiments on animals. The new legislation modifies the working of the previous Act but still allows painful experiments. Crucially (as Montefiore points out) the 'guidelines' were not published prior to the parliamentary debate itself.

21 C. S. Lewis, 'Vivisection' in Walter Hooper (ed.), *Undeceptions: Essays on Theology and Ethics* (Geoffrey Bles 1954); *First and Second Things* (Fount 1985), p. 81; his italics.

22 A. Linzey, *Animal Rights: A Christian Assessment* (SCM Press 1976), p. 21.

23 P. Green, *The Problem of Right Conduct: A Textbook on Christian Ethics* (Longman & Co 1936), p. 272.

24 J. Rickaby, *Moral Philosophy* (1901), extract in Tom Regan and Peter Singer (ed.), *Animal Rights and Human Obligations* (New Jersey: Prentice-Hall 1976), p. 179; my italics.

25 W. H. Thorpe, *Animal Nature and Human Nature* (Methuen 1974), p. 320.

26 K. Ward, *The Living God* (SPCK 1984), pp. 26, 27.

27 Rickaby, in Regan and Singer, op. cit., p. 179; my italics.

28 J. M. Gustafson, *Theology and Ethics* (Basil Blackwell 1981), p. 96.

29 A. Schweitzer, *My Life and Thought*, ET C. T. Campion (Allen & Unwin 1933), p. 271.

30 A. Schweitzer, *Civilization and Ethics*, ET C. T. Campion (Allen & Unwin 1967), p. 216.

31 Ecclesiastes 3.19–22.

32 Psalm 104.29–31 (RSV).

33 Joel 2.28 (RSV).

34 Acts 2.17.

35 Mark 1.13 (RSV).

36 Romans 8.23 (RSV).

37 M. Luther, *Lectures on Romans*, ed. and ET Wilhelm Pauck, The Library of Christian Classics, vol. XV (SCM Press 1961), p. 237.

38 Genesis 9.15, 16 (RSV).

39 Leviticus 17.11 (RSV).

40 Isaiah 66.23 and 40.5 (RSV).

41 1 Corinthians 15.39.

42 Ephesians 2.15 (RSV). Tertullian is one of the church Fathers who specifically defends the resurrection of the flesh. The 'universe' is seen as 'a parable of the resurrection'. While agreeing with Paul that there are different kinds of flesh, it is the same substance that will be redeemed. *Treatise on the Resurrection*, ed., ET and comm. Ernest Evans (SPCK 1960), p. 35 (para. 13) and pp. 156–7 (para. 52).

43 W. Bowling, cited in Keith Thomas, *Man and the Natural World:*

Changing Attitudes in England 1500–1800 (Penguin Books 1984), p. 139.

44 John 6.54 (RSV); 55 (AV).

45 See Gerhard von Rad, *Genesis: A Commentary*, ET J. H. Marks (SCM Press 1961), pp. 55f.

46 J. Bentham, *The Principles of Morals and Legislation* (1789), chapter XVII, section 1, extract in Regan and Singer, op. cit., p. 130.

47 R. G. Frey, 'What has Sentiency to do with the Possession of Rights?' in David Paterson and R. D. Ryder (ed.) *Animals' Rights—A Symposium* (Centaur Press 1979), pp. 106–11.

48 Frey, *Interests and Rights*, p. 47.

49 ibid., p. 161. For a critique, see James Gaffney, 'The Relevance of Animal Experimentation to Roman Catholic Ethical Methodology' in Tom Regan (ed.), *Animal Sacrifices: Religious Perspectives on the Use of Animals in Science* (Philadelphia: Temple University Press 1986), pp. 165f.

50 Revelation 21.4 (RSV).

51 Regan, *The Case for Animal Rights*, p. 243.

52 ibid., p. 78.

53 *Report of the Panel of Enquiry into Shooting and Angling 1976–1979*, chaired by Lord Medway (Horsham 1980), p. 52; my italics. The Report is odd in a number of ways, since on the one hand the evidence reviewed (pp. 3–11) does not appear to support the strong recommendations, and despite its conclusions the Report does not actually oppose shooting or angling on the other. Anglers are simply asked to 'review' their 'appreciation of the sport in the light of the evidence presented' (p. 53).

54 Regan, *The Case for Animal Rights*, p. 366.

55 Frey, 'What has Sentiency to do with the Possession of Rights?' in Paterson and Ryder (ed.), *Animals' Rights—A Symposium*, p. 108. Discussed by A. Linzey, 'Moral Education and Reverence of Life' in David Paterson (ed.), *Humane Education—A Symposium* (Humane Education Council 1981), p. 120.

56 Psalm 36.6 (AV); 'beast' (*behemat*) here refers primarily to cattle and, by implication, to all land animals.

57 K. Lorenz, 'Letter to Williams' in *On Aggression*, ET M. Latzke (Methuen 1966), p. 54; cited in Stephen R. L. Clark, *The Moral Status of Animals* (Clarendon Press 1977), p. 38.

58 A. S. Gunn, 'Traditional Ethics and the Moral Status of Animals', *Environmental Ethics*, 5.2 (Summer 1983), p. 145. I am grateful to Chris Langley for this reference.

59 ibid.

60 See Francoise Hampson and Andrew Linzey, *Theology, Law and the Use of Armed Force* (Crook Academic, forthcoming), for a discussion of the value of international law relating to armed conflict.

61 Gunn, op. cit., pp. 149–50.

62 ibid., p. 150.
63 ibid., p. 152; his italics.
64 ibid.
65 Hebrews 11.1, from E. L. Mascall, *Grace and Glory* (SPCK 1961), p. 40.
66 Julian of Norwich, *Revelations of Divine Love*, chapter 5, cited and discussed in E. L. Mascall, *Grace and Glory* (SPCK 1961), pp. 49f.
67 A. Pope, 'Of Cruelty to Animals' in Rosalind Vallance (ed.) *A Hundred English Essays* (Thomas Nelson & Sons 1950), p. 159.
68 K. Barth, *CD* III/4, 'The Command of God the Creator' (T. & T. Clark 1961), pp. 255–6.
69 e.g., John 4.23 (RSV).
70 K. Barth, *Ethics*, ed. Dietrich Braun, ET G. W. Bromiley (T. & T. Clark 1982), p. 142.
71 See Peter Singer, 'The Parable of the Fox and the Unliberated Animals', *Ethics*, 88.2 (January 1978), and Regan, *The Case for Animal Rights*, pp. 219f for a discussion and critique.
72 B. Häring, *The Law of Christ: Moral Theology for Clergy and Laity*, vol. 2 (Mercier Press 1963), pp. 361–2.
73 E. Carpenter, 'Christian Faith and the Moral Aspect of Hunting' in P. Moore (ed.), *Against Hunting: A Symposium* (Gollancz 1965), p. 136.

Chapter 6: Ways of Liberation (I)

1 Last two estimates from Sidney Glendin, 'The Use of Animals in Science', in Tom Regan (ed.), *Animal Sacrifices: Religious Perspectives on the Use of Animals in Science* (Philadelphia: Temple University Press 1986), p. 15.
2 Cited in Edward Carpenter *et al.*, *Animals and Ethics* (Watkins 1980), p. 21.
3 H. S. Salt, *Seventy Years Among the Savages* (London: Allen & Unwin; New York: T. Seltzer, Inc. 1921). Salt was a remarkable man who anticipated in his writings almost all of the humanitarian reforms of this century. See especially his *Animals' Rights Considered in Relation to Social Progress*, preface by Peter Singer (Centaur Press 1980) which, while not the first, is undoubtedly one of the best.
4 Cited in David Henshaw, 'Animal Liberationists declare war on their own species' in *The Listener* (19 June 1968), p. 5.
5 R. Lee, cited in Henshaw, ibid. I corresponded with Ronnie Lee during one of his periods of imprisonment for ALF activity. I believe him to be a person of considerable conviction and integrity. I am only sorry that he appears to have given up his commitment to non-violence.
6 Romans 3.23 (RSV).
7 Mark 10.18 (NEB).
8 J. S. Mill, cited in Tom Regan, *The Case for Animal Rights*

(Berkeley, California: University of California Press 1983), preface page.

9 G. B. Shaw, 'Killing for Sport' and 'The Doctor's Dilemma' in *Prefaces* (Constable and Co. 1934), pp. 144, 258–9.

10 A. Schweitzer, *Civilization and Ethics*, ET by C. T. Campion (Allen & Unwin 1967), p. 221.

11 Isaiah 6.7 (NEB).

12 K. Ward, 'Changing Ethical Values: A Christian Assessment', *Today's Church and Today's World* (The Lambeth Conference 1978 Preparatory Articles) (CIO Publishing 1977), p. 74.

13 Plato, *The Republic*, ET F. M. Cornford (Oxford University Press 1969), Part VII, 518, p. 232.

14 Isaiah 11.6–9 (NEB).

15 I have benefited from a lecture by Stephen R. L. Clark given at Essex University which helpfully distinguished between 'hurts', 'harms', 'pains', 'suffering', 'wrongs' and 'injuries' to animals. Although my own formulations are slightly different, I acknowledge my debt to his clarity of thought.

16 H. Primatt, *A Dissertation on the Duty of Mercy and the Sin of Cruelty to Brute Animals* (T. Constable 1834), p. 288; his emphases.

17 ibid, p. 289.

18 St Francis of Sales, *Introduction to the Devout Life*, ET Michael Day (Burns and Oates 1956), p. 173.

19 See, e.g., Jean Grou's peculiar assertion that Jesus himself 'renounced even the most innocent pleasure', *Manual for Interior Souls* (Burns Oates & Washbourne 1892), p. 9.

20 H. Vaughan, 'The World' in Helen Gardner (ed.), *The Metaphysical Poets* (Penguin Books 1964), p. 271. See also Andrew Marvell's 'Dialogue Between the Resolved Soul and the Created Pleasure', ibid., pp. 237–40.

21 *Extracts from the Minutes and Epistles of the Yearly Meeting of the Religious Society of Friends held in London, from its first institution to the present time, relating to Christian Doctrine, Practice and Discipline* (Friends Book Depository 1862), section XVI, p. 105.

22 Cited by James Turner, *Reckoning with the Beast: Animals, Pain and Humanity in the Victorian Mind* (Baltimore and London: Johns Hopkins University Press 1980), p. 20.

23 Cited in *Man in his Living Environment: An Ethical Assessment* (CIO Publishing 1970), pp. 24–5.

24 J. Rickaby, *Moral Philosophy* (1901), extract in Tom Regan and Peter Singer (ed.), *Animal Rights and Human Obligations* (New Jersey: Prentice-Hall 1976), p. 179.

25 T. Veblen, *Theory of the Leisure Class* (1899), p. 257. I am grateful to Peter J. Wexler for this reference.

26 The following passage from the Annual Report of the Universities Federation for Animal Welfare, 1970–1 (p. 9) makes clear the anomaly: 'UFAW takes no sides in the various controversies which

occur over the activities of foxhunters . . . except to assert that foxhunting does not control foxes in any locality and is quite impractical in areas where foxes are a pest. On one estate in East Anglia, the gamekeeper kills on average 80 foxes per year by humanely acceptable methods, but he leaves 2–3 foxes in selected coverts to keep the foxhunting fraternity happy.'

27 T. More, *The Complete Works*, eds. E. Surtz and J. H. Hexter, The Yale Edition of the Complete Works of St Thomas More, 4 vols. (New Haven and London: Yale University Press 1965), vol. 4, *Utopia* (1965); on farming p. 115 and commentary pp. 388–9; on desisting from sacrifice p. 235; on hunting p. 171.

28 A. Linzey, 'The Place of Animals in Creation—A Christian View' in Regan (ed.), *Animal Sacrifices*, pp. 139–40.

29 *Wildlife and Countryside Act 1981* (HMSO 1985), schedule 7, section 12, para 1, p. 75. The Act is an extraordinary mixture of narrow philanthropy and farmers' license.

30 Isaiah 2.4 (RSV).

31 M. Lerner, *America as a Civilization* (New York: Simon & Shuster 1957), p. 812.

32 A. Linzey, 'Moral Education and Reverence for Life' in David Paterson (ed.), *Humane Education—A Symposium* (Humane Education Council 1981), p. 123.

33 J. Hick, *Evil and the God of Love* (Collins 1968), p. 254.

34 See n. 24 above.

35 T. Regan, unpublished address at a 'One Day National Consultation on the Rights of Animals', University of Essex, May 1986.

36 Regan makes the point at length in his *Case for Animal Rights*, pp. 262f.

37 E. F. Schumacher, *Small is Beautiful: A Study of Economics as if People Mattered* (Abacus Books 1974), p. 88.

38 *Animals and Ethics*, p. 21.

39 *Animals and Ethics*, p. 21–2.

40 Runcie, 'Statement by the Archbishop of Canterbury on Animal Welfare Matters' (Lambeth Palace 1981), p. 2; see appendix for extract.

41 See M. S. Dawkins, *Animal Suffering: The Science of Animal Welfare* (London and New York: Chapman & Hall 1980).

42 *Animals and Ethics*, p. 19.

43 Primatt, op. cit., p. 136; his emphases.

44 *Animals and Ethics*, p. 24.

45 Bishop of Dudley, cited in *Church Times*, 29 August 1986, p. 16.

46 Cited in letter from Church Commissioners, 9 September 1986, p. 1.

47 'Is there any credit balance for the battery hen, denied almost all natural functioning, all normal environment, lapsing steadily into deformity and disease, for the whole of her existence? It is in the battery shed and the broiler house, not in the wild, that we find the true parallel to Auschwitz. Auschwitz is a purely human invention.'

John Austin Baker, Bishop of Salisbury, sermon preached in York Minster, 28 September 1986, *ACC Service for Animal Welfare* (Animal Christian Concern 1986), p. 3.

48 Uses listed by Glendin, op. cit., p. 16.

49 ibid.

50 H. Montefiore, review of *Animal Rights* in *Theology* (January 1977), pp. 72–3.

51 C. S. Lewis, 'Vivisection' in *Undeceptions: Essays in Theology and Ethics*, edited by Walter Hooper (Geoffrey Bles 1954), p. 183; *First and Second Things* (Fount 1985), p. 82; my italics.

52 Indeed this moral distinction amounts to what Lewis calls man being 'the Christ, of the animals', *The Problem of Pain* (Fontana Books 1967), p. 66.

53 Rasher, cited in Jacques Delarue, *The History of the Gestapo*, ET Mervyn Savill (Macdonald & Co. 1964), p. 262; my italics. I am grateful to Nicholas Garrard for this reference.

54 Cited in ibid.

55 N. Uezono, cited in Robert Whymant, 'The Brutal Truth about Japan', the *Guardian*, 14 August 1982, p. 15.

56 ibid.

57 ibid.

58 E. Hill, cited in Whymant, op. cit.

59 *Report of the Committee of Inquiry into Human Fertilization and Embryology* (HMSO 1984), p. 84.

60 ibid., p. 62.

61 ibid.

62 ibid., p. 63.

63 For a history see E. Westacott, *A History of Vivisection and Anti-Vivisection* (C. W. Daniel Co. 1949).

64 W. D. M. Paton, 'Some Notes on Experiments Recently Criticised', *RDS Paper No. 1* (Research Defence Society, no date). Paton objects to the original letter of the RSPCA which claimed that the RDS 'automatically defend[s] all animal experiments of whatever sort'. It would be interesting to learn of any experiment currently performed which the RDS opposes.

65 P. Singer, *Practical Ethics* (Cambridge University Press 1979), p. 58.

66 G. B. Shaw, 'The Doctor's Dilemma' in *Prefaces*, p. 262.

67 R. G. Frey, *Rights, Killing and Suffering* (Basil Blackwell 1983), p. 115.

68 ibid.

69 Hans Ruesch, *Slaughter of the Innocent* (Futura Publications 1979), p. 35.

70 'These tapes were nothing short of horrific. They showed conscious animals fighting to free themselves from their restraints before being subjected to "injury". Researchers laughed and joked as they played with brain-damaged monkeys. A struggling animal was showered with acid by an incompetent handler. Researchers

smoked as they operated on the brains of sentient monkeys,' John Robins, 'Pennsylvania Primates', *Black Beast*, No. 1 (Summer 1985), p. 9.

71　A. Flew, 'Torture: Could the End Justify the Means?', *Crucible* (January 1974), p. 23. Discussed in A. Linzey, *Animal Rights: A Christian Assessment* (SCM Press 1976), pp. 55–7.

72　Lewis, 'Vivisection', p. 186; *First and Second Things*, p. 83.

73　ibid., *First and Second Things*, p. 84.

74　*The Proposed International Guidelines for Biochemical Research Involving Human Subjects* (a joint project of the World Health Organization and Council for Organizations of Medical Sciences) (Geneva 1982), p. 22, para 1f. The reference is to article III.4 (the final provision of the declaration). Also discussed in Linzey, 'The Place of Animals in Creation—A Christian View', in T. Regan (ed.), *Animal Sacrifices*, p. 138. I am grateful to J. M. Finnis for this reference.

75　Information provided by the International Society for Animal Rights shows that only six states have legislation providing for protection of animals in private and public shelters, 'A Chart Further Clarifying State Laws Restricting or Prohibiting the Release of Shelter Animals for Research or Related Purposes', ISAR (September, 1986).

76　D. H. Smyth, *Alternatives to Animal Experiments* (Scolar Press 1978).

77　C. Roberts, *The Scientific Conscience: Reflections on the Modern Biologist and Humanism* (Centaur Press 1974), p. 46.

78　B. Brophy, 'In Pursuit of a Fantasy', in Stanley and Roslind Godlovitch and John Harris (ed.), *Animals, Men and Morals: An Enquiry into the Maltreatment of Non-Humans* (Gollancz 1971), p. 144.

79　*Animals and Ethics*, p. 30.

80　ibid., p. 32.

81　Those in any doubt should consult F. Jean Winter, *Facts about Furs* (Washington, DC: Animal Welfare Institute; Horsham, Sussex: RSPCA, 1973), which provides an excellent factual survey.

82　'Canada's Northern Bishops' in *Prairie Messenger* (Benedictine Monks of St Peter's Abbey, Muenster, Saskatchewan), reprinted under the heading 'Northern Bishops Seek Resurgence of Fur Trapping', *Fur Age Weekly*, 8 December 1985, p. 4. I am grateful to Ethel Thurston for this reference.

83　ibid.

84　ibid.

85　ibid.

86　ibid.

87　'Fur Trapping: The Lost Innocence', RSPCA (1984) p. 4.

88　'Answers to Criticism: Fake Fur Versus Real Fur', *Fur Age Weekly*, 8 December 1985.

89　Northern Bishops, cited in ibid.

181

Chapter 7: Ways of Liberation (II)

1 See Diana Spearman, 'The Moral Achievement of the RSPCA', *New Society*, 30 May 1974, p. 507.

2 'Policies on Animal Welfare', RSPCA (November 1984), p. 3.

3 ibid., p. 23.

4 Bill Jordan and Stefan Ormrod, *The Last Great Wild Beast Show: A Discussion on the Failure of British Animal Collections* (Constable 1978), p. 18.

5 RSPCA (Policies), p. 16.

6 Psalm 50.10–11 (NEB).

7 Psalm 148.9–14 (NEB).

8 Jordan and Ormrod, op. cit., p. 16.

9 The Work of the Education Unit of the Royal Zoological Society of Scotland is at least one exception. It has run enterprising 'ZooEd Programmes' with the specific aim of fostering 'an interest and understanding of the many aspects of animal life both at home and abroad', 'Zooed Services' (1980), p. 1.

10 Cited in Paul Vodden, 'Dolphin Shows in Britain—the Future', *RSPCA Today* (Autumn/Winter 1986), pp. 14–15; their italics.

11 A. Leopold, *A Sand Country Almanac* (New York: Oxford University Press 1949), p. 217; cited and discussed in Tom Regan, *The Case for Animal Rights* (Berkeley, California: University of California Press 1983), p. 361.

12 Regan, ibid., pp. 362, 361.

13 ibid., p. 363; his italics.

14 RSPCA Wildlife Department, *The Tortoise Trade* (RSPCA 1979), p. 14. Happily the importation of tortoises into Britain has now been restricted.

15 Edward Carpenter *et al.*, *Animals and Ethics* (Watkins 1980), p. 26.

16 JACOPIS, 'The Case for a Dog Warden Service on a National Basis' (Joint Advisory Committee on Pets in Society, April 1980), p. 6. I am grateful to Ruth Plant for this reference.

17 Information obtainable from the Vegetarian Society (UK), Parkdale, Dunham Road, Altrincham, Cheshire, WA14 4QG.

18 'Whenever an animal is in any way forced into the service of man, everyone of us must be concerned with the suffering which for that reason it has to undergo', Schweitzer, *Civilization and Ethics*, ET C. T. Campion (Allen & Unwin 1967), p. 222.

19 RSPCA 'Policies', p. 5.

20 BSAVA, cited in ibid.

21 R. D. Ryder, 'Pets are Good for People' (originally an address given to the annual congress of the British Small Animals Veterinary Association, April, 1973), Pet Food Manufacturers' Association (1974).

22 A. Linzey, *Animal Rights: A Christian Assessment* (SCM Press 1976), p. 68.

23 M. Midgley, *Animals and Why They Matter: A Journey Around the Species Barrier* (Penguin Books 1983), p. 25; her italics.

24 For example, research on 'The Control of Foxes in Scottish Forests' by R. Hewson and H. H. Kolb concludes: 'The need for a uniformly high level of control of foxes is questionable . . . control may only take off a constant proportion of the population. All animal populations produce offspring surplus to their annual breeding density and it would seem inefficient if control were largely to remove this surplus in competition with natural controls, particularly if these controls operate at a season of the year . . . when foxes are doing less mischief', *Scottish Forestry*, 28.4 (October 1974), p. 281.

25 'The Killing of the Harp Seal Pups, 1978' (report by W. J. Jordan following an investigation, 7–12 March, in the Magdalen Islands during the annual seal hunt), RSPCA (April 1978), pp. 3–7.

26 RSPCA 'Policies', pp. 14–15.

27 Edward Carpenter *et al.*, *Animals and Ethics* (Watkins 1980), p. 12.

28 Stephen R. L. Clark, *The Moral Status of Animals* (Clarendon Press 1977), pp. 82–3; his italics.

29 ibid., p. 82; his italics.

30 RSPCA 'Policies', p. 14.

31 Genesis 1.29 (NEB).

32 Isaiah 11.9 (NEB).

33 Genesis 9.3 (NEB).

34 A. Phillips, *Lower than the Angels: Questions Raised by Genesis 1–11* (Bible Reading Fellowship 1983), p. 48.

35 Genesis 9.4 (NEB).

36 Phillips, op. cit.

37 K. Barth, *Church Dogmatics*, III/4, *The Doctrine of Creation* ('The Command of God the Creator') (T. & T. Clark 1961), p. 354.

38 *Report on the Welfare of Livestock when Slaughtered by Religious Methods*, Farm Animal Welfare Council (HMSO 1985), p. 19. The Report recommended that 'legislative provisions which permit slaughter without stunning of animals (including poultry) by Jews and Muslims . . . be repealed within the next three years' (p. 25).

39 International Jewish Vegetarian Society, 853–855 Finchley Road, London NW11 8LX.

40 St Richard, cited in Alban Butler, *Lives of the Saints*, revised by Herbert Thurston and Donald Attwater (New York: P. J. Kennedy & Sons 1946) and in Ambrose Agius, *God's Animals* (Catholic Study Circle for Animal Welfare 1970), p. 51.

41 Barth, op. cit., p. 355.

42 The Lifestyle Movement, 'A Commitment to Personal Change' (The Lifestyle Movement 1984), p. 2.

43 E. Burke, cited in 'Live more simply so that all of us may simply live', (The Lifestyle Movement 1984), p. 11.

44 *The Rule of St Benedict*, ET Justin McCann (Sheed & Ward 1976), chapter 39, p. 46.

45 Enough Campaign, 'One Man's Meat . . .' (Enough Campaign 1986), p. 1.
46 ibid.
47 See especially Frey R. Ellis and V. M. E. Montegriffo, 'The Health of Vegans' in Frank Wakes (ed.), *Plant Foods for Human Nutrition* 2.2 (1970).
48 W. R. Inge, 'The Rights of Animals' in *Lay Thoughts of a Dean* (New York and London: The Knickerbocker Press 1926), p. 199.
49 Clark, op. cit., p. 183.
50 ibid, Preface.
51 *New Scientist*, 13 January 1972, cited by Jon Wynne-Tyson, *Food for a Future: The Complete Case for Vegetarianism* (Centaur Press 1979), p. 109.
52 *Report of the Brambell Committee* (HMSO 1965), cited by Wynne-Tyson, ibid., p. 108.
53 Wynne-Tyson, ibid., p. 107.
54 See Christine Townend, *Pulling the Wool: A New Look at the Australian Wool Industry* (Hale & Iremonger 1985), esp. pp. 65–75 for details of the gruesome practice of 'mulesing'.
55 Beauty Without Cruelty Limited, Avebury Avenue, Tonbridge TN9 1TL, UK and 175 West 12th Street, Suite 16G, New York 10011, USA.
56 A. Linzey, 'The Place of Animals in Creation—A Christian View' in T. Regan (ed.), *Animal Sacrifices: Religious Perspectives on the Use of Animals in Science* (Philadelphia: Temple University Press 1986), p. 140.
57 A. Schweitzer, *My Life and Thought: An Autobiography*, ET C. T. Campion (Allen & Unwin 1933), pp. 279–80. Also cited and discussed in A. Linzey, 'Moral Education and Reverence for Life' in David Paterson (ed.), *Humane Education—A Symposium* (Humane Education Council 1981), p. 124.

Guide to Further Reading

Agius, Ambrose, *God's Animals*, foreword by Cardinal Heenan (Catholic Study Circle for Animal Welfare 1970).
A useful compendium of Roman Catholic authorities.

Allchin, A. M., *Wholeness and Transfiguration Illustrated in the Lives of St Francis of Assisi and St Seraphim of Sarov* (SLG Press 1974).
Illustrates the concern for animals shown by these two figures.

Attfield, Robin, *The Ethics of Environmental Concern* (Basil Blackwell 1983).
A new philosophical treatment justifying the Christian view of stewardship but stopping short of animal rights.

Black, John, *Man's Dominion: The Search for Ecological Responsibility* (Edinburgh University Press 1970).
One of the first environmental books with detailed discussion of the Genesis sagas.

Board for Social Responsibility, *Man in his Living Environment: An Ethical Assessment*, Working Party Report of the Church Assembly of the Church of England (CIO Publishing 1970).
One of the best church reports, detailed with imaginative ethical discussion.

Board for Social Responsibility, *Our Responsibility for the Living Environment*: A Report of the General Synod Board for Social Responsibility of the Church of England (Church House Publishing 1986).
Greatly inferior to the 1970 report which it is supposed to replace. Altogether slight and insufficiently theological.

Carpenter, Edward *et al.*, *Animals and Ethics* (Watkins 1980).
A factual statement with ethical discussion by a working party of biologists and theologians.

Childress, James F. and Macquarrie, John (eds), *A New Dictionary of Christian Ethics* (Philadelphia and London: Westminster and SCM Press 1986).
Contains significant new entries on 'animals', 'environmental ethics' and 'vegetarianism'.

Clark, Stephen R. L., *The Moral Status of Animals* (The Clarendon Press 1977).
An outstanding work containing many insights into the Christian understanding of animals. Rigorous but lively.

Cobb Jr, John, *Is It Too Late? A Theology of Ecology* (Beverly Hills, California: Bruce 1972).
A pioneering work relating theology to environmental issues.

Dawkins, Marian Stamp, *Animal Suffering: The Science of Animal Welfare* (London and New York: Chapman & Hall 1980).
A scientific and largely unsuccessful attempt to provide criteria for measuring suffering in animals.

Derr, Thomas Sieger, *Ecology and Human Liberation* (Geneva: WSCF Books 1973).
A sadly anthropocentric understanding of creation.

Duffy, Maureen, *Men and Beasts: An Animal Rights Handbook* (Paladin Books 1984).
A popular presentation for animal rights activists. Its treatment of the Christian tradition is dismissive.

Farm Animal Welfare Council, *Report On the Welfare of Livestock when Slaughtered by Religious Methods* (HMSO 1985).
A report by the Government's expert committee on farming which concludes that religious methods of slaughter are appreciably more inhumane than other methods. Altogether a model report comprising hard evidence, detailed documentation and firm ethical discussion.

Frey, R. G., *Interests and Rights: The Case Against Animals* (The Clarendon Press 1980).
The first philosophical work in recent times against animal rights.

——, *Rights, Killing and Suffering: Moral Vegetarianism and Applied Ethics* (Basil Blackwell 1983).
Takes issue with many of the pro-animal arguments.

Galloway, A. D., *The Cosmic Christ* (Nisbet & Sons 1951).
A pioneering and much overlooked study of the tradition about the cosmic significance of Christ.

Godlovitch, Stanley and Roslind, and Harris, John (eds), *Animals, Men and Morals: An Enquiry into the Maltreatment of Non-Humans* (Gollancz 1971).
The original collection of essays which started the philosophical discussion about animals.

Griffiths, Richard, *The Human Use of Animals* (Grove Books 1982).
A thoroughgoing critique of animal rights from a conservative evangelical position.

Harrison, Ruth, *Animal Machines* (Vincent Stuart 1964).
The first book to question the morality of intensive farming and to document the evidence.

186

Hendry, George S., *Theology of Nature* (Philadelphia: Westminster Press 1980).
A full and sometimes insightful discussion but with little focus on animals.

Hick, John, *Evil and the God of Love* (Collins 1968).
Contains Hick's well-known theodicy about animal pain.

Hume, C. W., *The Status of Animals in the Christian Religion* (Universities Federation for Animal Welfare 1957).
Makes the case for kindness to animals but insufficiently theological.

Jordon, Bill and Ormrod, Stefan, *The Last Great Wild Beast Show: A Discussion on the Failure of British Animal Collections* (Constable 1978).
A detailed critique of zoos from people with expert knowledge.

Lewis, C. S., *The Problem of Pain* (Fontana Books 1967).
Chapter 9 gives Lewis's sympathetic discussion of animal suffering and his defence of animal 'resurrection'.

Linzey, Andrew, *Animal Rights: A Christian Assessment* (SCM Press 1976).
The first defence of animal rights in Christian moral terms.

——, *The Status of Animals in the Christian Tradition* (Woodbrooke College 1985).
A simple account of twelve ideas that have influenced Christian attitudes to animals.

Linzey, Andrew and Wexler, Peter J., *Heaven and Earth: Essex Essays in Theology and Ethics* (Churchman Publishing 1986).
Contains Tom Regan's essay on killing for food.

Magel, Charles R., *A Bibliography on Animal Rights and Related Matters* (Washington, DC: University Press of America 1981).
A comprehensive and invaluable guide to the debate.

Mason, James and Singer, Peter, *Animal Factories* (New York: Crown 1980).
A well-documented critique of the use of animals in intensive farming.

Midgley, Mary, *Beast and Man: The Roots of Human Nature* (Harvester Press 1979).
A philosophical analysis of the supposed difference between animal and human nature.

——, *Animals and Why They Matter: A Journey Around the Species Barrier* (Penguin Books 1983).
A qualified defence of animals, also critical of other philosophers.

Miller, H. and Williams, W. (eds), *Ethics and Animals* (New Jersey: Humana Press 1983).
Another collection of philosophical papers on animals.

Moltmann, Jürgen, *God in Creation: An Ecological Doctrine of Creation*, ET Margaret Kohl (SCM Press 1985).
An outstanding work with vital insights and connections for those concerned for a theology of animals.

Montefiore, Hugh (ed.), *Man and Nature* (Collins 1975).
The Report of the working party set up by Archbishop Ramsey in 1971 containing a joint statement and individual essays. Some of the best theological discussion so far but it does not take up animal issues in any detail.

Morris, Richard K. and Fox, Michael W. (eds), *On the Fifth Day: Animal Rights and Human Ethics* (Washington, DC: Acropolis Press 1978).
Another significant collection of papers, philosophical and pragmatic, on animal rights.

Moule, C. F. D., *Man and Nature in the New Testament: Some Reflections on Biblical Ecology* (Athlone Press 1964).
A slight discussion with summary treatment of the non-human.

Passmore, John, *Man's Responsibility for Nature: Ecological Problems and Western Traditions* (Duckworth 1974).
Passmore defends the biblical material from the charge of despotism but also argues against animal rights.

Paterson, David, (ed.), *Humane Education—A Symposium* (Humane Education Council 1981).
A collection of pioneering essays in humane education.

Paterson, David and Ryder, Richard D. (eds), *Animals' Rights—A Symposium* (Centaur Press 1979).
A lively collection of essays of varying quality presented to the Cambridge Symposium of 1977.

Paton, W. D. M., *Man and Mouse* (The Clarendon Press 1984).
A defence of animal experimentation by a practising scientist.

Porritt, Jonathan, *Seeing Green: The Politics of Ecology Explained*, foreword by Petra Kelly (Basil Blackwell 1984).
A spirited defence of Green perspectives with some discussion of animals.

Primatt, Humphry, *A Dissertation on The Duty of Mercy and the Sin of Cruelty to Brute Animals* (T. Constable 1934).
One of the first specifically theological attempts to defend the extension of moral duties to animals.

Regan, Tom, *All That Dwell Therein: Essays on Animal Rights and Environmental Ethics* (Berkeley, California: University of California Press 1982).
Shows the intellectual development of Regan's *Case for Animal Rights*.

——, *The Case for Animal Rights* (Berkeley, California: University of California Press 1983).
Without doubt the most impressive philosophical case for animals so far. Lucid, detailed and rigorous.

——, (ed.), *Animal Sacrifices: Religious Perspectives on the Use of Animals in Science*, introduction by John Bowker (Philadelphia: Temple University Press 1986).
A collection of papers given by representatives of the major world religions at the London conference in 1983.

Regan, Tom and Singer, Peter (eds), *Animal Rights and Human Obligations* (New Jersey: Prentice-Hall 1976).
An excellent collection of readings both historical and contemporary comprising arguments for and against animal exploitation.

Ryder, Richard D., *Victims of Science: The Use of Animals in Research*, forewords by Richard Adams and Muriel, Lady Dowding (National Anti-Vivisection Society ²1983).
A revised edition of the 1975 book which renewed concern for laboratory animals.

Salt, Henry S., *Animals' Rights Considered in Relation to Social Progress*, preface by Peter Singer (Centaur Press 1980).
A reprint of Salt's pioneering work. It may be a little ironical that Singer should write the commending preface since he does not believe that animals have rights.

Santmire, H. Paul, *The Travail of Nature: The Ambiguous Ecological Promise of Christian Theology* (Philadelphia: Fortress Press 1985).
An impressive and sympathetic treatment of 'the land motif' and wholistic thinking through centuries of Christian theology.

Schumacher, E. F., *Small is Beautiful: A Study of Economics as if People Mattered* (Abacus Books 1974).
His most celebrated work comprising his defence of the 'meta-economic value' of animals.

Schweitzer, Albert, *My Life and Thought: An Autobiography*, ET C. T. Campion (Allen & Unwin 1933).
Contains some of his moving statements about reverence for life.

——, *Civilization and Ethics*, ET C. T. Campion (A. & C. Black 1967).
His classic work on reverence for life.

——, *Reverence for Life*, ET R. H. Fuller, foreword by D. E. Trueblood (SPCK 1970).
A collection of sermons.

Singer, Peter, *Animal Liberation: A New Ethics for Our Treatment of Animals* (Jonathan Cape 1976).
One of the first comprehensive animal books and widely acclaimed. However, little understanding is shown of Christian theology.

——, *Practical Ethics* (Cambridge University Press 1979).
A thoroughgoing utilitarian view of ethics especially sympathetic to animals.

——, (ed.), *In Defence of Animals* (Basil Blackwell 1986).
A collection of essays by philosophers and activists of varied quality.

Sperlinger, David (ed.), *Animals in Research* (John Wiley & Sons 1980).
A factual survey with critical discussion.

Stewart Jr, Claude Y., *Nature in Grace: A Study in the Theology of Nature*, NABPR Dissertation Series, No. 3 (Macon, Georgia: Mercer University Press 1983).
An impressive work of scholarship which defends the idea that all creation is open to the working of God's grace.

Stone, C., *Can Trees Have Standing? Towards Legal Rights for Natural Objects* (New York: Avon Books 1975).
Reviews recent law suits and discusses their implications.

Thomas, Keith, *Man and The Natural World: Changing Attitudes in England 1500–1800* (Penguin Books 1984).
An exemplary work by an accomplished historian. It contains detailed examples of the changes of attitude towards animals during this period.

Torrance, T. F., *Divine and Contingent Order* (Oxford University Press 1981).
Includes sensitive discussions of animal pain and man's part in the redemption of creation.

Townend, Christine, *Pulling The Wool: A New Look at the Australian Wool Industry* (Sydney: Hale & Iremonger 1985).
A challenging and detailed critique of the cruelty involved in the Australian wool industry.

Turner, E. S., *All Heaven in a Rage* (Michael Joseph 1964).
A lively historical study of the birth of the humane movement.

Turner, James, *Reckoning with the Beast: Animals, Pain and Humanity in the Victorian Mind* (Baltimore and London: Johns Hopkins University Press 1980).
A thorough historical study showing the strengths and weaknesses of the emerging animal protection societies in the nineteenth century.

Vanstone, W. H., *Love's Endeavour, Love's Expense: The Response of Being to the Love of God*, foreword by H. A. Williams (Darton, Longman & Todd 1977).
Defends the view that nature and animals respond actively to the love of God.

Vyvyan, John, *In Pity and In Anger* (Michael Joseph 1964).

——, *The Dark Face of Science* (Michael Joseph 1971).
Two-volume history of the movement against animal experimentation.

Ward, Keith, *Rational Theology and the Creativity of God* (Basil Blackwell 1982).
Contains his interesting defence of animal immortality.

Wesley, John, *Sermons on Several Occasions*, 4 vols. with biographical note by J. Beecham (Wesleyan Conference Office 1874), vol. ii (1874).
Comprises his famous sermon, 'The General Deliverance', on the future life for animals.

Wynne-Tyson, Jon, *Food for a Future: The Complete Case for Vegetarianism* (Centaur Press 1979).
A popular statement of the case for vegetarianism, though generally weak on the religious aspects.

——, (ed.), *The Extended Circle: A Dictionary of Humane Thought* (Centaur Press 1986).
The first dictionary devoted to animal issues. An invaluable reference book.

Index

9870